S0-BOG-100

The Major Essays
of
Henry David Thoreau

The Major Essays
of
Henry David Thoreau

edited by
Richard Dillman

Whitston Publishing Company, Inc.
Albany, New York
2001

Copyright © 2001
Richard Dillman

Library of Congress Control Number 00-132994

ISBN 0-87875-523-3

Printed in the United States of America

Contents

Thoreau's Achievements as an Essayist

Known to most readers as the author of *Walden: Or Life in The Woods*, Henry David Thoreau is also one of America's most important and influential essayists, a fact that is often obscured by the power and popularity of his masterpiece. During the period from 1843 to 1862, Thoreau often published his essays in important periodicals before they appeared in collections or before they were collected by his editors for posthumous publication. *The Maine Woods*, for example, began as a collection of narrative essays published partly in popular periodicals. Thoreau's essays and their ideas were often tested in nineteenth-century literary and political journals. Many of his essays began as journal entries written in his fourteen volume journal, and many of these entries were later expanded into lectures that were read on the lyceum circuit, at times in heated political and rhetorical situations. These lectures were often revised as essays or transformed into much longer works like *Walden*, a book that strikes many scholars as a collection of related essays. For example, several chapters of *Walden*, such as "Economy" or "Spring," are often anthologized as distinct literary essays. Scholarly attempts to comprehend the unity of *Walden* often fail because individual chapters often operate as essays on single topics or groups of related topics. Why can "Economy," for example, be read as a sharp critique of the nineteenth-century cult of progress? Why can "Spring," moreover, be easily read as a euphoric tribute to the power of seasonal change and the myth of renewal? These essay-like chapters often followed the journal to lecture to essay pattern of development.

Thoreau's reputation as a skilled writer of nonfiction prose in the essay form places him among the most influential essayists in the American literary tradition. His contributions equal or surpass those of Benjamin Franklin, Ralph Waldo

Emerson, H. L. Mencken, E. B. White, Wendell Berry, Annie Dillard, and others. His essays explore many of the same issues as those of Emerson, but his style and approach are profoundly different. Some of his essays respond to real historical events; some question the ethics and values of American life, and some are gentle and entertaining excursions, while others address serious issues of natural history in which Thoreau demonstrates his understanding of botany, biology, and the foundations of ecology. The sheer range of his work is impressive; his essays range across forms and topics, moods and tones, and rhetorical purposes. Thoreau, often with a clear sense of audience, may attempt to persuade, to educate, to amuse, and to entertain. He is a virtuoso writing across the range of essay forms and exhibiting impressive variety within the essay genre.

Thoreau's essays frequently address major issues of his day and ours, and he often speaks to current generations more powerfully than he did to his own. He used the essay format to critique the power of government, to condemn slavery, to honor the martyr John Brown, to examine the ways that his peers earned their livings, and to analyze the nature of reformers. His essays on political and ethical topics seem timeless, while they are also historically important. "Civil Disobedience" is the classic American statement on civil disobedience and passive resistence that has influenced generations of Americans as well as Martin Luther King and Mahatma Gandhi in their struggles against oppression. Thoreau, who was fascinated with political and economic issues that were related to his strong belief in self-reliance and individualism, used his essays to critique government and community suppression of individual liberty. He also used his political and ethical essays to persuade his readers and listeners to embrace important moral and ethical positions such as opposition to slavery and resistence to irresponsible government behavior.

Thoreau also wrote narrative essays that followed the journey or excursion pattern. Journey essays, for example, were collected to become the *Maine Woods, Cape Cod* and *A Yankee in Canada.* The prototype of these longer works, however, appeared in informal essays like "A Winter Walk" or "Walking." These pieces are informal, casual, and suggestive. In each piece, the act of walking suggests larger meanings, issues and themes; for each composition, therefore, the outward journey becomes, at least in part, the inward journey. Both follow a formal movement related to the walking theme, and both are also exploratory and often richly symbolic. The act of walking inspires the senses, suggesting topics to the narrators for mini-sermons, analysis, and discussions. Here Thoreau develops a close relationship with his readers as he attempts to persuade them to share his journey and his discoveries. Implicit in the formal structures of these compositions is the idea that readers will share the journey and open themselves to new insights. Thoreau's excursions are designed to help stimulate new thoughts in his readers' minds.

Thoreau also wrote natural history essays. As a naturalist and close observer of nature, he was easily attracted to natural history writing. Thoreau filled his journals with observations about the plants, flowers, insects, animals, geography, and the seasonal changes in New England. He valued keen observation, precise measurement, and careful classification. He worked part-time as a surveyor of property and wood-lots in and around Concord, and even *Walden*, particularly the ponds chapters, contains several examples of his interest in measurement and quantification. The essay form provided an appropriate outlet for these interests. He wrote such essays as "The Natural History of Massachusetts," a work of empirical exposition, and "Autumnal Tints," a combination of botanical knowledge, observation, and poetic vision, in the natural history mode. He wrote as scientist and humanist in these essays, which are often precise, visual, sensual, and richly metaphorical.

At times, Thoreau seems to embody the principles of poetic sensibility that Emerson elucidates in "The Poet." In his prose, he is often poetic, able to synthesize the disparate, fragmented parts of experience or to unify the fragmented landscape. He seems to develop "meter-making arguments" in poetic prose, to be Emerson's "seer" and "language maker" who shows us reality amidst appearances ("The Poet" 9, 21, 36). At other times, he seems like the embodiment of Emerson's American scholar as expressed in the essay of the same name. He is Emerson's "man thinking," who thinks honestly and openly about important themes ("The American Scholar" 84). Despite his wide reading and learning, Thoreau does not make his essays overly allusive. Instead, he uses the tropes of everyday experience; he makes natural facts suggest higher meanings. He helps the stones, forests, and mountains to speak to us. Instead of theorizing about the qualities of a poet, Thoreau, in his essays, exemplifies Emerson's concept of the poet.

Thoreau the essayist is also Thoreau the master rhetorician who uses effective rhetorical techniques to achieve his effects and develop his arguments. It is reasonable to view Thoreau's prose as governed by rhetorical strategies common in his time but used uniquely for his own ends and situations. I will present an overview of the strategies and techniques that mark his style and approach to help clarify his rhetorical practice. Throughout the essays, Thoreau is a master symbolist who uses the natural world for symbols and tropes, and who takes his symbols from the forests, lakes, trails, and basic features of common life. We can read his essays as collections of natural symbols that suggest, define, and encompass complex situations. In addition to his rich and skillful use of metaphors drawn from the natural world, Thoreau effectively uses synecdoches, a figure in which the part is used for the whole or the whole is used for the part. This is also the rhetorical figure behind Thoreau's microcosms in which the small and the typical represent the general or the universal; Walden Pond, for example, represents all the principles of nature.

Thoreau is a master of precise, imagistic description, frequently using concrete, specific and sensual language to support his propositions or expand his ideas. He seldom leaves us at an abstract conceptual level but instead clarifies and amplifies his abstractions in ways that allow readers to see, feel, understand, and, at times, to hear the material. These sensual descriptions are remarkable for their clarity, their visual metaphors, and for the meticulously developed structural patterns that often function in poetic and meditative fashions. Thoreau often brings his readers closer to a subject by providing collections of images that invite his audience to meditate on the subject at hand.

Thoreau frequently uses other techniques in his more persuasive and argumentative essays such as those on politics and ethical themes. Often reasoning syllogistically, he will move the reader from proposition to proposition, sometimes without supporting evidence for his premises. His well-formed propositions stand out in memorable ways, often appearing as aphorisms and other forms of sententia common to his style. At times, such propositions will be the lead sentences for whole paragraphs; at other times, they will belong to strings of related propositions that are stacked together for rhetorical power.

Thoreau is the master of the sentence, perhaps his most effective unit of discourse. His development of other units of discourse pales in comparison to his skill with these polished and often much revised sentences. I speak here of the sentence in an earlier sense as a capsule of wisdom, a unit of discourse that is usually compact, suggestive, and sententious. He mastered at least three forms of sententious sentences and the anti-Ciceronian period, known today as the cumulative sentence.

Thoreau frequently used three types of suggestive and compact sentences—paradox, aphorism, and proverb. He frequently used paradoxical statements to shock and disrupt conventional thinking and to urge his readers to see a different perspective on his subjects. These paradoxes are of two types—the self-contradictory statement that upon closer examination contains unexpected forms of truth and the compact statement that contradicts conventional or received opinion. The second type has a kind of jarring effect and often appears as unexpected and initially disconcerting. Ultimately both types of paradoxes help readers restructure their thinking about Thoreau's topics in new or different ways. They help readers develop new angles of vision. Sometimes his paradoxes are stated aphoristically, but his aphorisms are often not paradoxes but short, compact, and suggestive sentences instead that have at least the aura of wisdom. Such sententious sentences are easily remembered, highly polished, emphatic, and declarative, suggesting more than they say. The third type is the proverb in which Thoreau states his points in the style of folk or traditional wisdom, presented in laconic, and colloquial sentences. Proverb style sentences appear occasionally in the essays but more frequently in *Walden*. Finally, Thoreau masterfully uses the cumulative sentence or the anti-Ciceronian period, often presenting readers with short declarative sentences followed by long strings of descriptive modifiers that are frequently visual and concrete. What happens in these sentences is this: the main statement which is often general and abstract is clarified and amplified by additions that follow the initial statement called the kernal sentence. Thus statements are embellished, amplified, and copiously developed in ways that draw readers into Thoreau's versions of the natural world or into his arguments.

Thoreau's essays also possess a pronounced oral quality. That is they have qualities common to lectures or sermons. An example of this oral feel is an often obvious appeal to specific audiences, particularly in those essays concerned with political, economic, and ethical questions and those designed to be persuasive. Several essays in this collection have this feel of oral address to a specific group or to people who share specific values typical of the Concord, Massachusetts area around 1850. Remembering that Thoreau often delivered these essays as lectures to identifiable audiences helps explain the genesis of this audience awareness. Concord residents who attended his lectures were often conservative, rural people, who admired tradition, the work ethic, frugality, and conformity. Certainly people who shared Thoreau's views attended his lectures, but his essays are loaded with arguments and images aimed at those who would disagree. I am not saying that he changed his viewpoints to pander to his audiences but rather that he simply used strategies that would make some of his controversial ideas more persuasive to listeners and readers. At times, he uses elements of the sermon form to make his points, presenting parables, exempla, and quotations from diverse scriptural traditions. Most importantly, he attempted to tell the truth as he saw it, thus allowing readers to accept or reject his arguments.

Thoreau did not always organize his essays consistently. They often seem to follow an organic form in which each essay's arrangement follows and evolves from the content instead of the content simply following the form. Thoreau does not appear to develop a pattern of organization and then fill it with ideas. Form in a specific sense does not precede content. Substance generates form, and his pattern of organization appears artless and genuine. Many of the essays are rather loosely organized by contemporary standards of expository prose. The walking essays follow the progression of the walk or brief journey; "The Succession of Forest Trees" follows the progress of biological development of the new forest, and "Autumnal Tints" follows the pattern by which deciduous trees change color in the fall. Moreover, Thoreau has a strong sense of the expectations that he creates in his readers' minds, and he often strives to meet these expectations. His form seems organic and nearly spontaneous. It seems to evolve in a way that is analogous to the growth of a tree or leaf or even to that of the melting sandbank in the "Spring" chapter of *Walden* (304-308).

I have chosen the most significant of Thoreau's individual essays for this collection, grouping them according to the three types discussed earlier: reform essays on political and ethical behavior, informal essays on walking, and the natural history essays. I have tried to represent the range of his achievements with the essay genre, presenting a variety of forms, styles, subjects, and interests, and I have selected essays that help illustrate his progressive development as a writer, with the earliest published in 1843, at the start of his writing career, and the latest published in 1863, nearly a year after his death. In this collection will appear essays like "Civil Disobedience" that possess great historical significance, essays that have influenced later writers and thinkers, informal essays like "Walking" that are classics in their genre, and essays illustrating Thoreau's strong scientific bent and interests. The essays in this volume often appear individually in anthologies, and are seldom found grouped together. I have also deliberately omitted works originally published as essays that later became sections or chapters of book length published works. "Ktaadn" and "Chesuncook," both of which were published separately as essays, were later collected and published as part of *The Maine Woods*," and sections of *Cape Cod*, like "The Shipwreck," appeared originally as short prose. These essays are know as parts of these larger works and are best understood in the full context of these volumes. I have also avoided pieces that were so heavily edited after his death that they carry the editor's imprint and voice. In these pieces, Thoreau's original intentions easily become lost or obscured.

Section I
Reform Essays: Politics and Ethics

"Paradise To Be Regained" (1843) is a review of a book popular in the 1840's, J. A. Etzler's *The Paradise within the Reach of all Men, without Labour, by Powers of Nature and Machinery. An Address to All Intelligent Men* (Part First, Second English Edition, published in London in 1842). At the suggestion of R.W. Emerson, who also wished to publish the review in *The Dial*, Thoreau submitted this piece to J. L. Sullivan, who published it in the *Democratic Review* in November of 1843. Etzler's monograph developed the view that an earthly paradise is possible if mankind would only harness the wind, the tides, and the sun, live in communal dwellings, and communize most economic activities. Doing so would relieve humanity of most forms of labor.   Such thinking, to be sure, was anathema to Thoreau and other transcendentalists, and in this essay Thoreau develops his theory of self-culture, essentially holding that true social reform comes from the individual and that economic or political systems do not reform humanity but instead limit our individual freedom and creativity.   Systems imposed from above by social reformers or by governments stifle individual efforts to live creative lives.   Thoreau felt we must begin by reforming willing individuals.   For example, when many individuals are reformed, then society will begin to be reformed. This essay pre-dates and foreshadows the argument developed in "Civil Disobedience" that "That Government is best that governs least" (47).   This review may be regarded as one of Thoreau's responses to the socialist experiments of his time, specifically to the utopian socialist experiments of the mid Nineteenth Century such as the Brook Farm Community, where Hawthorne temporarily resided, the Fruitlands Community in Massachusetts, the Owenite communities in Indiana, and the Oneida Community in New York, among others.   The social reform movement and varied forms of utopian socialism were widespread in the 1840s.   Thoreau may also have had the Fourierists in mind in this essay (Harding and Meyer 38), particularly the many Fourierist communities with their phalanx style organization.   To Thoreau, Etzler advocated directing mankind's energies in the wrong direction, away from spiritual improvement towards a mere mechanical improvement.   In Etzler's world, real work, particularly physical work, would be devalued, and the dignity of real labor diminished.   We would have, then, improved means to unimproved ends.

As an early 1843 essay, "Paradise to be Regained" has the hallmarks of a novice writer who is learning his craft.   It has a certain roughness; the paragraphs seem too loosely organized, and his long strings of rhetorical questions become tedious. Thoreau arrives at his own views on the issues rather indirectly. The essay is a response to another text, instead of a formal, critical review.   The first two-thirds of the essay are responses to sections of Etzler's book, and the final quarter presents some of Thoreau's thoughts on how people should live.   Thoreau was no supporter of over-simplified solutions to humanity's complex problems, and this essay illustrates his impatience with utopian schemes.

"Civil Disobedience" (1849) or "Resistance to Civil Government" is partly a reponse to Thoreau's arrest for failure to
pay his poll tax in 1846. Thoreau was arrested and jailed for non-
payment of his poll tax in the summer of 1846, and during the
evening of his jailing someone, probably his Aunt Maria, paid
the tax, and he was released. Thoreau had stopped paying his tax
in 1842 or 43 to protest against slavery, but his protest was ig-
nored for several years. Sam Staples, the Concord jailor, arrested
him illegally because the normal way to settle such disputes was
for the authorities to seize enough personal property to pay the
fine, and Thoreau had more than enough personal property.
Because he was bailed out in untimely fashion, he used this essay as a vehicle to publicize his ideas and his protest. First presented as a lecture in two parts, it was presented before the Concord Lyceum with the title of "The Relation of the Individual to
the State" in January and February of 1848. It was first printed
with the title "Resistance to Civil Government" in May 1849 in
Elizabeth Peabody's periodical *Aesthetic Papers*. After Thoreau's
death in 1862, the essay was included in his collected works under the title of "Civil Disobedience."

While the ideas in "Civil Disobedience" are not new and
can be traced back to classical Greece, Thoreau states them in a
compelling and persuasive way. Next to *Walden*, "Civil Disobedience" is the most widely known of Thoreau's works, having a
widespread international readership. He emphasizes the specific
circumstances of his own situation, relating it to contemporary
political events, and using the narrative to explore the conflict
between the individual conscience and the power of the state.
Thoreau asks how the individual whose personal moral and
ethical beliefs conflict with those of the state can have an impact
on state policy. He attempted to answer this by outlining the elements of a theory of civil disobedience that was capable of crip-
pling the machinery of government. His approach is nonvio-
lent and passive. By making this strong statement about the necessity of civil disobedience, he created a document of enormous
importance in American and world history. Gandhi used it as a
text for his civil disobedience campaigns in India and Africa; it
was a handbook for political action used by the British labor
party in its early days; it was frequently cited by Martin Luther
King, Jr., during the civil rights campaigns in the American
South. During the sixties and early seventies, it was also used by
the anti-Vietnam War movement as inspiration for its sit-ins

and demonstrations. In 1989 it played a role in the pro-democracy demonstrations in Tien An Mien Square in Peking with tragic results. Chinese students educated in the West had become familiar with "Civil Disobedience." In the essay, Thoreau also presented much of his general theory of government. This very conservative position basically argues that government functions should be severely limited and that the government often interferes with individual liberty and potential achievement. Thoreau thus proposes a theory of minimal government.

"Civil Disobedience" represents Thoreau's mature prose style. It is well organized, rhetorically effective and written at the same time that he was writing *Walden*. Paradoxes and aphorisms abound, and sententious phrasing is common. His striking metaphors help carry the power of his argument; he compares the state to a huge machine complete with gears and levers, and he compares the civilly disobedient to impediments who bring this machine to a clumsy halt. Thoreau moves us from general principles to concrete respresentation of his philosophy in the graphic description of his night in jail that slows the essay's rhythm and invites readers to quietly meditate on his themes. He moves us from general to specific and then back to general principles again. His personal situation is both symbol and synecdoche for the more abstract conflict of individual conscience and state power.

"Civil Disobedience" is also concerned with ethical questions. Thoreau probes questions of the individual's relationship to other individuals, the individual's relationship to humanity in general, and the individual's relationship to institutions with the power to intimidate and control. Moreover, he also raises the issue of the individual's relationship to war. Do citizens, he asks, have the obligation to financially support wars with which they do not agree by paying taxes that may directly or indirectly support these wars? A similar issue surfaced during the Vietnam War when some people withheld all or part of their taxes to register their dissent from the war effort. This essay, moreover, even asks readers to consider the ethics of tax policy.

"Slavery in Massachusetts," the next essay, was delivered in part on July 4, 1854, at an anti-slavery convention in Framingham, Massachusetts, and first published in *The Liberator* on July 21, 1854. The abolitionist William Lloyd Garrison publically burned a copy of the constitution at this convention to symbolically protest against slavery. Thoreau objected to the recent arrest of the fugitive slave Anthony Burns and his return to slavery in Virginia. A major portion of the essay is derived from his journal entries at the time of Burn's arrest, while a significant portion is also dervived from the journal entries of early summer 1851 when another fugitive slave named Symms was arrested in Massachusetts. The finished essay itself is also exceptionally well organized. Considering the urgency of his topic, Thoreau exhibits great rhetorical control in developing several persuasive arguments against slavery. Employing his common paradoxical approach to truth, he demonstrates that the citizens of Massachusetts are paradoxically slaves themselves and that by honoring the fugitive slave law they also accept slavery in their own state. This essay reflects Thoreau's growing impatience with the federal government's approach to the slavery question and with northern efforts to compromise with the South over slavery. Thoreau was very close to the abolitionist movement, particularly since his mother often harbored fugitive slaves in the Thoreau home, and he himself alludes in the "Visitors" chapter of *Walden* to harboring escaped slaves in his cabin (152). His main argument is that we must obey the higher moral law that holds slavery to be unjust, immoral, and obscene. This higher law takes precedence over state and federal law and the constitution. In transcendentalist fashion, these higher laws are known intuitively. He sees constitutionality as an ephemeral and transitory test of justice and right created only by men. Thoreau again expresses ethical and moral positions. If citizens adhere to the state endorsement of the Fugitive Slave Act, then they are complicit in the immoral and unethical act of supporting slavery. They indirectly support slavery, while they may not consciously do so. The legal standing of an unjust law makes citizens, even those of good-will, complicit in the injustice.

"Slavery in Massachusetts" is polemical, hard-hitting, and loaded with powerful metaphors and analogies used to attack slavery and the federal government's approach to it. Well-developed arguments, probing rhetorical questions, and historical narrative comprise Thoreau's main techniques here. This essay is an important document in abolitionist literature, while it also embodies the same political theory as "Civil Disobedience." A government that tolerates slavery has betrayed the trust of the governed, and it should be altered or abolished, and citizens, moreover, should refuse to cooperate with such a state. Much of Thoreau's language is strong, especially towards the conclusion when he declares that "My thoughts are murder to the state and involuntarily go plotting against her" (80). He expresses his increasing impatience with the absence of reform on the slavery issue.

In "A Plea for Captain John Brown," published 6 years after "Slavery in Massachusetts," Thoreau has lost patience with non-violence. The first of three essays on John Brown, this essay was first delivered as an impassioned lecture on October 30, 1859, at the Concord Town Hall in response to Brown's arrest and the attack on Harper's Ferry. Thoreau, who had met Brown twice through his friend F. B. Sanborn, had been impressed with the radical abolitionist. He sprang quickly to Brown's defense after Harper's Ferry, and he personally called a meeting in the Concord Town Hall to defend him. On November 1, 1859, he repeated the speech at Theodore Parker's temple in Boston as a last minute substitute for Frederick Douglass, and on November third he delivered the same lecture in Worchester, Massachusetts. Thoreau, abandoning his original plan to print the lecture as a pamphlet to raise money for Brown's family, allowed the revised lecture to be printed as an essay in 1860 in James Redpath's collection *Echoes of Harper's Ferry*. In supporting Brown's act of violence against slavery, Thoreau seems to contradict his often stated theory of individual reform and non-violent behavior. He portrays Brown as a true transcendentalist in tune with a higher law, a true son of New England soil, and as an American Christ figure willing to lay down his life for higher laws. Brown is depicted as a man in tune with the higher laws mentioned in "Slavery in Massachusetts," and as a man of integrity willing to let his life represent his beliefs.

"A Plea for Captain John Brown" has less emotional control than "Slavery in Massachusetts." The essay is emotional and impassioned, reflecting the incendiary circumstances that it addresses. The essay reflects Thoreau's evolving thoughts on slavery and politics, the growing national impatience with slavery, his impatience with genteel elements of the abolitionist movement, and the dynamic historical events surrounding the Harper's Ferry incident. Thoreau is not at all the contemplative philosopher of *Walden* but a man of action identifying closely with another man of action. Circumstances force him to take rhetorical action to help abolish slavery and support justice. Thoreau's persona is aroused and angry. Despite his impassioned tone, however, Thoreau is very careful to appeal to his potentially skeptical audience in this piece, when he associates Brown with revolutionary war heros and with traditional New England values in the essay's first few pages.

Ralph Waldo Emerson also delivered two lectures on John Brown that were subsequently published in a variety of sources. The first titled "Speech at a Meeting to Aid John Brown's Family" was delivered on November 18, 1859 at the Tremont Temple in Boston and subsequently published in Boston newspapers and eventually in James Redpath's *Echoes of Harper's Ferry* in 1860. The second titled "John Brown" was delivered in Salem, Massachusetts, in January 1860 and first published in Redpath's *Echoes of Harper's Ferry* in 1860. They bear little relationship to Thoreau's John Brown essays, except that the second piece touches on some of the commonplaces about Brown's life and character that Thoreau mentions. The first lecture is a direct appeal for aid to assist Brown's family, and the second is a short, rather undeveloped set of remarks on John Brown. There seems to be little connection between "A Plea for Captain John Brown" and Emerson's published speeches. These speeches both appear in the 1995 collection titled *Emerson's Antislavery Writings*, edited by Len Gougen and Joel Myerson.

"After the Death of John Brown," the second of Thoreau's essays on Brown, has little literary value, and it is included in this collection for historical reasons. It is a brief eulogy read at the Concord memorial services for Brown on the day of his execution, December 2, 1859. The third John Brown essay, "The Last Days of John Brown," was written for the memorial services held in North Elba, New York, on July 4, 1860, when Brown was interred there. This piece was derived from his journal entries of November and December 1859, during the period of the John Brown affair. R. J. Hunter read the essay as a speech for the memorial service since Thoreau was unable to attend, and in July 1860 it was printed in essay form in William Lloyd Garrison's *Liberator*. "The Last Days of John Brown" is relatively short and written in a contemplative, almost meditative style. It has the qualities of a eulogy intended to be read at the memorial service, but it is also very self-expressive and similar to sections of his journal. Here he thinks aloud about the circumstances surrounding Brown's death and about the public reaction to those events. He was very disappointed in the reaction of many of his fellow citizens to Brown's death, and he chastises them in this piece for their inability to comprehend the higher law that motivated Brown. They lack insight and intuition; their beliefs do not reflect the transcendentalist ideals of perception and understanding. He also depicts Brown as a fine writer able to express profound moral sentiments in vernacular language. Brown did not need a Harvard education in rhetoric to speak his version of the truth. Thoreau, at this juncture, mentions the great rule of composition on which he would insist were he a professor of rhetoric—"To speak the truth" (107). "The Last Days of John Brown" is significantly different in tone and purpose than the impassioned and persuasive "Plea for Captain John Brown."

"Life Without Principle," the last essay in the first section, provides a powerful summation of political, economic and ethical themes that Thoreau explored throughout his writing life. Published in October 1863, over a year after his death, in the *Atlantic Monthly*, he prepared this essay for publication in his final months. Many ideas in this work appeared in Thoreau's journals for 1851-1855, and an earlier draft was composed as a lecture titled "Getting a Living" as early as 1854. "Life Without Principle" is intense, concentrated, and highly aphoristic in style, full of the concentrated, succinct sentences known as sententia—aphorisms and compact paradoxes. Thoreau stressed the theme that a life spent working for money only and not principle can only lead downward. He indirectly expresses his concern about disturbing contemporary developments like the growth of industrialism and the factory system and their impact on the commercial and agrarian society of the Concord area. He critiques the visible effects of industrial capitalism and the forms of employment and labor that this system fostered. The effects of division of labor on workers particularly bothered him. He argues for self-reliance and advocates working as an advocation in which the goal is to perform high quality work and not merely to earn money. The person totally immersed in his or her employment, indeed loving his or her task, would be a Thoreauvian ideal in this essay, analogous to the "Artist of Kouroo" in the final chapter of *Walden* (326-327).

Thoreau's reform essays consistently address ethical issues. He raises questions about the individual's relationship to and responsibilities for less fortunate people like the victims of slavery, of war, or of the emergent industrial system. He also encourages his readers to think carefully about the citizen's relationship to government and its institutions. In all of these essays, he argues that a humane and just life that can be achieved by making principled, ethical and moral choices. Such choices will ultimately enhance everyone's dignity. Thoreau also moves intellectually from advocating non-violent protest in "Resistance to Civil Government" to implicitly endorsing violence to end slavery in "A Plea for Captain John Brown."

Section II
Informal Essays: Excursions

Section II, "The Informal Essays: Excursions," include three essays emphasizing the process of walking. Walking here is used metaphorically as a counter for such things as traveling and external and internal exploration. Thoreau was an avid reader of travel books and accounts of explorations like the *Journals of Lewis and Clark*. He also traveled himself on excursions to such places as the Maine wilderness, Cape Cod, and Quebec which he chronicled in such longer works as *The Maine Woods, Cape Cod*, and *A Yankee in Canada*. "A Walk to Wachusett" (1843) and "A Winter Walk" (1843) are early works that represent Thoreau's writing while he was learning his craft, and "Walking" is a mature, well-developed essay that includes some of his most memorable passages and engaging explorations of several topics. As informal essays, these compositions have a charm that reflects minimal distance between the persona and audience. The tone of each is informal; their rhetoric lacks the intensity of his political essays, and their form usually follows the journey pattern. The speaker in each essay narrates the progress of walks or small excursions, and he shows us several sights that heighten our awareness of the sensory qualities of the natural world. At times, he encourages readers to experience nature vicariously through his descriptions, while he also entertains them with wit and humor, and, at other times, he encourages them to explore philosophical topics like the symbolic meaning of the American West. All three walking essays follow a loose, organic form popular among romantic writers.

First published in *The Boston Miscellany* in January 1843, "A Walk to Wachusett," recounts a walking excursion that Thoreau took with Richard Fuller, Margaret Fuller's brother, in July of 1842, to the top of Mt. Wachusett near Worchester, Massachusetts. Following his usual practice, he used journal materials in composing this essay. He follows the journey or excursion organization, and he speaks in the familiar we. Thoreau's rhetoric is informal but marred at times by some overly formal phrasing and an overly abstract quality. This early essay lacks the concreteness and specificity typical of much of his later work. Numerous classical allusions permeate the essay, and this journey to Mount Wachusett resembles an excursion through a pastoral Greek landscape. The pastoral imagery is consistent, and he portrays rural citizens as stylized rustics. He stresses the differences between life seen from the plain and life seen from the mountain, and he creates the expectation that the hikers will experience some type of enlightenment at the mountain top. However, this disappointing enlightenment consists of large unified vistas and more pastoral imagery. Nevertheless, Thoreau realistically points out that there "was little of the sublimity and grandeur which belong to mountain scenery" (141). This early essay is an informal, fast-paced journey from the plain to the mountain top and back.

"A Winter Walk," the second walking essay in this section, which evolved primarily from his journal for 1841, was first published in *The Dial* in October 1843 and edited extensively by Emerson who objected to the paradoxical nature of some of Thoreau's phrasing (Harding and Meyer 37). This essay anticipates some of the richly textured nature description in *Walden*, but it is nevertheless an apprenticeship essay that shows Thoreau learning his craft. The essay is abstract, at times breezy in manner, and fast paced. Thoreau uses a familiar tone with his readers, and he uses the conventions of winter pastorals or winter idylls. He celebrates winter's pleasures, particularly those experienced after a fresh snow fall. Thoreau observes the crisp snow, the first travelers, the happy farmers, the frozen rivers and ponds, and the active ice skaters as he walks through a winter landscape. The essay gradually reveals a crisp, clean, invigorating and attractive winter scene. Allusions from classical mythology also permeate the essay.

"Walking" is by far the strongest of the three walking essays. Published in the *Atlantic Monthly* in June 1862, a month after his death, this selection is composed mainly of journal materials from 1850-1852. Thoreau delivered the lecture form of the essay in 1851, 1852, 1856, and 1857, and he eventually split it into two lectures. He revised the essay in the last few months of his life, submitting it to the *Atlantic* on March 11, 1862. "Walking" can be viewed as two compositions fused into one essay. The first section on walking discusses the joys of walking as an art, as spiritual journey, and as spontaneous behaviour. This section is witty, sometimes playful, and sometimes serious. He seriously explores the concept and promise of the American West as symbol and myth, alluding to America's westward movement and to the concept of the frontier. He celebrates the American landscape's power to inspire the imagination.

The second part of "Walking" is a discussion of the wild in which Thoreau argues for the value of wilderness and urges civilized people to return to the wild for sustenance and recreation. Contained here are evocative passages useful to environmental groups like the Sierra Club that effectively project the value of wilderness. This section contains the famous line "in wildness is the preservation of the world" (174) that was used as the title of a Sierra Club photographic study by Eliot Porter that illustrates passages from Thoreau's work. "Walking" is loosely organized and casually structured around the walking metaphor. The essay's main strength, however, lies in the strong evocative passages on diverse topics that can stand alone as unified prose compositions. Walking as a physical activity leads to intellectual explorations of several topics. Thoreau completes the essay by returning to the sauntering theme that began the essay.

Section III
Natural History Essays

Thoreau's natural history essays reveal a different side of Thoreau's mind. The essays in this third section present Thoreau as the poet-naturalist and synthesizer of nineteenth-century science and humanist thought. He reveals his interests in botany, biology, and natural history, and he reveals the classificatory and empirical side of his personality. Thoreau, we must recognize, was a professional surveyor who made his living through measuring and careful observation, an avocation that provided him with the leisure to pursue his explorations and his writing. As a scientific thinker, Thoreau, as Loren Eiseley points out in "Thoreau's Vision of the Natural World," is an anticipator and forerunner of the process philosophers who have

largely dominated the Twentieth Century. He stands at the border between existent and potential nature" (224). Eiseley identifies Thoreau as laying the foundations of the then unnamed science of ecology in his recognition of the flux, movement, and in-
tegration of the natural world (234).

The earliest natural history essay in this collection, "Natural History of Massachusetts," was first published in *The Dial* in
July 1842 and was derived from journal entries from 1837 to
1842. On the surface, this essay appears to be a review of a
Commonwealth of Massachusetts publication titled *Reports—
On the Fishes, Reptiles, and Birds, the Herbacious Plants and
Quadrupeds; the Insects Injurious to Vegetation; and the In-
vertabrate Animals of Massachusetts* put together by a state scientific committee. The composition is a nature essay combined
with several of Thoreau's own poems. Thoreau expresses joy in
the natural world, while he also provides a broad survey of the
natural features of Massachusetts which he often describes in a
poetic and enthusiastic tone. He discusses the birds of Massachusetts, the state's rivers, some of its small animals; its fish,
its turtles and snakes, its plants, and some of its coastal features.
In the last few pages, Thoreau finally discusses the report that he
intended to review, finding a few flaws, but essentially praising
the report for its specificity, detail, and pioneering role in cata-
loguing the natural history of the commonwealth.

"The Succession of Forest Trees" was first delivered to the
Middlesex Agricultural Society in Concord in September, 1860,
and first printed in the *New York Tribune* on October 6, 1860. It,
too, is derived from his journal, this time covering the period
from 1852 to 1860. This essay was also printed in the *Transactions
of the Middlesex Agricultural Society* for 1860 and reprinted in
abridged form in the *Eighth Annual Report of the Secretary of
the Massachusetts Board of Agriculture* for 1860. Thoreau, in
this essay, identifies the principle of tree succession in cut-over
or burnt forest areas, explaining the principle of succession
clearly and fully, while he also credits the naturalists Bartram
and Loudon for their ideas on this scientific principle. Although
Thoreau did not discover the principle of tree succession, his essay was the first well-developed presentation of the idea
(Harding and Meyer 59). He accumulated the data for his study
from his many years as a surveyor of woodlots and farms in the
Concord area—an activity that brought him in contact with
forests in various stages of development. As a naturalist, he was

caught in an ironic dilemma in his role as a surveyor of forests and woodlots destined in most cases for harvest, but his observations led him to insights into the principles of forest ecology. Thoreau's essay is precise, scientifically accurate, and as tightly organized as technical exposition. Thoreau, however, does not hesitate to add wit and charm to lighten this discussion and relax his audience. He begins with some carefully crafted ironic references to himself and adds some typical Thoreauvian puns and suggestive phrasing before delving into technical exposition. The essay's persona seems to be a humourous scientist rather than a poet-naturalist. He declares that anyone may come to "the Cattle Show, even a transcendentalist," refers to himself as one "who is distinguished for his oddity," and he makes several references to his work as a surveyor, mentioning instances in which his presence on a farm or woodlot surprised the landowner. He exclaims that "I have several times shown the proprietor the shortest way out of his woodlot" (213). He concludes the essay by returning to the humorous tone with a short narrative about his prize winning yellow squash, one of which weighed 123 1/2 pounds, and a short discussion of the symbolic meaning of seeds.

In "Autumnal Tints," Thoreau performs the role of the poet-naturalist at his best. Derived from his journal of 1851-1858 and used as a lecture as early as 1839, "Autumnal Tints" was published posthumously in October 1862 in the *Atlantic Monthly* and revised for publication in the last few months of his life. Fortunately, he was able to correct the proofs before his death. The essay itself is a poetic, imagistic account of the movement and types of New England fall foliage that stresses the dynamics of the fall color changes. It is both a feast of color and an optimistic celebration of Autumn. Throughout this essay, he deliberately uses subtitles to identify his topics and his transitions. He discusses "the Purple Grasses," "the Red Maple," "The Elm," "Fallen Leaves," "The Sugar Maple," and the "Scarlet Oak" at some length. While Thoreau's tone is upbeat and optimistic throughout this work, he occasionally assumes an elegaic tone consistent with his autumnal concerns, as when he declares that "When the leaves fall, the whole earth is a cemetary pleasant to walk in. I love to wander and muse over them in their graves" (240).

"Wild Apples," the final essay, originally delivered as a lecture before the Concord Lyceum on February 8, 1860, was first

published in November 1862 in the *Atlantic Monthly*. It is derived primarily from journal entries primarily from 1850 to
1852, and it was revised continuously until publication. It even
includes observations of the wild crab apple tree made during
his Minnesota journey in 1861. "Wild Apples" is a tightly organized composition that also relies on sub-headings to help establish its organization. The essay begins with "The History of the
Apple tree," and considers other topics like "The Wild Apple,"
"The Crab," "How the Wild Apple Grows," "The Fruit and its
Flavor," "Their Beauty," "The Naming of Them," "The Last
Gleaning," and "The Frozen-Thawed Apple." He begins the essay by tracing the mythological history of the apple in ancient
Greek and Roman mythology, and discussing its appearance in
the Old Testament and in the Scandinavian *Prose Eddas*. He
then proceeds to discuss the factual history of the apple in America. Thoreau gives a seemingly insignificant topic a mythic and
universal significance that seems to paint the apple's history as
courageous and heroic. In the remainder of the essay, he exhibits an encyclopedic knowledge of apples that reflects his com-
petence as a natural historian. "Wild Apples" included several
typical Thoreauvian themes—love of the landscape, delight in
natural processes, symbolic use of natural objects, fascination
with the derivation of names and words, and a concern with
travel and walking. He treats both his love of the land and his
fascination with wild apples in the same affectionate manner.

Thoreau's natural history essays have also attracted much
recent scholarly attention. The recent increase in interest in nature writing as a literary form and in natural history as a theme
and subject for literature has also helped attract readers and
scholars to Thoreau's treatment of nature in these essays and in
his more comprehensive works like *Walden* and *The Maine
Woods*. Moreover, the new critical approach of ecocriticism,
through which critics examine literature to explicate ecological
or environmental concerns and issues, has found a rich field for
analyis in Thoreau's work. The rapid growth after 1990 of the
Association for the Study of Literature and the Environment has
also contributed to the evolution of an academic culture that
values natural history writing.

Several recent books exemplify this new interest in
Thoreau as a nature writer and natural historian. Scott Slovic's
Seeking Awareness in American Nature Writing (1992) devotes
a chapter to Thoreau's modes of perceiving the natural world in

his journals, and Laura Dassow Walls explores Thoreau's scientific beliefs and attitudes as well as his relationship to nineteenth-century natural science in her 1995 book *Seeking New Worlds: Henry David Thoreau and Nineteenth-Century Natural Science.* Futhermore, Lawrence Buell's *The Environmental Imagination: Thoreau: Nature Writing, and the Formation of American Culture* (1995) has been very influential in calling scholarly attention to Thoreau's environmental imagination in *Walden* and the natural history essays. Buell offers a discussion of environmental and ecological themes in Thoreau's works that re-evaluates Thoreau's achievements in light of his treatment of ecological themes and concepts.

Thoreau made important contributions to the essay tradition in America. He established what I would call a Thoreauvian tradition in American literary nonfiction. In the Twentieth Century, for instance, many authors of literary nonfiction whose works are book length essays or collections of essays have produced works resembling Thoreau's in theme, style, viewpoint, or attitude. At times these essayists critique industrial culture, explore natural history or pursue environmental topics. I do not wish to overstate the case, arguing for too direct an influence, but these authors have all read Thoreau and have taken him to heart. Within this tradition, I would place Annie Dillard in *Pilgrim at Tinker Creek,* John McPhee in some of his works like *Survival of the Bark Canoe* and *The Pine Barrens,* Edward Abbey in *Down the River* and many others works, Aldo Leopold in *Sand County Almanac,* Loren Eiseley in numerous essays and books, E. B. White in numerous essays, and Edward Hoagland in *Journey to the Century Before, Walking the Dead Diamond River* and others works. Additional authors, too numerous to mention here, are certainly associated with this Thoreauvian tradition. Thoreau's concerns and his approachs to writing are still very much alive.

These are Thoreau's specific contributions to the American essay tradition. In his essays, he treated the land and natural objects as natural facts that became metaphors and symbols. Indeed, all nature became metaphor in Thoreau's hands. He was able to extract maximum meaning from nature's minutia, seeing apples, say, in universal ways, seeing the local, the regional, and the particular as symbolic and broadly significant. He also helped develop the essay as a vehicle for social criticism in which social and political injustices could be carefully and powerfully criticized and dissected. Significantly, his critiques of specific government policies are also carefully integrated with theory in an unobtrusive way. The specific examples that he uses are presented as embodying his political and ethical philosophies or as somehow supporting his philosophical positions. He skillfully blends philosophy and example, general and specific, in apparently seamless ways. Thoreau the essayist is also the master of often-imitated clear, precise concrete description.

Thoreau's range of styles and topics is also part of his legacy. He is not simply a natural historian; he is also social critic, informal essayist, polemicist, and architect of poetic prose in his essays and frequently in his journals. As a master of informal prose, he uses techniques from that genre in nearly all forms of his essays. Attractive, relaxed personas appear in several essays, and his penchant for wit and wordplay are common, as in the introduction to the otherwise serious "Succession of Forest Trees." Of all the elements of the essay form, Thoreau is most adept at the sentence; indeed, he is a virtuoso with sentence form, frequently using the ancient technique of sententia when he carefully crafts compact, pithy, suggestive aphorisms and paradoxes. Short, compact, suggestive sentences are his trademark, and the essays are full of memorable sentences that in an earlier age would have found their way into commonplace books. His approach to truth and understanding in the essay is often paradoxical, and he uses the aphorism as the main vehicle for expressing these paradoxes. Thoreau, in the essays, also frequently uses the cumulative sentence form, mentioned earlier, which is ideal for narrative and descriptive writing. These long sentences tend to follow a pattern in which the main idea of the sentence is stated as an independent clause to start the sentence and is then followed by modifying phrases, clauses, and words that often copiously amplify the main idea. These modifiers often create images and perspectives that successfully develop the main idea in a way that enriches the texture of his prose. Such sentences, commonly associated with Faulkner's prose, frequently add a very visual and sensory quality to Thoreau's representational writing, while they also help involve readers in the content of his essays.

In his journals and in his correspondence, Thoreau frequently stated his opinions on his writing and on prose writing in general. While a full explication of his philosophy of writing is more complex than the scope of this essay allows, a brief explanation of some of his main ideas on writing may cast some light on his rhetorical practice in the essays. Thoreau felt that writers must possess great personal integrity. They must speak for themselves and not for others, and they must have an authentic personal voice reflected in their choice of subject matter and themes. He was skeptical of writers who simply gave the public whatever it seemed to desire. The true writer, he thought, must be sincere, honest, and forthright (J 3:99, 157, in 1851). This approach is clearly evident in *Walden* and in several essays in this collection like "Civil Disobedience," and "A Plea for Captain John Brown." The effective writer will be able to use the integrity of his own life and beliefs as rhetorical capital for honest writing as Thoreau did in "Civil Disobedience," for example, as he recounts his time in jail. For a more detailed discussion of Thoreau's philosophy of writing and rhetoric, see my 1993 book *Essays on Henry David Thoreau: Rhetoric, Style, and Audience*.

He also felt that the effective writer must be a keen observer and student of life and nature. In his journals, he repeatedly refers to writers as seers and examiners, arguing that the abilty to see and experience the world deeply is a major source of the writer's power. "A man must see before he can say," he tells us in 1854 (J 6:236-237). However, he believed that objective observation is only myth, revealing his lack of faith in the Lockean notion of empirical perception. He saw perception as subjective and mediated. Facts could be perceived in such a way as to make them mythological and universal in significance. To the open, inquiring mind, small facts suggest large ideas (J 3:85, 1851). Thoreau's essays are full of careful observation and understanding of nature and natural facts expressed mythologically and universally. His metaphorical and synecdochic use of natural images provides another example.

Related to this notion of perception is his theory of the writer's journal. As the previous discussion illustrates, he used his journal extensively to provide material for his lectures and published essays, and he was so very conscious of the role his journals played in his own composing processes that he developed a philosophy for their use. Basically, he thought of the journal as a seed bed for ideas (J 2: 101, in 1850) and as a "nest-egg by the side of which more [ideas] will be laid" (J 3:217, in 1852). He also defined the journal as a record of experiences and growth, not a preserve of things well done or said (J 8: 134, in

1856). It was a place to test new ideas and thoughts as well as a place for unplanned writing. Journal writers should not, he felt, choose their subjects strategically or too meticulously plan their entries. He wrote what moved him on a given day, and he recorded thoughts related to his experiences. Significantly, he speaks of his journal as a route to discovery, where a writer might metaphorically, at least, discover the wealth of India (*J* 1: 182, in 1841).

On prose style, Thoreau was an organicist who believed that style often derived from thought. The writer's most important task was to discover and effectively write the truth; style would follow but not precede the truth, and the writer's subject would be more important than ornament or decoration. He clearly reacted against the neo-classical idea of style as ornament or decoration. He favored a plain style, at least philosophically, that reflected the vocabulary and rhythms of popular speech, and he often spoke well of the speaking and writing styles of farmers and laborers. In essence, he took a romantic, transcendentalist approach to style in which the honest writer or speaker would be concerned with the truth first, and the appropriate expression of the writer's subject would take precedence over artifice and the ornaments of style. Such a style would seem natural and partake of colloquial rhetoric, drawing its rhythms from the speech of farmers and laborers, and be populist in spirit (*J* 3:278-279, in 1852; *J* 1:342-344, in 1842). In 1852, he tells us that "I do not believe that any writer who considered the ornaments and not the truth simply, ever succeeded" (*J* 3:278-279).

Related to style are Thoreau's thoughts on sentences, perhaps, his most effective unit of composition. He claims that sentences should be simple and suggestive, having "The strength and compactness of masonry" and in which "simplicity is exuberant" (*J* 1:343, in 1842). He also claimed that "Every natural form—palm leaves and acorns, oak leaves and sumach and dodder are untranslatable aphorisms" (*J* 1:380, 1845). His comments appear to describe the compact aphoristic sentences common throughout his essays.

Finally, the selection of essays presented here provides the best of Thoreau's rich achievements in this form. Some of the essays anticipate *Walden* (1854), while others represent his mature and evolving thought. Some reflect his deeply held political convictions, while still others reveal his interest in and knowledge of natural history. Here I have presented Thoreau the political, ethical, and economic philosopher, Thoreau the meditative hiker and saunterer, and Thoreau the natural historian and poet-naturalist.

List of Works Cited

Buell, Lawrence. *The Environmental Imagination: Thoreau, Nature Writing, and the Formation of American Culture.* Cambridge: Harvard University Press, 1995.

Dillman, Richard. *Essays on Henry David Thoreau: Rhetoric, Style, and Audience.* West Cornwall, Connecticut: Locust Hill Press, 1993.

—. "Thoreau's Psychological Rhetoric." Diss. University of Oregon, 1978. Much of the theoretical foundation for Thoreau's rhetoric is drawn from this source.

Eiseley, Loren. "Thoreau's Vision of the Natural World." *The Star Thrower.* Intro. by W. H. Auden. New York: Harcourt, Brace, Jovanovich, 1978.

Emerson, Ralph Waldo. "The American Scholar." *Nature Addresses and Lectures. The Complete Works of Ralph Waldo Emerson.* Vol. IV. Boston: Houghton Mifflin Company, 1903. 79-115.

—. "The Poet." *Essays by Ralph Waldo Emerson, Second Series. The Complete Works of Ralph Waldo Emerson.* Vol. III. Boston: Houghton Mifflin Company, 1903. 1-42.

Harding, Walter and Michael Meyer. *The New Thoreau Handbook.* New York: New York University Press, 1980. All basic factual information on the essays, including dates and circumstances of publication and the history of the essays as journal entries and lectures, is from this volume.

Porter, Eliot. *From Henry David Thoreau, "In Wildness is the Preservation of the World."* New York: Sierra Club, Ballantine Books, 1962.

Slovic, Scott. *Seeking Awareness in American Nature Writing: Henry Thoreau, Annie Dillard, Edward Abbey, Wendell Berry, Barry Lopez.* Salt Lake City: University of Utah Press, 1992.

Thoreau, Henry David. *The Journal of Henry David Thoreau.* Ed. Bradford Torrey and Francis H. Allen. 14 vols. New York: Dover, 1962. Thoreau's *Journal* is referred to as *J* in internal citations.

—. *Walden.* Princeton: Princeton University Press, 1973.

Walls, Laura Dassow. *Seeing New Worlds: Henry David Thoreau and Nineteenth-Century Natural Science.* Madison: The University of Wisconsin Press, 1995.

Suggested Bibliography for Thoreau's Essays

Albrecht, Robert. "Conflict and Resolution: "Slavery in Massachusetts." *ESQ: Journal of the American Renaissance* 19 (1973): 179-188.

—. "Thoreau and His Audience: 'A Plea For Captain John Brown.'" *American Literature* 32 (1961): 393-402.

Berger, Michael. "The Saunterer's Vision: Henry Thoreau's Epiphany of Forest Dynamics in 'The Dispersion of Seeds.'" *The Concord Saunterer* 4 (1996): 45-71.

Buell, Lawrence. *The Environmental Imagination: Thoreau, Nature Writing, and the Formation of American Culture.* Cambridge: Harvard University Press, 1995.

—. *Literary Transcendentalism: Style and Vision in the American Renaissance.* Ithaca: Cornell University Press, 1973.

Burbick, Joan. *Thoreau's Alternative History: Changing Perspectives on Nature, Culture, and Language.* Philadelphia: University of Pennsylvania Press, 1987.

Cameron, Sharon. *Writing Nature: Henry David Thoreau's Journal.* Chicago: University of Chicago Press, 1989.

Channing, Edward T. *Lectures Read to the Seniors at Harvard College.* Eds. Dorothy Anderson and Waldo Braden. Carbondale: Southern Illinois University Press, 1968.

Dillman, Richard. *Essays on Henry David Thoreau: Rhetoric Style and Audience.* West Cornwall, Connecticut, Locust Hill Press, 1993.

—. "The Long Shadow of Thoreau: The Thoreauvian Tradition in Twentieth-Century American Nonfiction." *Essays on Henry David Thoreau: Rhetoric, Style, and Audience.* West Cornwall, Connecticut: Locust Hill Press, 1993.

—. "Thoreau's Harvard Education in Rhetoric and Composition: 1833-37." *Thoreau Journal Quarterly* 8.3 and 4 (1981): 47-62.

—. "Thoreau's Philosophy of Audience." *The Bucknell Review* 31.2 (1988): 74-85.

—. "Thoreau's Philosophy of Rhetorical Invention." *The Bucknell Review* 31.2 (1988): 60-73.

—. "Thoreau's Psychological Rhetoric." Diss. University of Oregon, 1978.

—. "Thoreau's Philosophy of Style." *The Bucknell Review* 31.2 (1988): 86-96.

Duban, James. "Conscience and Consciousness: The Liberal Christian Context of Thoreau's Political Ethics." *The New England Quarterly* 60 (1987): 208-222.

Duban, James. "Garrison and Dymond: Unbending Firmness of Mind." *American Literature* 57 (1985): 309-317

Eiseley, Loren. "Thoreau's Vision of the Natural World." *The Star Thrower.* Intro. by W. H. Auden. New York: Harcourt, Brace, Jovanovich, 1978.

Fink, Steven. "Thoreau and His Audience in 'Natural History of Massachusetts.'" *The Bucknell Review* 28 (1983): 65-80.

Friesen, Carl. "Thoreau's Sauntering: The Adventure of the Day." *The Concord Saunterer* 2, new series (1994): 21-31.

Fuller, David. "Correcting the Newspapers: Thoreau and 'A Plea for Captain John Brown.'" *The Concord Saunterer* 5, new series (1997): 165-175.

Golemba, Henry. *Thoreau's Wild Rhetoric.* New York: New York University Press, 1990.

—. "Unreading Thoreau." *American Literature* 60 (1988): 385-401.

Gura, Phillip. "Henry Thoreau and the Wisdom of Words." *New England Quarterly* 52 (1979): 38-54.

—. "Language and Meaning: An American Tradition." *American Literature* 53 (1981): 1-21.

Harding, Walter. *The Days of Henry David Thoreau: A Biography.* New York: Dover Publications, 1962.

—. "The Influence of Thoreau's Lecturing on His Writing." *Bulletin of the New York Public Library* 60 (1956): 74-80.

—. and Michael Meyer. *The New Thoreau Handbook.* New York: New York University Press, 1980.

—. "Thoreau on the Lecture Platform." *New England Quarterly* 24 (1951): 365-375.

Hildebidle, John. *A Naturalist's Liberty.* Cambridge: Harvard University Press, 1983.

Hoag, Ronald, Wesley. "Thoreau's Later Natural History Writings." *The Cambridge Companion To Henry David Thoreau.* Ed. Joel Myerson. Cambridge: Cambridge University Press, 1995. 152-170.

Hoeltje, Hubert H. "Thoreau as Lecturer." *New England Quarterly* 19 (1946): 485-494.

Kritzberg, Barry. "Thoreau. Slavery, and 'Resistance to Civil Government.'" *Massachusetts Review* 30 (1989): 535-565.

Orth, Michael. "The Prose Style of Henry David Thoreau" *Language and Style* 7 (1974): 36-52.

Richardson, Robert. *Henry Thoreau: A Life of the Mind.* Berkeley: University of California Press, 1986.

Schneider, Richard, ed. *Approaches to Teaching Thoreau's Walden and Other Works.* New York: Modern Language Association of America, 1996.

Simpson, Jeffrey. "Thoreau: The Walking Muse." *ESQ: A Journal of the American Renaissance* 37 (1991): 1-33.

Slovic, Scott. *Seeking Awareness in American Nature Writing: Henry Thoreau, Annie Dillard, Edward Abbey, Wendell Berry, Barry Lopez.* Salt Lake City: University of Utah Press, 1992.

Stull, William. "Action from Principle: Thoreau's Transcendental Economics." *English Language Notes* 22 (1984): 58-62.

Van Anglen, Kevin. "True Pulpit Power: 'The Natural History of Massachusetts' and the Problem of Cultural Authenticity." *Studies in the American Renaissance.* Ed. Joel Myerson. Charlottesville: University of Virginia Press, 1990. 119-147.

Walls, Laura, Dassow. *Seeing New Worlds: Henry David Thoreau and Nineteenth-Century Natural Science.* Madison: University of Wisconsin Press, 1995.

West, Michael. "Charles Kraitsir's Influence Upon Thoreau's Theory of Language." *ESQ: Journal of the American Renaissance* 4 (1973): 262-274.

—. "Thoreau and the Language Theories of the French Enlightenment." *Journal of English Literary History* 51 (1984): 747-770.

Yu, Ning. "'The Poem of Concord' and the Structure of Thoreau's 'Natural History of Massachuetts.'" *Colby Quarterly* 31 (1995): 68-78.

A Note on The Text

The essays in this collection originally appeared in the periodicals mentioned in the critical introduction. The texts for the essays in this collection are from the standard 1906 *Walden* or Manuscript Edition of Thoreau's works. The political and ethical essays are from the "Miscellanies" section of Volume 4, and the informal walking essays and the natural history essays are from the "Excursions" section of Volume 5. The full citation is *The Writings of Henry David Thoreau*. Walden Edition. Vols. 4 and 5. Boston: Houghton Mifflin, 1906.

Section I

Reform Essays:
Politics and Ethics

PARADISE (TO BE) REGAINED[1]
1843

We learn that Mr. Etzler is a native of Germany, and originally published his book in Pennsylvania, ten or twelve years
ago; and now a second English edition, from the original American one, is demanded by his readers across the water, owing, we
suppose, to the recent spread of Fourier's doctrines. It is one of
the signs of the times. We confess that we have risen from reading this book with enlarged ideas, and grander conceptions of
our duties in this world. It did expand us a little. It is worth attending to, if only that it entertains large questions. Consider
what Mr. Etzler proposes:—

"Fellow-men! I promise to show the means of creating a
paradise within ten years, where everything desirable for human
life may be had by every man in superabundance, without labor,
and without pay; where the whole face of nature shall be
changed into the most beautiful forms, and man may live in the
most magnificent palaces, in all imaginable refinements of lux-
ury, and in the most delightful gardens; where he may accomplish, without labor, in one year, more than hitherto could be
done in thousands of years; may level mountains, sink valleys,
create lakes, drain lakes and swamps, and intersect the land
everywhere with beautiful canals, and roads for transporting
heavy loads of many thousand tons, and for traveling one thousand miles in twenty-four hours; may cover the ocean with
floating islands movable in any desired direction with immense
power and celerity, in perfect security, and with all comforts and
luxuries, bearing gardens and palaces, with thousands of families, and provided with rivulets of sweet water; may explore the
interior of the globe, and travel from pole to pole in a fortnight;
provide himself with means, unheard of yet, for increasing his
knowledge of the world, and so his intelligence; lead a life of

continual happiness, of enjoyments yet unknown: free himself
from almost all the evils that afflict mankind, except death, and
even put death far beyond the common period of human life,
and finally render it less afflicting. Mankind may thus live in
and enjoy a new world, far superior to the present, and raise
themselves far higher in the scale of being."

It would seem from this and various indications beside,
that there is a transcendentalism in mechanics as well as in
ethics. While the whole field of the one reformer lies beyond
the boundaries of space, the other is pushing his schemes for the
elevation of the race to its utmost limits. While one scours the
heavens, the other sweeps the earth. One says he will reform
himself, and then nature and circumstances will be right. Let us
not obstruct ourselves, for that is the greatest friction. It is of little importance though a cloud obstruct the view of the astronomer compared with his own blindness. The other will reform nature and circumstances, and then man will be right.
Talk no more vaguely, says he, of reforming the world,—I will
reform the globe itself. What matters it whether I remove this
humor out of my flesh, or this pestilent humor from the fleshy
part of the globe? Nay, is not the latter the more generous
course? At present the globe goes with a shattered constitution
in its orbit. Has it not asthma, and ague, and fever, and dropsy,
and flatulence, and pleurisy, and is it not afflicted with vermin?
Has it not its healthful laws counteracted, and its vital energy
which will yet redeem it? No doubt the simple powers of nature, properly directed by man, would make it healthy and a paradise; as the laws of man's own constitution but wait to be
obeyed, to restore him to health and happiness. Our panaceas
cure but few ails, our general hospitals are private and exclusive.
We must set up another Hygeia than is now worshipped. Do
not the quacks even direct small doses for children, larger for
adults, and larger still for oxen and horses? Let us remember
that we are to prescribe for the globe itself.

This fair homestead has fallen to us, and how little have
we done to improve it, how little have we cleared and hedged
and ditched! We are too inclined to go hence to a "better land,"
without lifting a finger, as our farmers are moving to the Ohio
soil; but would it not be more heroic and faithful to till and redeem this New England soil of the world? The still youthful
energies of the globe have only to be directed in their proper
channel. Every gazette brings accounts of the untutored freaks of

the wind,—shipwrecks and hurricanes which the mariner and planter accept as special or general providences; but they touch our consciences, they remind us of our sins. Another deluge would disgrace mankind. We confess we never had much respect for that antediluvian race. A thoroughbred business man cannot enter heartily upon the business of life without first looking into his accounts. How many things are now at loose ends! Who knows which way the wind will blow to-morrow? Let us not succumb to nature. We will marshal the clouds and restrain tempests; we will bottle up pestilent exhalations; we will probe for earthquakes, grub them up, and give vent to the dangerous gas; we will disembowel the volcano, and extract its poison, take its seed out. We will wash water, and warm fire, and cool ice, and underprop the earth. We will teach birds to fly, and fishes to swim, and ruminants to chew the cud. It is time we had looked into these things.

And it becomes the moralist, too, to inquire what man might do to improve and beautify the system; what to make the stars shine more brightly, the sun more cheery and joyous, the moon more placid and content. Could he not heighten the tints of flowers and the melody of birds? Does he perform his duty to the inferior races? Should he not be a god to them? What is the part of magnanimity to the whale and the beaver? Should we not fear to exchange places with them for a day, lest by their behavior they should shame us? Might we not treat with magnanimity the shark and the tiger, not descend to meet them on their own level, with spears of shark's teeth and bucklers of tiger's skin? We slander the hyena; man is the fiercest and cruelest animal. Ah! he is of little faith; even the erring comets and meteors would thank him, and turn his kindness in their kind.

How meanly and grossly do we deal with nature! Could we not have a less gross labor? What else do these fine inventions suggest,—magnetism, the daguerreotype, electricity? Can we not do more than cut and trim the forest?—can we not assist in its interior economy, in the circulation of the sap? Now we work superficially and violently. We do not suspect how much might be done to improve our relation to animated nature even; what kindness and refined courtesy there might be.

There are certain pursuits which, if not wholly poetic and true, do at least suggest a nobler and finer relation to nature than we know. The keeping of bees, for instance, is a very slight interference. It is like directing the sunbeams. All nations, from the remotest antiquity, have thus fingered nature. There are Hymettus and Hybla, and how many bee-renowned spots beside! There is nothing gross in the idea of these little herds,—their hum like the faintest low of kine in the meads. A pleasant reviewer has lately reminded us that in some places they are led out to pasture where the flowers are most abundant. "Columella tells us," says he, "that the inhabitants of Arabia sent their hives into Attica to benefit by the later-blowing flowers." Annually are the hives, in immense pyramids, carried up the Nile in boats, and suffered to float slowly down the stream by night, resting by day, as the flowers put forth along the banks; and they determine the richness of any locality, and so the profitableness of delay, by the sinking of the boat in the water. We are told, by the same reviewer, of a man in Germany, whose bees yielded more honey than those of his neighbors, with no apparent advantage; but at length he informed them, that he had turned his hives one degree more to the east, and so his bees, having two hours the start in the morning, got the first sip of honey. True, there is treachery and selfishness behind all this, but these things suggest to the poetic mind what might be done.

Many examples there are of a grosser interference, yet not without their apology. We saw last summer, on the side of a mountain, a dog employed to churn for a farmer's family, traveling upon a horizontal wheel, and though he had sore eyes, an alarming cough, and withal a demure aspect, yet their bread did get buttered for all that. Undoubtedly, in the most brilliant successes, the first rank is always sacrificed. Much useless traveling of horses, *in extenso*, has of late years been improved for man's behoof, only two forces being taken advantage of,—the gravity of the horse, which is the centripetal, and his centrifugal inclination to go ahead. Only these two elements in the calculation. And is not the creature's whole economy better economized thus? Are not all finite beings better pleased with motions relative than absolute? And what is the great globe itself but such a wheel,—a larger treadmill,—so that our horse's freest steps over prairies are oftentimes balked and rendered of no avail by the earth's motion on its axis? But here he is the central agent and motive-power; and, for variety of scenery, being provided with a window in front, do not the ever-varying activity and fluctuating energy of the creature himself work the effect of the most varied scenery on a country road? It must be confessed that horses at present work too exclusively for men, rarely men for hones; and the brute degenerates in man's society.

It will be seen that we contemplate a time when man's will shall be law to the physical world, and he shall no longer be deterred by such abstractions as time and space, height and depth, weight and hardness, but shall indeed be the lord of creation. "Well," says the faithless reader, "'life is short, but art is long'; where is the power that will effect all these changes?" This it is the very object of Mr. Etzler's volume to show. At present, he would merely remind us that there are innumerable and immeasurable powers already existing in nature, unimproved on a large scale, or for generous and universal ends, amply sufficient for these purposes. He would only indicate their existence, as a surveyor makes known the existence of a water-power on any stream; but for their application he refers us to a sequel to this book, called the "Mechanical System." A few of the most obvious and familiar of these powers are the Wind, the Tide, the Waves, the Sunshine. Let us consider their value.

First, there is the power of the Wind, constantly exerted over the globe. It appears from observation of a sailing-vessel, and from scientific tables, that the average power of the wind is equal to that of one horse for every one hundred square feet. We do not attach much value to this statement of the comparative power of the wind and horse, for no common ground is mentioned on which they can he compared. Undoubtedly, each is incomparably excellent in its way, and every general comparison made for such practical purposes as are contemplated, which gives a preference to the one, must be made with some unfairness to the other. The scientific tables are, for the most part, true only in a tabular sense. We suspect that a loaded wagon, with a light sail, ten feet square, would not have been blown so far by the end of the year, under equal circumstances, as a common racer or dray horse would have drawn it. And how many crazy structures on our globe's surface, of the same dimensions, would wait for dry-rot if the traces of one horse were hitched to them, even to their windward side? Plainly this is not the principle of comparison. But even the steady and constant force of the horse may be rated as equal to his weight at least. Yet we should prefer to let the zephyrs and gales bear, with all their weight, upon our fences, than that Dobbin, with feet braced, should lean ominously against them for a season.

Nevertheless, here is an almost incalculable power at our disposal, yet how trifling the use we make of it! It only serves to turn a few mills, blow a few vessels across the ocean, and a few trivial ends besides. What a poor compliment do we pay to our indefatigable and energetic servant!

Men having discovered the power of falling water, which, after all, is comparatively slight, how eagerly do they seek out and improve these *privileges*! Let a difference of but a few feet in level he discovered on some stream near a populous town, some slight occasion for gravity to act, and the whole economy of the neighborhood is changed at once. Men do indeed speculate about and with this power as if it were the only privilege. But meanwhile this aerial stream is falling from far greater heights with more constant flow, never shrunk by drought, offering mill-sites wherever the wind blows; a Niagara in the air, with no Canada side;—only the application is hard.

There are the powers, too, of the Tide and Waves, constantly ebbing and flowing, lapsing and relapsing, but they serve man in but few ways. They turn a few tide-mills, and perform a few other insignificant and accidental services only. We all perceive the effect of the tide; how imperceptibly it creeps up into our harbors and rivers, and raises the heaviest navies as easily as the lightest chip. Everything that floats must yield to it. But man, slow to take nature's constant hint of assistance, makes slight and irregular use of this power, in careening ships and getting them afloat when aground.

This power may be applied in various ways. A large body, of the heaviest materials that will float, may first be raised by it, and being attached to the end of a balance reaching from the land, or from a stationary support fastened to the bottom, when the tide falls the whole weight will be brought to bear upon the end of the balance. Also, when the tide rises, it may be made to exert a nearly equal force in the opposite direction. It can be employed wherever a *point d'appui* can be obtained.

Verily, the land would wear a busy aspect at the spring and neap tide, and these island ships, these *terrae infirmae*, which realize the fables of antiquity, affect our imagination. We have often thought that the fittest locality for a human dwelling was on the edge of the land, that there the constant lesson and impression of the sea might sink deep into the life and character of the landsman, and perhaps impart a marine tint to his imagination. It is a noble word, that *mariner*,—one who is conversant with the sea. There should he more of what it signifies in each of us. It is a worthy country to belong to,—we look to see him not disgrace it. Perhaps we should be equally mariners and terreners, and even our Green Mountains need some of that sea-green to be mixed with them.

The computation of the power of the Waves is less satisfactory. While only the average power of the wind and the average height of the tide were taken before, now the extreme height of the waves is used, for they are made to rise ten feet above the level of the sea, to which, adding ten more for depression, we have twenty feet, or the extreme height of a wave. Indeed, the power of the waves, which is produced by the wind blowing obliquely and at disadvantage upon the water, is made to be, not only three thousand times greater than that of the tide, but one hundred times greater than that of the wind itself, meeting its object at right angles. Moreover, this power is measured by the area of the vessel, and not by its length mainly, and it seems to be forgotten that the motion of the waves is chiefly undulatory, and exerts a power only within time limits of a vibration, else the very continents, with their extensive coasts, would soon be set adrift.

Finally, there is the power to be derived from Sunshine, by the principle on which Archimedes contrived his burning-mirrors, a multiplication of mirrors reflecting the rays of the sun upon the same spot, till the requisite degree of heat is obtained. The principal application of this power will be to the boiling of water and production of steam. So much for these few and more obvious powers, already used to a trifling extent. But there are innumerable others in nature, not described nor discovered. These, however, will do for the present. This would be to make the sun and the moon equally our satellites. For, as the moon is the cause of the tides, and the sun the cause of the wind, which, in turn, is the cause of the waves, all the work of this planet would be performed by these far influences.

"We may store up water in some eminent pond, and take out of this store, at any time, as much water through the outlet as we want to employ, by which means the original power may react for many days after it has ceased. . . . Such reservoirs of moderate elevation or size need not be made artificially, but will be found made by nature very frequently, requiring but little aid for their completion. They require no regularity of form. Any valley, with lower grounds in its vicinity, would answer the purpose. Small crevices may be filled up. Such places may be eligible for the beginning of enterprises of this kind."

The greater the height, of course, the less water required. But suppose a level and dry country; then hill and valley, and "eminent pond," are to be constructed by main force; or, if the springs are unusually low, then dirt and stones may be used, and the disadvantage arising from friction will he counterbalanced by their greater gravity. Nor shall a single rood of dry land be sunk in such artificial ponds as may be wanted, but their surfaces "may be covered with rafts decked with fertile earth, and all kinds of vegetables which may grow there as well as anywhere else."

And, finally, by the use of thick envelopes retaining the heat, and other contrivances, "the power of steam caused by sunshine may react at will, and thus be rendered perpetual, no matter how often or how long the sunshine may be interrupted."

Here is power enough, one would think, to accomplish somewhat. These are the Powers below. O ye mill-wrights, ye engineers, ye operatives and speculators of every class, never again complain of a want of power: it is the grossest form of infidelity. The question is, not how we shall execute, but what. Let us not use in a niggardly manner what is thus generously offered.

Consider what revolutions are to be effected in agriculture. First, in the new country a machine is to move along, taking out trees and stones to any required depth, and piling them up in convenient heaps; then the same machine, "with a little alteration," is to plane the ground perfectly, till there shall be no hills nor valleys, making the requisite canals, ditches, and roads as it goes along. The same machine, "with some other little alterations," is then to sift the ground thoroughly, supply fertile soil from other places if wanted, and plant it; and finally the same machine, "with a little addition," is to reap and gather in the crop, thresh and grind it, or press it to oil, or prepare it any way for final use. For the description of these machines we are referred to "Etzler's Mechanical System," pages 11 to 27. We should be pleased to see that "Mechanical System." We have great faith in it. But we cannot stop for applications now.

Who knows but by accumulating the power until the end of the present century, using meanwhile only the smallest allowance, reserving all that blows, all that shines, all that ebbs and flows, all that dashes, we may have got such a reserved accumulated power as to run the earth off its track into a new orbit, some summer, and so change the tedious vicissitude of the seasons? Or, perchance, coming generations will not abide the dissolution of the globe, but, availing themselves of future inventions in aerial locomotion, and the navigation of space, the entire race may migrate from the earth, to settle some vacant and more western planet, it may be still healthy, perchance unearthy, not composed of dirt and stones, whose primary strata only are strewn, and where no weeds are sown. It took but little art, a simple application of natural laws, a canoe, a paddle, and a sail of matting, to people the isles of the Pacific, and a little more will people the shining isles of space. Do we not see in the firmament the lights carried along the shore by night, as Columbus did? Let us not despair nor mutiny.

"The dwellings also ought to be very different from what is known, if the full benefit of our means is to be enjoyed. They are to be of a structure for which we have no name yet. They are to be neither palaces, nor temples, nor cities, but a combination of all, superior to whatever is known.

"Earth may be baked into bricks, or even vitrified stone by heat,—we may bake large masses of any size and form, into stone and vitrified substance of the greatest durability, lasting even thousands of years, out of clayey earth, or of stones ground to dust, by the application of burning-mirrors. This is to be done in the open air without other preparation than gathering the substance, grinding and mixing it with water and cement, moulding or casting it, and bringing the focus of the burning-mirrors of proper size upon the same."

The character of the architecture is to be quite different from what it ever has been hitherto; large solid masses are to be baked or cast in one piece, ready shaped in any form that may be desired. The building may, therefore, consist of columns two hundred feet high and upwards, of proportionate thickness, and of one entire piece of vitrified substance; huge pieces are to be moulded so as to join and hook on to each other firmly by proper joints and folds, and not to yield in any way without breaking.

"Foundries, of any description, are to be heated by burning-mirrors, and will require no labor, except the making of the first moulds and the superintendence for gathering the metal and taking the finished articles away."

Alas! in the present state of science, we must take the finished articles away; but think not that man will always be the victim of circumstances.

The countryman who visited the city, and found the streets cluttered with bricks and lumber, reported that it was not yet finished; and one who considers the endless repairs and reforming of our houses might well wonder when they will be done. But why may not the dwellings of men on this earth be built, once for all, of some durable material, some Roman or Etruscan masonry, which will stand, so that time shall only adorn and beautify them? Why may we not finish the outward world for posterity, and leave them leisure to attend to the inner? Surely, all the gross necessities and economies might be cared for in a few years. All might be built and baked and stored up, during this, the term-time of the world, against the vacant eternity, and the globe go provisioned and furnished, like our public vessels, for its voyage through space, as through some Pacific Ocean, while we would "tie up the rudder and sleep before the wind," as those who sail from Lima to Manilla.

But, to go back a few years in imagination, think not that life in these crystal palaces is to bear any analogy to life in our present humble cottages. Far from it. Clothed, once for all, in some "flexible stuff," more durable than George Fox's suit of leather, composed of "fibres of vegetables," "glutinated" together by some "cohesive substances," and made into sheets, like paper, of any size or form, man will put far from him corroding care and the whole host of ills.

"The twenty-five halls in the inside of the square are to be each two hundred feet square and high; the forty corridors, each one hundred feet long and twenty wide; the eighty galleries, each from 1,000 to 1,250 feet long; about 7,000 private rooms, the whole surrounded and intersected by the grandest and most splendid colonnades imaginable; floors, ceilings, columns, with their various beautiful and fanciful intervals, all shining, and reflecting to infinity all objects and persons, with splendid lustre of all beautiful colors, and fanciful shapes and pictures.

"All galleries, outside and within the halls, are to be provided with many thousand commodious and most elegant vehicles, in which persons may move up and down like birds, in perfect security, and without exertion. . . . Any member may procure himself all the common articles of his daily wants, by a short turn of some crank, without leaving his apartment.

"One or two persons are sufficient to direct the kitchen business. They have nothing else to do but to superintend the cookery, and to watch the time of the victuals being done, and then to remove them, with the table and vessels, into the dining-hall, or to the respective private apartments, by a slight motion of the hand at some crank. . . . *Any very extraordinary desire of person may be satisfied by going to the place where the thing is to be had; and anything that requires a particular preparation in cooking or baking may be done by the person who desires it.*"

This is one of those instances in which the individual genius is found to consent, as indeed it always does, at last, with the universal. This last sentence has a certain sad and sober truth, which reminds us of the scripture of all nations. All expression of truth does at length take this deep ethical form. Here is hint of a place the most eligible of any in space, and of a servitor, in comparison with whom all other helps dwindle into insignificance. We hope to hear more of him anon, for even a Crystal Palace would be deficient without his invaluable services.

And as for the environs of the establishment:—

"There will be afforded the most enrapturing views to be fancied, out of the private apartments, from the galleries, from the roof, from its turrets and cupolas,—gardens, as far as the eye can see, full of fruits and flowers, arranged in the most beautiful order, with walks, colonnades, aqueducts, canals, ponds, plains, amphitheatres, terraces, fountains, sculptural works, pavilions, gondolas, places for public amusement, etc., to delight the eye and fancy, the taste and smell. . . . The walks and roads are to be paved with hard vitrified large plates, so as to be always clean from all dirt in any weather or season. . . .

"The walks may be covered with porticoes adorned with magnificent columns, statues, and sculptural works; all of vitrified substance, and lasting forever. At night the roof and the inside and outside of the whole square are illuminated by gas-light, which, in the mazes of many-colored crystal-like colonnades and vaultings, is reflected with a brilliancy that gives to the whole a lustre of precious stones, as far as the eye can see. Such are the future abodes of men. . . . Such is the life reserved to true intelligence, but withheld from ignorance, prejudice, and stupid adherence to custom."

Thus is Paradise to be Regained, and that old and stern decree at length reversed. Man shall no more earn his living by the sweat of his brow. All labor shall be reduced to "a short turn of some crank," and "taking the finished articles away." But there is a crank,—oh, how hard to be turned! Could there not he a crank upon a crank,—an infinitely small crank?—we would fain inquire. No,—alas! not. But there is a certain divine energy in every man, but sparingly employed as yet, which may be called the crank within,—the crank after all,—the prime mover in all machinery,—quite indispensable to all work. Would that we might get our hands on its handle! In fact, no work can be shirked. It may be postponed indefinitely, but not infinitely. Nor can any really important work he made easier by coöperation or machinery. Not one particle of labor now threatening any man can he routed without being performed. It cannot be hunted out of the vicinity like jackals and hyenas. It will not run. You may begin by sawing the little sticks, or you may saw the great sticks first, but sooner or later you must saw them both.

We will not be imposed upon by this vast application of forces. We believe that most things will have to he accomplished still by the application called Industry. We are rather pleased, after all, to consider the small private, but both constant and accumulated, force which stands behind every spade in the field. This it is that makes the valleys shine, and the deserts really bloom. Sometimes, we confess, we are so degenerate as to reflect with pleasure on the days when men were yoked like cattle, and drew a crooked stick for a plow. After all, the great interests and methods were the same.

It is a rather serious objection to Mr. Etzler's schemes, that they require time, men and money, three very superfluous and inconvenient things for an honest and well-disposed man to deal with. "The whole world," he tells us, "might therefore be really changed into a paradise, within less than ten years, commencing from the first year of an association for the purpose of constructing and applying the machinery." We are sensible of a startling incongruity when time and money are mentioned in this connection. The ten years which are proposed would be a tedious while to wait, if every man were at his post and did his duty, but quite too short a period, if we are to take time for it. But this fault is by no means peculiar to Mr. Etzler's schemes.

There is far too much hurry and bustle, and too little patience and privacy, in all our methods, as if something were to be accomplished in centuries. The true reformer does not want time, nor money, nor coöperation, nor advice. What is time but the stuff delay is made of? And depend upon it, our virtue will not live on the interest of our money. He expects no income, but outgoes; so soon as we begin to count the cost, the cost begins. And as for advice, the information floating in the atmosphere of society is as evanescent and unserviceable to him as gossamer for clubs of Hercules. There is absolutely no common sense; it is common nonsense. If we are to risk a cent or a drop of our blood, who then shall advise us? For ourselves, we are too young for experience. Who is old enough? We are older by faith than by experience. In the unbending of the arm to do the deed there is experience worth all the maxims in the world.

"It will now be plainly seen that the execution of the proposals is not proper for individuals. Whether it be proper for government at this time, before the subject has become popular, is a question to be decided; all that is to be done is to step forth, after mature reflection, to confess loudly one's conviction, and to constitute societies. Man is powerful but in union with many. Nothing great, for the improvement of his own condition, or that of his fellow-men, can ever be effected by individual enterprise."

Alas! this is the crying sin of the age, this want of faith in the prevalence of a man. Nothing can be effected but by one man. He who wants help wants everything. True. This is the condition of our weakness, but it can never be the means of our recovery. We must first succeed alone, that we may enjoy our success together. We trust that the social movements which we witness indicate an aspiration not to be thus cheaply satisfied. In this matter of reforming the world, we have little faith in corporations; not thus was it first formed.

But our author is wise enough to say that the raw materials for the accomplishment of his purposes are "iron, copper, wood, earth chiefly, and a union of men whose eyes and understanding are not shut up by preconceptions." Ay, this last may be what we want mainly,—a company of "odd fellows" indeed.

"Small shares of twenty dollars will be sufficient"—in all, from "200,000 to 300,000"—"to create the first establishment for a whole community of from 3,000 to 4,000 individuals"; at the end of five years we shall have a principal of 200 millions of dollars, and so paradise will be wholly regained at the end of the tenth year. But, alas! the ten years have already elapsed, and there are no signs of Eden yet, for want of the requisite funds to begin the enterprise in a hopeful manner. Yet it seems a safe investment. Perchance they could be hired at a low rate, the property being mortgaged for security, and, if necessary, it could be given up in any stage of the enterprise, without loss, with the fixtures.

But we see two main difficulties in the way: first, the successful application of the powers by machinery (we have not yet seen the "Mechanical System"), and, secondly, which is infinitely harder, the application of man to the work by faith. This it is, we fear, which will prolong the ten years to ten thousand at least. It will take a power more than "80,000 times greater than all the men on earth could effect with their nerves" to persuade men to use that which is already offered them. Even a greater than this physical power must be brought to bear upon that moral power. Faith, indeed, is all the reform that is needed; it is itself a reform. Doubtless, we are as slow to conceive of Paradise as of Heaven, of a perfect natural as of a perfect spiritual world. We see how past ages have loitered and erred. "Is perhaps our generation free from irrationality and error? Have we perhaps reached now the summit of human wisdom, and need no more to look out for mental or physical improvement?" Undoubtedly, we are never so visionary as to be prepared for what the next hour may bring forth.

Μελλει το θειου δ' εστι τοιουτον φυσει.

The Divine is about to be, and such is its nature. In our wisest moments we are secreting a matter, which, like the lime of the shell-fish, incrusts us quite over, and well for us if, like it, we cast our shells from time to time, though they be pearl and of fairest tint. Let us consider under what disadvantages Science has hitherto labored before we pronounce thus confidently on her progress.

Mr. Etzler is not one of the enlightened practical men, the pioneers of the actual, who move with the slow, deliberate tread of science, conserving the world; who execute the dreams of the last century, though they have no dreams of their own; yet he deals in the very raw but still solid material of all inventions. He has more of the practical than usually belongs to so bold a schemer, so resolute a dreamer. Yet his success is in theory, and not in practice, and he feeds our faith rather than contents our understanding. His book wants order, serenity, dignity, everything,—but it does not fail to impart what only man can impart to man of much importance, his own faith. It is true his dreams are not thrilling nor bright enough, and he leaves off to dream where he who dreams just before the dawn begins. His castles in the air fall to the ground, because they are not built lofty enough; they should be secured to heaven's roof. After all, the theories and speculations of men concern us more than their puny accomplishment. It is with a certain coldness and languor that we loiter about the actual and so-called practical. How little do the most wonderful inventions of modern times detain us. They insult nature. Every machine, or particular application, seems a slight outrage against universal laws. How many fine inventions are there which do not clutter the ground? We think that those only succeed which minister to our sensible and animal wants, which bake or brew, wash or warm, or the like. But are those of no account which are patented by fancy and imagination, and succeed so admirably in our dreams that they give the tone still to our waking thoughts? Already nature is serving all those uses which science slowly derives on a much higher and grander scale to him that will he served by her. When the sunshine falls on the path of the poet, he enjoys all those pure benefits and pleasures which the arts slowly and partially realize from age to age. The winds which fan his cheek waft him the sum of that profit and happiness which their lagging inventions supply.

The chief fault of this book is, that it aims to secure the greatest degree of gross comfort and pleasure merely. It paints a Mahometan's heaven, and stops short with singular abruptness when we think it is drawing near to the precincts of the Christian's,—and we trust we have not made here a distinction without a difference. Undoubtedly if we were to reform this outward life truly and thoroughly, we should find no duty of the inner omitted. It would be employment for our whole nature; and what we should do thereafter would be as vain a question as to ask the bird what it will do when its nest is built and its brood reared. But a moral reform must take place first, and then the necessity of the other will be superseded, and we shall sail and plow by its force alone. There is a speedier way than the "Mechanical System" can show to fill up marshes, to drown the roar of the waves, to tame hyenas, secure agreeable environs, diversify the land, and refresh it with "rivulets of sweet water," and that is by the power of rectitude and true behavior. It is only for a little while, only occasionally, methinks, that we want a garden. Surely a good man need not be at the labor to level a hill for the sake of a prospect, or raise fruits and flowers, and construct floating islands, for the sake of a paradise. He enjoys better prospects than lie behind any hill. Where an angel travels it will be paradise all the way, but where Satan travels it will be burning marl and cinders. What says Veeshnoo Sarma? "He whose mind is at ease is possessed of all riches. Is it not the same to one whose foot is inclosed in a shoe, as if the whole surface of the earth were covered with leather?"

He who is conversant with the supernal powers will not worship these inferior deities of the wind, waves, tide, and sunshine. But we would not disparage the importance of such calculations as we have described. They are truths in physics, because they are true in ethics. The moral powers no one would presume to calculate. Suppose we could compare the moral with the physical, and say how many horse-power the force of love, for instance, blowing on every square foot of a man's soul, would equal. No doubt we are well aware of this force; figures would not increase our respect for it; the sunshine is equal to but one ray of its heat. The light of the sun is but the shadow of love. "The souls of men loving and fearing God," says Raleigh, "receive influence from that divine light itself, whereof the sun's clarity, and that of the stars, is by Plato called but a shadow. *Lumen est umbra Dei, Deus est Lumen Luminis*. Light is the shadow of God's brightness, who is the light of light," and, we may add, the heat of heat. Love is the wind, the tide, the waves, the sunshine. Its power is incalculable; it is many horse-power. It never ceases, it never slacks; it can move the globe without a resting-place; it can warm without fire; it can feed without meat; it can clothe without garments; it can shelter without roof; it can make a paradise within which will dispense with a paradise without. But though the wisest men in all ages have labored to publish this force, and every human heart is, sooner or later, more or less, made to feel it, yet how little is actually applied to social ends! True, it is the motive-power of all successful social machinery; but as in physics we have made the elements do only a little drudgery for us,—steam to take the place of a few horses, wind of a few oars, water of a few cranks and hand-mills,—as the mechanical forces have not yet been generously and largely applied to make the physical world answer to the ideal, so the power of love has been but meanly and sparingly applied, as yet. It has patented only such machines as the almshouse, the hospital, and the Bible Society, while its infinite wind is still blowing, and blowing down these very structures too, from time to time. Still less are we accumulating its power, and preparing to act with greater energy at a future time. Shall we not contribute our shares to this enterprise, then?

Note

[1] *The Paradise within the Reach of all Men, without Labor, by Powers of Nature and Machinery. An Address to all intelligent Men.* In Two Parts. By J. A. Etzler. Part First. Second English Edition. London. 1842. Pp. 55.

CIVIL DISOBEDIENCE
1849

I heartily accept the motto, "That government is best which governs least"; and I should like to see it acted up to more rapidly and systematically. Carried out, it finally amounts to this, which also I believe,—"That government is best which governs not at all"; and when men are prepared for it, that will be the kind of government which they will have. Government is at best but an expedient; but most governments are usually, and all governments are sometimes, inexpedient. The objections which have been brought against a standing army, and they are many and weighty, and deserve to prevail, may also at last be brought against a standing government. The standing army is only an arm of the standing government. The government itself, which is only the mode which the people have chosen to execute their will, is equally liable to be abused and perverted before the people can act through it. Witness the present Mexican war, the work of comparatively a few individuals using the standing government as their tool; for, in the outset, the people would not have consented to this measure.

This American government,—what is it but a tradition, though a recent one, endeavoring to transmit itself unimpaired to posterity, but each instant losing some of its integrity? It has not the vitality and force of a single living man; for a single man can bend it to his will. It is a sort of wooden gun to the people themselves. But it is not the less necessary for this; for the people must have some complicated machinery or other, and hear its din, to satisfy that idea of government which they have. Governments show thus how successfully men can be imposed on, even impose on themselves, for their own advantage. It is excellent, we must all allow. Yet this government never of itself furthered any enterprise, but by the alacrity with which it got out of its way. *It* does not keep the country free. *It* does not settle the West. *It* does not educate. The character inherent in the American people has done all that has been accomplished; and it would have done somewhat more, if the government had not sometimes got in its way. For government is an expedient by which men would fain succeed in letting one another alone; and, as has been said, when it is most expedient, the governed are most let alone by it. Trade and commerce, if they were not made of india-rubber, would never manage to bounce over the obstacles which legislators are continually putting in their way; and, if one were to judge these men wholly by the effects of their actions and not partly by their intentions, they would deserve to be classed and punished with those mischievous persons who put obstructions on the railroads.

But, to speak practically and as a citizen, unlike those who call themselves no-government men, I ask for, not at once no government, but *at once* a better government. Let every man make known what kind of government would command his respect, and that will be one step toward obtaining it.

After all, the practical reason why, when the power is once in the hands of the people, a majority are permitted, and for a long period continue, to rule is not because they are most likely to be in the right, nor because this seems fairest to the minority, but because they are physically the strongest. But a government in which the majority rule in all cases cannot be based on justice, even as far as men understand it. Can there not be a government in which majorities do not virtually decide right and wrong, but conscience?—in which majorities decide only those questions to which the rule of expediency is applicable? Must the citizen ever for a moment, or in the least degree, resign his conscience to the legislator? Why has every man a conscience, then? I think that we should be men first, and subjects afterward. It is not desirable to cultivate a respect for the law, so much as for the right. The only obligation which I have a right to assume is to do at any time what I think right. It is truly enough said that a corporation has no conscience; but a corporation of conscientious men is a corporation *with* a conscience. Law never made men a whit more just; and, by means of their respect for it, even the well-disposed are daily made the agents of injustice. A common and natural result of an undue respect for law is, that you may see a file of soldiers, colonel, captain, corporal, privates, powder-monkeys, and all, marching in admirable

order over hill and dale to the wars, against their wills, ay,
against their common sense and consciences, which makes it
very steep marching indeed, and produces a palpitation of the
heart. They have no doubt that it is a damnable business in
which they are concerned; they are all peaceably inclined. Now,
what are they? Men at all? or small movable forts and magazines, at the service of some unscrupulous man in power? Visit
the Navy-Yard, and behold a marine, such a man as an American government can make, or such as it can make a man with its
black arts,—a mere shadow and reminiscence of humanity, a
man laid out alive and standing, and already, as one may say,
buried under arms with funeral accompaniments, though it may
be,—

> "Not a drum was heard, not a funeral note,
>   As his corse to the rampart we hurried;
> Not a soldier discharged his farewell shot
>   O'er the grave where our hero we buried."

The mass of men serve the state thus, not as men mainly,
but as machines, with their bodies. They are the standing army,
and the militia, jailers, constables, *posse comitatus*, etc. In most
cases there is no free exercise whatever of the judgment or of the
moral sense; but they put themselves on a level with wood and
earth and stones; and wooden men can perhaps be manufac-
tured that will serve the purpose as well. Such command no
more respect than men of straw or a lump of dirt. They have the
same sort of worth only as horses and dogs. Yet such as these
even are commonly esteemed good citizens. Others—as most
legislators, politicians, lawyers, ministers, and office-holders—
serve the state chiefly with their heads; and, as they rarely make
any moral distinctions, they are as likely to serve the devil,
without *intending* it, as God. A very few—as heroes, patriots,
martyrs, reformers in the great sense, and *men*—serve the state
with their consciences also, and so necessarily resist it for the
most part; and they are commonly treated as enemies by it. A
wise man will only be useful as a man, and will not submit to be
"clay," and "stop a hole to keep the wind away," but leave that
office to his dust at least:—

> "I am too high-born to he propertied.
> To be a secondary at control,
> Or useful serving-man and instrument
> To any sovereign state throughout the world."

He who gives himself entirely to his fellow-men appears to them useless and selfish; but he who gives himself partially to them is pronounced a benefactor and philanthropist.

How does it become a man to behave toward this American government to-day? I answer, that he cannot without disgrace be associated with it. I cannot for an instant recognize that political organization as *my* government which is the *slave's* government also.

All men recognize the right of revolution; that is, the right to refuse allegiance to, and to resist, the government, when its tyranny or its inefficiency are great and unendurable. But almost all say that such is not the case now. But such was the case, they think, in the Revolution of '75. If one were to tell me that this was a bad government because it taxed certain foreign commodities brought to its ports, it is most probable that I should not make an ado about it, for I can do without them. All machines have their friction; and possibly this does enough good to counterbalance the evil. At any rate, it is a great evil to make a stir about it. But when the friction comes to have its machine, and oppression and robbery are organized, I say, let us not have such a machine any longer. In other words, when a sixth of the population of a nation which has undertaken to be the refuge of liberty are slaves, and a whole country is unjustly overrun and conquered by a foreign army, and subjected to military law, I think that it is not too soon for honest men to rebel and revolutionize. What makes this duty the more urgent is the fact that the country so overrun is not our own, but ours is the invading army.

Paley, a common authority with many on moral questions, in his chapter on the "Duty of Submission to Civil Government," resolves all civil obligation into expediency; and he proceeds to say that "so long as the interest of the whole society requires it, that is, so long as the established government cannot be resisted or changed without public inconveniency, it is the will of God . . . that the established government be obeyed,—and no longer. This principle being admitted, the justice of every particular case of resistance is reduced to a computation of the quantity of the danger and grievance on the one side, and of the probability and expense of redressing it on the other." Of this, he says, every man shall judge for himself. But Paley appears never to have contemplated those cases to which the rule of expediency does not apply, in which a people, as well as an individual, must do justice, cost what it may. If I have unjustly wrested a plank from a drowning man, I must restore it to him though I drown myself. This, according to Paley, would be inconvenient. But he that would save his life, in such a case, shall lose it. This people must cease to hold slaves, and to make war on Mexico, though it cost them their existence as a people.

In their practice, nations agree with Paley; but does any one think that Massachusetts does exactly what is right at the present crisis?

> "A drab of state, a cloth-o'-silver slut,
> To have her train borne up, and her soul trail in the dirt."

Practically speaking, the opponents to a reform in Massachusetts are not a hundred thousand politicians at the South, but a hundred thousand merchants and farmers here, who are more interested in commerce and agriculture than they are in humanity, and are not prepared to do justice to the slave and to Mexico, *cost what it may*. I quarrel not with far-off foes, but with those who, near at home, coöperate with, and do the bidding of, those far away, and without whom the latter would be harmless. We are accustomed to say, that the mass of men are unprepared; but improvement is slow, because the few are not materially wiser or better than the many. It is not so important that many should be as good as you, as that there be some absolute goodness somewhere; for that will leaven the whole lump. There are thousands who are *in opinion* opposed to slavery and to the war, who yet in effect do nothing to put an end to them; who, esteeming themselves children of Washington and Franklin, sit down with their hands in their pockets, and say that they know not what to do, and do nothing; who even postpone the question of freedom to the question of free trade, and quietly read the prices-current along with the latest advices from Mexico, after dinner, and, it may be, fall asleep over them both. What is the price-current of an honest man and patriot to-day? They hesitate, and they regret, and sometimes they petition; but they do nothing in earnest and with effect. They will wait, well disposed, for others to remedy the evil, that they may no longer have it to regret. At most, they give only a cheap vote, and a feeble countenance and God-speed, to the right, as it goes by them. There are nine hundred and ninety-nine patrons of virtue to one virtuous man.

But it is easier to deal with the real possessor of a thing than with the temporary guardian of it.

All voting is a sort of gaming, like checkers or back-gammon, with a slight moral tinge to it, a playing with right and wrong, with moral questions; and betting naturally accompanies it. The character of the voters is not staked. I cast my vote, perchance, as I think right; but I am not vitally concerned that that right should prevail. I am willing to leave it to the majority.
Its obligation, therefore, never exceeds that of expediency. Even voting *for the right is doing* nothing for it. It is only expressing to men feebly your despite that it should prevail. A wise man will not leave the right to the mercy of chance, nor wish it to prevail through the power of the majority. There is but little virtue in the action of masses of men. When the majority shall at length vote for the abolition of slavery, if will be because they are indifferent to slavery, or because there is but little slavery left to be abolished by their vote. *They* will then be the only slaves. Only *his* vote can hasten the abolition of slavery who asserts his own freedom by his vote.

I hear of a convention to be held at Baltimore, or elsewhere, for the selection of a candidate for the Presidency, made up chiefly of editors, and men who are politicians by profession; but I think, what is it to any independent, intelligent, and respectable man what decision they may come to? Shall we not have the advantage of his wisdom and honesty, nevertheless? Can we not count upon some independent votes? Are there not many individuals in the country who do not attend conventions? But no: I find that the respectable man, so called, has immediately drifted from his position, and despairs of his country, when his country has more reason to despair of him. He forthwith adopts one of the candidates thus selected as the only *available* one, thus proving that he is himself *available* for any purposes of the demagogue. His vote is of no more worth than that of any unprincipled foreigner or hireling native, who may have been bought. O for a man who is a *man*, and, as my neighbor says, has a bone in his back which you cannot pass your hand through! Our statistics are at fault: the population has been returned too large. How many *men* are there to a square thousand miles in this country? Hardly one. Does not America offer any inducement for men to settle here? The American has dwindled into an Odd Fellow,—one who may be known by the development of his organ of gregariousness, and a manifest lack of intellect and cheerful self-reliance; whose first and chief concern, on coming into the world, is to see that the almshouses are in good repair; and, before yet he has lawfully donned the virile garb, to collect a fund for the support of the widows and orphans that may be; who, in short, ventures to live only by the aid of the Mutual Insurance Company, which has promised to bury him decently.

It is not a man's duty, as a matter of course, to devote himself to the eradication of any, even the most enormous, wrong; he may still properly have other concerns to engage him; but it is his duty, at least, to wash his hands of it, and, if he gives it no thought longer, not to give it practically his support. If I devote myself to other pursuits and contemplations, I must first see, at least, that I do not pursue them sitting upon another man's shoulders. I must get off him first, that he may pursue his contemplations too. See what gross inconsistency is tolerated. I have heard some of my townsmen say, "I should like to have them order me out to help put down an insurrection of the slaves, or to march to Mexico;—see if I would go"; and yet these very men have each, directly by their allegiance, and so indirectly, at least, by their money, furnished a substitute. The soldier is applauded who refuses to serve in an unjust war by those who do not refuse to sustain the unjust government which makes the war; is applauded by those whose own act and authority he disregards and sets, at naught; as if the state were penitent to that degree that it hired one to scourge it while it sinned, but not to that degree that it left off sinning for a moment. Thus, under the name of Order and Civil Government, we are all made at last to pay homage to and support our own meanness. After the first blush of sin comes its indifference; and from immoral it becomes, as it were, *un*moral, and not quite unnecessary to that life which we have made.

The broadest and most prevalent error requires the most disinterested virtue to sustain it. The slight reproach to which the virtue of patriotism is commonly liable, the noble are most likely to incur. Those who, while they disapprove of the character and measures of a government, yield to it their allegiance and support are undoubtedly its most conscientious supporters, and so frequently the most serious obstacles to reform. Some are petitioning the State to dissolve the Union, to disregard the requisitions of the President. Why do they not dissolve it themselves,—the union between themselves and the State,—and refuse to pay their quota into its treasury? Do not they stand in the same relation to the State that the State does to the Union? And have not the same reasons prevented the State from resisting the Union which have prevented them from resisting the State?

How can a man be satisfied to entertain an. opinion merely, and enjoy *it*? Is there any enjoyment in it, if his opinion is that he is aggrieved? If you are cheated out of a single dollar by your neighbor, you do not rest satisfied with knowing that you are cheated, or with saying that you are cheated, or even with petitioning him to pay you your due; but you take effectual steps at once to obtain the full amount, and see that you are never cheated again. Action from principle, the perception and the performance of right, changes things and relations; it is essentially revolutionary, and does not consist wholly with anything which was. It not only divides States and churches, it divides families; ay, it divides the *individual*, separating the diabolical in him from the divine.

Unjust laws exist: shall we be content to obey them, or shall we endeavor to amend them, and obey them until we have succeeded, or shall we transgress them at once? Men generally, under such a government as this, think that they ought to wait until they have persuaded the majority to alter them. They think that, if they should resist, the remedy would be worse than the evil. But it is the fault of the government itself that the remedy *is* worse than the evil. *It* makes it worse. Why is it not more apt to anticipate and provide for reform? Why does it not cherish its wise minority? Why does it cry and resist before it is hurt? Why does it not encourage its citizens to be on the alert to point out its faults, and *do* better than it would have them? Why does it always crucify Christ, and excommunicate Copernicus and Luther, and pronounce Washington and Franklin rebels?

One would think, that a deliberate and practical denial of its authority was the only offence never contemplated by government; else, why has it not assigned its definite, its suitable and proportionate, penalty? If a man who has no property refuses but once to earn nine shillings for the State, he is put in prison for a period unlimited by any law that I know, and determined only by the discretion of those who placed him there; but if he should steal ninety times nine shillings from the State, he is soon permitted to go at large again.

If the injustice is part of the necessary friction of the machine of government, let it go, let it go: perchance it will wear smooth,—certainly the machine will wear out. If the injustice has a spring, or a pulley, or a rope, or a crank, exclusively for itself, then perhaps you may consider whether the remedy will not be worse than the evil; but if it is of such a nature that it requires you to be the agent of injustice to another, then, I say, break the law. Let your life be a counter-friction to stop the machine. What I have to do is to see, at any rate, that I do not lend myself to the wrong which I condemn.

As for adopting the ways which the State has provided for remedying the evil, I know not of such ways. They take too much time, and a man's life will be gone. I have other affairs to attend to. I came into this world, not chiefly to make this a good place to live in, but to live in it, be it good or bad. A man has not everything to do, but something; and because he cannot do *everything*, it is not necessary that he should do *something* wrong. It is not my business to be petitioning the Governor or the Legislature any more than it is theirs to petition me; and if they should not hear my petition, what should I do then? But in this case the State has provided no way: its very Constitution is the evil. This may seem to be harsh and stubborn and unconciliatory; but it is to treat with the utmost kindness and consideration the only spirit that can appreciate or deserves it. So is all change for the better, like birth and death, which convulse the body.

I do not hesitate to say, that those who call themselves Abolitionists should at once effectually withdraw their support, both in person and property, from the government of Massachusetts, and not wait till they constitute a majority of one, before they suffer the right to prevail through them. I think that it is enough if they have God on their side, without waiting for that other one. Moreover, any man more right than his neighbors constitutes a majority of one already.

I meet this American government, or its representative, the State government, directly, and face to face, once a year—no more—in the person of its tax-gatherer; this is the only mode in which a man situated as I am necessarily meets it; and it then says distinctly, Recognize me; and the simplest, the most effectual, and, in the present posture of affairs, the indispensablest mode of treating with it on this head, of expressing your little satisfaction with and love for it, is to deny it then. My civil

neighbor, the tax-gatherer, is the very man I have to deal with,—
for it is, after all, with men and not with parchment that I quarrel,—and he has voluntarily chosen to be an agent of the government. How shall he ever know well what he is and does as
an officer of the government, or as a man, until he is obliged to
consider whether he shall treat me, his neighbor, for whom he
has respect, as a neighbor and well-disposed man, or as a maniac
and disturber of the peace, and see if he can get over this obstruc-
tion to his neighborliness without a ruder and more impetuous
thought or speech corresponding with his action. I know this
well, that if one thousand, if one hundred, if ten men whom I
could name,—if ten *honest* men only,—ay, if *one* HONEST man,
in this State of Massachusetts, *ceasing to hold slaves*, were actually to withdraw from this copartnership, and be locked up in
the county jail therefor, it would be the abolition of slavery in
America. For it matters not how small the beginning may seem
to be: what is once well done is done forever. But we love better
to talk about it: that we say is our mission. Reform keeps many
scores of newspapers in its service, but not one man. If my esteemed neighbor, the State's ambassador, who will devote his
days to the settlement of the question of human rights in the
Council Chamber, instead of being threatened with the prisons
of Carolina, were to sit down the prisoner of Massachusetts, that
State which is so anxious to foist the sin of slavery upon her sister,—though at present she can discover only an act of inhospi-
tality to be the ground of a quarrel with her,—the Legislature
would not wholly waive the subject the following winter.

Under a government which imprisons any unjustly, the
true place for a just man is also a prison. The proper place to-
day, the only place which Massachusetts has provided for her
freer and less desponding spirits, is in her prisons, to be put out
and locked out of the State by her own act, as they have already
put themselves out by their principles. It is there that the fugitive slave, and the Mexican prisoner on parole, and the Indian
come to plead the wrongs of his race should find them; on that
separate, but more free and honorable, ground, where the State
places those who are not *with* her, but *against* her,—the only
house in a slave State in which a free man can abide with honor.
If any think that their influence would be lost there, and their
voices no longer afflict the ear of the State, that they would not
be as an enemy within its walls, they do not know by how much
truth is stronger than error, nor how much more eloquently and

effectively he can combat injustice who has experienced a little in his own person. Cast your whole vote, not a strip of paper merely, but your whole influence. A minority is powerless while it conforms to the majority; it is not even a minority then; but it is irresistible when it clogs by its whole weight. If the alternative is to keep all, just men in prison, or give up war and slavery, the State will not hesitate which to choose. If a thousand men were not to pay their tax-bills this year, that would not be a violent and bloody measure, as it would be to pay them, and enable the State to commit violence and shed innocent blood. This is, in fact, the definition of a peaceable revolution, if any such is possible. If the tax-gatherer, or any other public officer, asks me, as one has done, "But what shall I do?" my answer is, "If you really wish to do anything, resign your office." When the subject has refused allegiance, and the officer has resigned his office, then the revolution is accomplished. But even suppose blood should flow. Is there not a sort of blood shed when the conscience is wounded? Through this wound a man's real manhood and immortality flow out, and he bleeds to an everlasting death. I see this blood flowing now.

I have contemplated the imprisonment of the offender, rather than the seizure of his goods,—though both will serve the same purpose,—because they who assert the purest right, and consequently are most dangerous to a corrupt State, commonly have not spent much time in accumulating property. To such the State renders comparatively small service, and a slight tax is wont to appear exorbitant, particularly if they are obliged to earn it by special labor with their hands. If there were one who lived wholly without the use of money, the State itself would hesitate to demand it of him. But the rich man—not to make any invidious comparison —is always sold to the institution which makes him rich. Absolutely speaking, the more money, the less virtue; for money comes between a man and his objects, and obtains them for him; and it was certainly no great virtue to obtain it. It puts to rest many questions which he would otherwise be taxed to answer; while the only new question which it puts is the hard but superfluous one, how to spend it. Thus his moral ground is taken from under his feet. The opportunities of living are diminished in proportion as what are called the "means" are increased. The best thing a man can do for his culture when he is rich is to endeavor to carry out those schemes which he entertained when he was poor. Christ answered the Herodians according to their condition. "Show me the tribute-money," said he;—and one took a penny out of his pocket;—if you use money which has the image of Cæsar on it, and which he has made current and valuable, that is, *if you are men of the State*, and gladly enjoy the advantages of Cæsar's government, then pay him back some of his own when he demands it. "Render therefore to Cæsar that which is Cæsar's, and to God those things which are God's,"—leaving them no wiser than before as to which was which; for they did not wish to know.

When I converse with the freest of my neighbors, I perceive that, whatever they may say about the magnitude and seriousness of the question, and their regard for the public tranquillity, the long and the short of the matter is, that they cannot spare the protection of the existing government, and they dread the consequences to their property and families of disobedience to it. For my own part, I should not like to think that I ever rely on the protection of the State. But, if I deny the authority of the State when it presents its tax-bill, it will soon take and waste all my property, and so harass me and my children without end. This is hard. This makes it impossible for a man to live honestly, and at the same time comfortably, in outward respects. It will not be worth the while to accumulate property; that would be sure to go again. You must hire or squat somewhere, and raise but a small crop, and eat that soon. You must live within yourself, and depend upon yourself always tucked up and ready for a start, and not have many affairs. A man may grow rich in Turkey even, if he will be in all respects a good subject: of the Turkish government. Confucius said: "If a state is governed by the principles of reason, poverty and misery are subjects of shame; if a state is not governed by the principles of reason, riches and honors are the subjects of shame." No: until I want the protection of Massachusetts to he extended to me in some distant Southern port, where my liberty is endangered, or until I am bent solely on building up an estate at home by peaceful enterprise, I can afford to refuse allegiance to Massachusetts, and her right to my property and life. It costs me less in every sense to incur the penalty of disobedience to the State than it would to obey. I should feel as if I were worth less in that case.

Some years ago, the State met me in behalf of the Church, and commanded me to pay a certain sum toward the support of a clergyman whose preaching my father attended, but never I myself. "Pay," it said, "or be locked up in the jail." I declined to pay. But, unfortunately, another man saw fit to pay it. I did not see why the schoolmaster should be taxed to support the priest, and not the priest the schoolmaster; for I was not the State's schoolmaster, but I supported myself by voluntary subscription. I did not see why the lyceum should not present its tax-bill, and have the State to back its demand, as well as the Church. However, at the request of the selectmen, I condescended to make some such statement as this in writing:—"Know all men by these presents, that I, Henry Thoreau, do not wish to be regarded as a member of any incorporated society which I have not joined." This I gave to the town clerk; and he has it. The State, having thus learned that I did not wish to be regarded as a member of that church, has never made a like demand on me since; though it said that it must adhere to its original presumption that time. If I had known how to name them, I should then have signed off in detail from all the societies which I never signed on to; but I did not know where to find a complete list.

I have paid no poll-tax for six years. I was put into a jail once on this account; for one night; and, as I stood considering the walls of solid stone, two or three feet thick, the door of wood and iron, a foot thick, and the iron grating which strained the light, I could not help being struck with the foolishness of that institution which treated me as if I were mere flesh and blood and bones, to be locked up. I wondered that it should have concluded at length that this was the best use it could put me to, and had never thought to avail itself of my services in some way. I saw that, if there was a wall of stone between me and my townsmen, there was a still more difficult one to climb or break through before they could get to be as free as I was. I did not for a moment feel confined, and the walls seemed a great waste of stone and mortar. I felt as if I alone of all my townsmen had paid my tax. They plainly did not know how to treat me, but behaved like persons who are underbred. In every threat and in every compliment there was a blunder; for they thought that my chief desire was to stand the other side of that stone wall. I could not but smile to see how industriously they locked the door on my meditations, which followed them out again without let or hindrance, and *they* were really all that was dangerous. As they could not reach me, they had resolved to punish my body; just as boys, if they cannot come at some person against whom they have a spite, will abuse his dog. I saw that the State was half-witted, that it was timid as a lone woman with her silver spoons, and that it did not know its friends from its foes, and I lost all my remaining respect for it, and pitied it.

Thus the State never intentionally confronts a man's sense, intellectual or moral, but only his body, his senses. It is not armed with superior wit or honesty, but with superior physical strength. I was not born to be forced. I will breathe after my own fashion. Let us see who is the strongest. What force has a multitude? They only can force me who obey a higher law than I. They force me to become like themselves. I do not hear of *men* being *forced* to live this way or that by masses of men. What sort of life were that to live? When I meet a government which says to me, "Your money or your life," why should I be in haste to give it my money? It may be in a great strait, and not know what to do: I cannot help that. It must help itself; do as I do. It is not worth the while to snivel about it. I am not responsible for the successful working of the machinery of society. I am not the son of the engineer. I perceive that, when an acorn and a chestnut fall side by side, the one does not remain inert to make way for the other, but both obey their own laws, and spring and grow and flourish as best they can, till one, perchance, overshadows and destroys the other. If a plant cannot live according to its nature, it dies; and so a man.

The night in prison was novel and interesting enough. The prisoners in their shirt-sleeves were enjoying a chat and the evening air in the doorway, when I entered. But the jailer said, "Come, boys, it is time to lock up"; and so they dispersed, and I heard the sound of their steps returning into the hollow apartments. My room-mate was introduced to me by the jailer as "a first-rate fellow and a clever man." When the door was locked, he showed me where to hang my hat, and how he managed matters there. The rooms were whitewashed once a month; and this one, at least, was the whitest, most simply furnished, and probably the neatest apartment in the town. He naturally wanted to know where I came from, and what brought me there; and, when I had told him, I asked him in my turn how he came there, presuming him to be an honest man, of course; and, as the world goes, I believe he was. "Why," said he, "they accuse me of burning a barn; but I never did it." As near as I could discover, he had probably gone to bed in a barn when drunk, and smoked his pipe there; and so a barn was burnt. He had the reputation of being a clever man, had been there some three months waiting for his trial to come on, and would have to wait as much longer;

but he was quite domesticated and contented, since he got his board for nothing, and thought that he was well treated.

He occupied one window, and I the other; and I saw that if one stayed there long, his principal business would be to look out the window. I had soon read all the tracts that were left there, and examined where former prisoners had broken out, and where a grate had been sawed off, and heard the history of the various occupants of that room; for I found that even here there was a history and a gossip which never circulated beyond the walls of the jail. Probably this is the only house in the town where verses are composed, which are afterward printed in a circular form, but not published. I was shown quite a long list of verses which were composed by some young men who had been detected in an attempt to escape, who avenged themselves by singing them.

I pumped my fellow-prisoner as dry as I could, for fear I should never see him again; but at length he showed me which was my bed, and left me to blow out the lamp.

It was like traveling into a far country, such as I had never expected to behold, to lie there for one night. It seemed to me that I never had heard the town clock strike before, nor the evening sounds of the village; for we slept with the windows open, which were inside the grating. It was to see my native village in the light of the Middle Ages, and our Concord was turned into a Rhine stream, and visions of knights and castles passed before me. They were the voices of old burghers that I heard in the streets. I was an involuntary spectator and auditor of whatever was done and said in the kitchen of the adjacent village inn,—a wholly new and rare experience to me. It was a closer view of my native town. I was fairly inside of it. I never had seen its institutions before. This is one of its peculiar institutions; for it is a shire town. I began to comprehend what its inhabitants were about.

In the morning, our breakfasts were put through the hole in the door, in small oblong-square tin pans, made to fit, and holding a pint of chocolate, with brown bread, and an iron spoon. When they called for the vessels again, I was green enough to return what bread I had left; but my comrade seized it, and said that I should lay that up for lunch or dinner. Soon after he was let out to work at haying in a neighboring field, whither he went every day, and would not be back till noon; so he bade me good-day, saying that he doubted if he should see me again.

When I came out of prison,—for some one interfered, and paid that tax,—I did not perceive that great changes had taken place on the common, such as he observed who went in a youth and emerged a tottering and gray-headed man; and yet a change had to my eyes come over the scene,—the town, and State, and country,—greater than any that mere time could effect. I saw yet more distinctly the State in which I lived. I saw to what extent the people among whom I lived could be trusted as good neighbors and friends; that their friendship was for summer weather only; that they did not greatly propose to do right; that they were a distinct race from me by their prejudices and superstitions, as the Chinamen and Malays are; that in their sacrifices to humanity they ran no risks, not even to their property; that after all they were not so noble but they treated the thief as he had treated them, and hoped, by a certain outward observance and a few prayers, and by walking in a particular straight though useless path from time to time, to save their souls. This may be to judge my neighbors harshly; for I believe that many of them are not aware that they have such an institution as the jail in their village.

It was formerly the custom in our village, when a poor debtor came out of jail, for his acquaintances to salute him, looking through their fingers, which were crossed to represent the grating of a jail window, "How do ye do?" My neighbors did not thus salute me, but first looked at me, and then at one another, as if I had returned from a long journey. I was put into jail as I was going to the shoemaker's to get a shoe which was mended. When I was let out the next morning, I proceeded to finish my errand, and, having put on my mended shoe, joined a huckleberry party, who were impatient to put themselves under my conduct; and in half an hour,—for the horse was soon tackled,—was in the midst of a huckleberry field, on one of our highest hills, two miles off, and then the State was nowhere to be seen. This is the whole history of "My Prisons."

I have never declined paying the highway tax, because I am as desirous of being a good neighbor as I am of being a bad subject; and as for supporting schools, I am doing my part to educate my fellow-countrymen now. It is for no particular item in the tax-bill that I refuse to pay it. I simply wish to refuse allegiance to the State, to withdraw and stand aloof from it effectually. I do not care to trace the course of my dollar, if I could, till it buys a man or a musket to shoot one with,—the dollar is innocent,—but I am concerned to trace the effects of my allegiance. In fact, I quietly declare war with the State, after my fashion, though I will still make what use and get what advantage of her I can, as is usual in such cases.

If others pay the tax which is demanded of me, from a sympathy with the State, they do but what they have already done in their own case, or rather they abet injustice to a greater extent than the State requires. If they pay the tax from a mistaken interest in the individual taxed, to save his property, or prevent his going to jail, it is because they have not considered wisely how far they let their private feelings interfere with the public good.

This, then, is my position at present. Buy one cannot be too much on his guard in such a case, lest his action be biased by obstinacy or an undue regard for the opinions of men. Let him see that he does only what belongs to himself and to the hour.

I think sometimes, Why, this people mean well, they are only ignorant; they would do better if they knew how: why give your neighbors this pain to treat you as they are not inclined to? But I think gain, This is no reason why I should do as they do, or permit others to suffer much greater pain of a different kind. Again, I sometimes say to myself, When many millions of men, without heat, without ill will, without personal feeling of any kind, demand of you a few shillings only, without the possibility, such is their constitution, of retracting or altering their present demand, and without the possibility, on your side, of appeal to any other millions, why expose yourself to this overwhelming brute force? You do not resist cold and hunger, the winds and the waves, thus obstinately; you quietly submit to a thousand similar necessities. You do not put your head into the fire. But just in proportion as I regard this as not wholly a brute force, but partly a human force, and consider that I have relations to those millions as to so many millions of men, and not of mere brute or inanimate things, I see that appeal is possible, first and instantaneously, from them to the Maker of them, and, secondly, from them to themselves. But if I put my head deliberately into the fire, there is no appeal to fire or to the Maker of fire, and I have only myself to blame. If I could convince myself that I have any right to be satisfied with men as they are, and to treat them accordingly, and not according, in some respects, to my requisitions and expectations of what they and I ought to be, then, like a good Mussulman and fatalist, I should endeavor to be satisfied with things as they are, and say it is the will of God. And, above all, there is this difference between resisting this and a purely brute or natural force, that I can resist this with some effect; but I cannot expect, like Orpheus, to change the nature of the rocks and trees and beasts.

I do not wish to quarrel with any man or nation. I do not wish to split hairs, to make fine distinctions, or set myself up as better than my neighbors. I seek rather, I may say, even an excuse for conforming to the laws of the land. I am but too ready to conform to them. Indeed, I have reason to suspect myself on this head; and each year, as the tax-gatherer comes round, I find myself disposed to review the acts and position of the general and State governments, and the spirit of the people, to discover a pretext for conformity.

> "We must affect our country as our parents,
> And if at any time we alienate
> Our love or industry from doing it honor,
> We must respect effects and teach the soul
> Matter of conscience and religion,
> And not desire of rule or benefit."

I believe that the State will soon be able to take all my work of this sort out of my hands, and then I shall be no better a patriot than my fellow-countrymen. Seen from a lower point of view, the Constitution, with all its faults, is very good; the law and the courts are very respectable; even this State and this American government are, in many respects, very admirable, and rare things, to be thankful for, such as a great many have described them; but seen from a point of view a little higher, they are what I have described them; seen from a higher still, and the highest, who shall say what they are, or that they are worth looking at or thinking of at all?

However, the government does not concern me much, and I shall bestow the fewest possible thoughts on it. It is not many moments that I live under a government, even in this world. If a man is thought-free, fancy-free, imagination-free, that which *is not* never for a long time appearing *to be* to him, unwise rulers or reformers cannot fatally interrupt him.

I know that most men think differently from myself; but those whose lives are by profession devoted to the study of these or kindred subjects content me as little any. Statesmen and legislators, standing so completely within the institution, never distinctly and nakedly hold it. They speak of moving society, but have no resting-place without it. They may be men of a certain experience and discrimination, and have no doubt invented ingenious and even useful systems, for which we sincerely thank them; but all their wit and usefulness lie within certain not very wide limits. They are wont to forget that the world is not governed by policy and expediency. Webster never goes behind government, and so cannot speak with authority about it. His words are wisdom to those legislators who contemplate no essential reform in the existing government; but for thinkers, and those who legislate for all time, he never once glances at the subject. I know of those whose serene and wise speculations on this theme would soon reveal the limits of his mind's range and hospitality. Yet, compared with the cheap professions of most reformers, and the still cheaper wisdom and eloquence of politicians in general, his are almost the only sensible and valuable words, and we thank Heaven for him. Comparatively, he is always strong, original, and, above all, practical. Still his quality is not wisdom, but prudence. The lawyer's truth is not Truth, but consistency or a consistent expediency. Truth is always in harmony with herself, and is not concerned chiefly to reveal the justice that may consist with wrong-doing. He well deserves to be called, as he has been called, the Defender of the Constitution. There are really no blows to be given by him but defensive ones. He is not a leader, but a follower. His leaders are the men of '87. "I have never made an effort," he says, "and never propose to make an effort; I have never countenanced an effort, and never mean to countenance an effort, to disturb the arrangement as originally made, by which the various States came into the Union." Still thinking of the sanction which the Constitution gives to slavery, he says, "Because it was a part of the original compact,—let it stand." Notwithstanding his special acuteness and ability, he is unable to take a fact out of its merely political relations, and behold it as it lies absolutely to be disposed of by the intellect,—what, for instance, it behooves a man to do here in America to-day with regard to slavery,—but ventures, or is driven, to make some such desperate answer as the following, while professing to speak absolutely, and as a private man,—

from which what new and singular code of social duties might be inferred? "The manner," says he, "in which the governments of those States where slavery exists are to regulate it is for their own consideration, under their responsibility to their constituents, to the general laws of propriety, humanity, and justice, and to God. Associations formed elsewhere, springing from a feeling of humanity, or any other cause, have nothing whatever to do with it. They have never received any encouragement from me, and they never will."[1]

They who know of no purer sources of truth, who have traced up its stream no higher, stand, and wisely stand, by the Bible and the Constitution, and drink at it there with reverence and humility; but they who behold where it comes trickling into this lake or that pool, gird up their loins once more, and continue their pilgrimage toward its fountain-head.

No man with a genius for legislation has appeared in America. They are rare in the history of the world. There are orators, politicians, and eloquent men, by the thousand; but the speaker has not yet opened his mouth to speak who is capable of settling the much-vexed questions of the day. We love eloquence for its own sake, and not for any truth which it may utter, or any heroism it may inspire. Our legislators have not yet learned the comparative value of free trade and of freedom, of union, and of rectitude, to a nation. They have no genius or talent for comparatively humble questions of taxation and finance, commerce and manufactures and agriculture. If we were left solely to the wordy wit of legislators in Congress for our guidance, uncorrected by the seasonable experience and the effectual complaints of the people, America would not long retain her rank among the nations. For eighteen hundred years, though perchance I have no right to say it, the New Testament has been written; yet where is the legislator who has wisdom and practical talent enough to avail himself of the light which it sheds on the science of legislation?

The authority of government, even such as I am willing to submit to,—for I will cheerfully obey those who know and can do better than I, and in many things even those who neither know nor can do so well,—is still an impure one: to be strictly just, it must have the sanction and consent of the governed. It can have no pure right over my person and property but what I concede to it. The progress from an absolute to a limited monarchy, from a limited monarchy to a democracy, is a progress toward a true respect for the individual. Even the Chinese philosopher was wise enough to regard the individual as the basis of the empire. Is a democracy, such as we know it, the last improvement possible in government? Is it not possible to take a step further towards recognizing and organizing the rights of man? There will never be a really free and enlightened State until the State comes to recognize the individual as a higher and independent power, from which all its own power and authority are derived, and treats him accordingly. I please myself with imagining a State at last which can afford to be just to all men, and to treat the individual with respect as a neighbor; which even would not think it inconsistent with its own repose if a few were to live aloof from it, not meddling with it, nor embraced by it, who fulfilled all the duties of neighbors and fellow-men. A State which bore this kind of fruit, and suffered it to drop off as fast as it ripened, would prepare the way for a still more perfect and glorious State, which also I have imagined, but not yet anywhere seen.

Note

[1] These extracts have been inserted since the lecture was read.

SLAVERY IN MASSACHUSETTS
1854

I lately attended a meeting of the citizens of Concord, expecting, as one among many, to speak on the subject of slavery in Massachusetts; but I was surprised and disappointed to find that what had called my townsmen together was the destiny of Nebraska, and not of Massachusetts, and that what I had to say would be entirely out of order. I had thought that the house was on fire, and not the prairie; but though several of the citizens of Massachusetts are now in prison for attempting to rescue a slave from her own clutches, not one of the speakers at that meeting expressed regret for it, not one even referred to it. It was only the disposition of some wild lands a thousand miles off which appeared to concern them. The inhabitants of Concord are not prepared to stand by one of their own bridges, but talk only of taking up a position on the highlands beyond the Yellowstone River. Our Buttricks and Davises and Hosmers are retreating thither, and I fear that they will leave no Lexington Common between them and the enemy. There is not one slave in Nebraska; there are perhaps a million slaves in Massachusetts.

They who have been bred in the school of politics fall now and always to face the facts. Their measures are half measures and makeshifts merely. They put off the day of settlement indefinitely, and meanwhile the debt accumulates. Though the Fugitive Slave Law had not been the subject of discussion on that occasion, it was at length faintly resolved by my townsmen, at an adjourned meeting, as I learn, that the compromise compact of 1820 having been repudiated by one of the parties, "therefore, . . . the Fugitive Slave Law of 1850 must be repealed." But this is not the reason why an iniquitous law should be repealed. The fact which the politician faces is merely that there is less honor among thieves than was supposed, and not the fact that they are thieves.

As I had no opportunity to express my thoughts at that meeting, will you allow me to do so here?

Again it happens that the Boston Court-House is full of armed men, holding prisoner and trying a MAN, to find out if he is not really a SLAVE. Does any one think that justice or God awaits Mr. Loring's decision? For him to sit there deciding still, when this question is already decided from eternity to eternity, and the unlettered slave himself and the multitude around have long since heard and assented to the decision, is simply to make himself ridiculous. We may be tempted to ask from whom he received his commission, and who he is that received it; what novel statutes he obeys, and what precedents are to him of authority. Such an arbiter's very existence is an impertinence. We do not ask him to make up his mind, but to make up his pack.

I listen to hear the voice of a Governor, Commander-in-Chief of the forces of Massachusetts. I hear only the creaking of crickets and the hum of insects which now fill the summer air. The Governor's exploit is to review the troops on muster days. I have seen him on horseback, with his hat off, listening to a chaplain's prayer. It chances that that is all I have ever seen of a Governor. I think that I could manage to get along without one. If he is not of the least use to prevent my being kidnapped, pray of what important use is he likely to be to me? When freedom is most endangered, he dwells in the deepest obscurity. A distinguished clergyman told me that he chose the profession of a clergyman because it afforded the most leisure for literary pursuits. I would recommend to him the profession of a Governor.

Three years ago, also, when the Sims tragedy was acted, I said to myself, There is such an officer, if not such a man, as the Governor of Massachusetts,—what has he been about the last fortnight? Has he had as much as he could do to keep on the fence during this moral earthquake? It seemed to me that no keener satire could have been aimed at, no more cutting insult have been offered to that man, than just what happened,—the absence of all inquiry after him in that crisis. The worst and the most I chance to know of him is that he did not improve that opportunity to make himself known, and worthily known. He could at least have *resigned* himself into fame. It appeared to be forgotten that there was such a man or such an office. Yet no doubt he was endeavoring to fill the gubernatorial chair all the while. He was no Governor of mine. He did not govern me.

But at last, in the present case, the Governor was heard from. After he and the United States government had perfectly succeeded in robbing a poor innocent black man of his liberty for life, and, as far as they could, of his Creator's likeness in his breast, he made a speech to his accomplices, at a congratulatory supper!

I have read a recent law of this State, making it penal for any officer of the "Commonwealth" to "detain or aid in the . . . detention," anywhere within its limits," of any person, for the reason that he is claimed as a fugitive slave." Also, it was a matter of notoriety that a writ of replevin to take the fugitive out of the custody of the United States marshal could not be served for want of sufficient force to aid the officer.

I had thought that the Governor was, in some sense, the executive officer of the State; that it was his business, as a Governor, to see that the laws of the State were executed; while, as a man, he took care that he did not, by so doing, break the laws of humanity; but when there is any special important use for him, he is useless, or worse than useless, and permits the laws of the State to go unexecuted. Perhaps I do not know what are the duties of a Governor; but if to be a Governor requires to subject one's self to so much ignominy without remedy, if it is to put a restraint upon my manhood, I shall take care never to be Governor of Massachusetts. I have not read far in the statutes of this Commonwealth. It is not profitable reading. They do not always say what is true; and they do not always mean what they say. What I am concerned to know is, that that man's influence and authority were on the side of the slaveholder, and not of the slave,—of the guilty, and not of the innocent,—of injustice, and not of justice. I never saw him of whom I speak; indeed, I did not know that he was Governor until this event occurred. I heard of him and Anthony Burns at the same time, and thus, undoubtedly, most will hear of him. So far am I from being governed by him. I do not mean that it was anything to his discredit that I had not heard of him, only that I heard what I did. The worst I shall say of him is, that he proved no better than the majority of his constituents would be likely to prove. In my opinion, he was not equal to the occasion.

The whole military force of the State is at the service of a Mr. Suttle, a slaveholder from Virginia, to enable him to catch a man whom he calls his property; but not a soldier is offered to save a citizen of Massachusetts from being kidnapped! Is this what all these soldiers, all this *training*, have been for these seventy-nine years past? Have they been trained merely to rob Mexico and carry back fugitive slaves to their masters?

These very nights I heard the sound of a drum in our streets. There were men *training* still; and for what? I could with an effort pardon the cockerels of Concord for crowing still, for they, perchance, had not been beaten that morning; but I could not excuse this rub-a-dub of the "trainers." The slave was carried back by exactly such as these; *i.e.*, by the soldier, of whom the best you can say in this connection is that he is a fool made conspicuous by a painted coat.

Three years ago, also, just a week after the authorities of Boston assembled to carry back a perfectly innocent man, and one whom they knew to be innocent, into slavery, the inhabitants of Concord caused the bells to be rung and the cannons to be fired, to celebrate their liberty,—and the courage and love of liberty of their ancestors who fought at the bridge. As if *those* three millions had fought for the right to be free themselves, but to hold in slavery three million others. Nowadays, men wear a fool's cap, and call it a liberty-cap. I do not know but there are some who, if they were tied to a whipping-post, and could but get one hand free, would use it to ring the bells and fire the cannons to celebrate *their* liberty. So some of my townsmen took the liberty to ring and fire. That was the extent of their freedom; and when the sound of the bells died away, their liberty died away also; when the powder was all expended, their liberty went off with the smoke.

The joke could be no broader if the inmates of the prisons were to subscribe for all the powder to be used in such salutes, and hire the jailers to do the firing and ringing for them, while they enjoyed it through the grating.

This is what I thought about my neighbors.

Every humane and intelligent inhabitant of Concord, when he or she heard those bells and those cannons, thought not with pride of the events of the 19th of April 1775, but with shame of the events of the 12th of April 1851. But now we have half buried that old shame under a new one.

Massachusetts sat waiting Mr. Loring's decision, as if it could in any way affect her own criminality. Her crime, the most conspicuous and fatal crime of all, was permitting him to be the umpire in such a case. It was really the trial of Massachusetts. Every moment that she hesitated to set this man free, every moment that site now hesitates to atone for her crime, she is convicted. The commissioner on her case is God; not Edward G. God, but simple God.

I wish thy countrymen to consider that whatever the human law may be, neither an individual nor a nation can ever commit the least act of injustice against the obscurest individual without having to pay the penalty for it. A government which deliberately enacts injustice, and persists in it, will at length even become the laughing-stock of the world.

Much has been said about American slavery, but I think that we do not even yet realize what slavery is. If I were seriously to propose to Congress to make mankind into sausages, I have no doubt that most of the members would smile at my proposition, and if any believed me to be in earnest, they would think that I proposed something much worse than Congress had ever done. But if any of them will tell me that to make a man into a sausage would be much worse—would be any worse—than to make him into a slave,—than it was to enact the Fugitive Slave Law,—I will accuse him of foolishness, of intellectual incapacity, of making a distinction without a difference. The one is just as sensible a proposition as the other.

I hear a good deal said about trampling this law under foot. Why, one need not go out of his way to do that. This law rises not to the level of the head or the reason; its natural habitat is in the dirt. It was born and bred, and has its life, only in the dust and mire, on a level with the feet; and he who walks with freedom, and does not with Hindoo mercy avoid treading on every venomous reptile, will inevitably tread on it, and so trample it under foot,—and Webster, its maker, with it, like the dirt-bug and its ball.

Recent events will be valuable as a criticism on the administration of justice in our midst, or, rather, as showing what are the true resources of justice in any community. It has come to this, that the friends of liberty, the friends of the slave, have shuddered when they have understood that his fate was left to the legal tribunals of the country to be decided. Free men have no faith that justice will be awarded in such a case. The judge may decide this way or that; it is a kind of accident, at best. It is evident that he is not a competent authority in so important a case. It is no time, then, to be judging according to his precedents, but to establish a precedent for the future. I would much rather trust to the sentiment of the people. In their vote you would get something of some value, at least, however small; but in the other case, only the trammeled judgment of an individual, of no significance, be it which way it might.

It is to some extent fatal to the courts, when the people are compelled to go behind them. I do not wish to believe that the courts were made for fair weather, and for very civil cases merely; but think of leaving it to any court in the land to decide whether more than three millions of people, in this case a sixth part of a nation, have a right to be freemen or not! But it has been left to the courts of *justice*, so called,—to the Supreme Court of the land,—and, as you all know, recognizing no authority but the Constitution, it has decided that the three millions are and shall continue to be slaves. Such judges as these are merely the inspectors of a pick-lock and murderer's tools, to tell him whether they are in working order or not, and there they think that their responsibility ends. There was a prior case on the docket, which they, as judges appointed by God, had no fight to skip; which having been justly settled, they would have been saved from this humiliation. It was the ease of the murderer himself.

The law will never make men free; it is men who have got to make the law free. They are the lovers of law and order who observe the law when the government breaks it.

Among human beings, the judge whose words seal the fate of a man furthest into eternity is not he who merely pronounces the verdict of the law, but he, whoever he may be, who, from a love of truth, and unprejudiced by any custom or enactment of men, utters a true opinion or *sentence* concerning him. He it is that *sentences* him. Whoever can discern truth has received his commission from a higher source than the chiefest justice in the world who can discern only law. He finds himself constituted judge of the judge. Strange that it should be necessary to state such simple truths!

I am more and more convinced that, with reference to any public question, it is more important to know what the country thinks of it than what the city thinks. The city does not *think* much. On any moral question, I would rather have the opinion

of Boxboro than of Boston and New York put together. When
the former speaks, I feel as if somebody *had* spoken, as if *humanity* was yet, and a reasonable being had asserted its fights,—as if
some unprejudiced men among the country's hills had at length
turned their attention to the subject, and by a few sensible words
redeemed the reputation of the race. When, in some obscure
country town, the farmers come together to a special town meeting, to express their opinion on some subject which is vexing the
land, that, I think, is the true Congress, and the most respectable
one that is ever assembled in the United States.

It is evident that there are, in this Commonwealth at least,
two parties, becoming more and more distinct,—the party of the
city, and the party of the country. I know that the country is
mean enough, but I am glad to believe that there is a slight difference in her favor. But as yet she has few if any organs
through which to express herself. The editorials which she
reads, like the news, come from the sea-board. Let us, the inhabitants of the country, cultivate self-respect. Let us not send to the
city for aught more essential than our broadcloths and groceries;
or, if we read the opinions of the city, let us entertain opinions of
our own.

Among measures to be adopted, I would suggest to make
as earnest and vigorous an assault on the press as has already
been made, and with effect, on the church. The church has
much improved within a few years; but the press is, almost
without exception, corrupt. I believe that in this country the
press exerts a greater and a more pernicious influence than the
church did in its worst period. We are not a religious people, but
we are a nation of politicians. We do not care for the Bible, but
we do care for the newspaper. At any meeting of politicians,—
like that at Concord the other evening, for instance,—how impertinent it would be to quote from the Bible! how pertinent to
quote from a newspaper or from the Constitution! The newspaper is a Bible which we read every morning and every afternoon,
standing and sitting, riding and walking. It is a Bible which every man carries in his pocket, which lies on every table and
counter, and which the mail, and thousands of missionaries, are
continually dispersing. It is, in short, the only book which
America has printed, and which America reads. So wide is its
influence. The editor is a preacher whom you voluntarily support. Your tax is commonly one cent daily, and it costs nothing
for pew hire. But how many of these preachers preach the

truth? I repeat the testimony of many an intelligent foreigner, as well as my own convictions, when I say, that probably no country was ever ruled by so mean a class of tyrants as, with a few noble exceptions, are the editors of the periodical press in *this* country. And as they live and rule only by their servility, and appealing to the worse, and not the better, nature of man, the people who read them are in the condition of the dog that returns to his vomit.

The *Liberator* and the *Commonwealth* were the only papers in Boston, as far as I know, which made themselves heard in condemnation of the cowardice and meanness of the authorities of that city, as exhibited in '51. The other journals, almost without exception, by their manner of referring to and speaking of the Fugitive Slave Law, and the carrying back of the slave Sims, insulted the common sense of the country, at least. And, for the most part, they did this, one would say, because they thought so to secure the approbation of their patrons, not being aware that a sounder sentiment prevailed to any extent in the heart of the Commonwealth. I am told that some of them have improved of late; but they are still eminently time-serving. Such is the character they have won.

But, thank fortune, this preacher can be even more easily reached by the weapons of the reformer than could the recreant priest. The free men of New England have only to refrain from purchasing and reading these sheets, have only to withhold their cents, to kill a score of them at once. One whom I respect told me that he purchased Mitchell's *Citizen* in the cars, and then threw it out the window. But would not his contempt have been more fatally expressed if he had not bought it?

Are they Americans? are they New-Englanders? are they inhabitants of Lexington and Concord and Framingham, who read and support the Boston *Post, Mail, Journal, Advertiser, Courier,* and *Times?* Are these the Flags of our Union? I am not a newspaper-reader, and may omit to name the worst.

Could slavery suggest a more complete servility than some of these journals exhibit? Is there any dust which their conduct does not lick, and make fouler still with its slime? I do not know whether the Boston *Herald* is still in existence, but I remember to have seen it about the streets when Sims was carried off. Did it not act its part well,—serve its master faithfully! How could it have gone lower on its belly? How can a man stoop lower than he is low? do more than put his extremities in the place of the head he has? than make his head his lower extremity? When I have taken up this paper with my cuffs turned up, I have heard the gurgling of the sewer through every column. I have felt that I was handling a paper picked out of the public gutters, a leaf from the gospel of the gambling-house, the groggery, and the brothel, harmonizing with the gospel of the Merchants' Exchange.

The majority of the men of the North, and of the South and East and West, are not men of principle. If they vote, they do not send men to Congress on errands of humanity; but while their brothers and sisters are being scourged and hung for loving liberty, while—I might here insert all that slavery implies and is—it is the mismanagement of wood and iron and stone and gold which concerns them. Do what you will, O Government, with my wife and children, my mother and brother, my father and sister, I will obey your commands to the letter. It will indeed grieve me if you hurt them, if you deliver them to overseers to be hunted by hounds or to be whipped to death; but, nevertheless, I will peaceably pursue my chosen calling on this fair earth, until perchance, one day, when I have put on mourning for them dead, I shall have persuaded you to relent. Such is the attitude, such are the words of Massachusetts.

Rather than do thus, I need not say what match I would touch, what system endeavor to blow up; but as I love my life, I would side with the light, and let the dark earth roll from under me, calling my mother and my brother to follow.

I would remind my countrymen that they are to be men first, and Americans only at a late and convenient hour. No matter how valuable law may be to protect your property, even to keep soul and body together, if it do not keep you and humanity together.

I am sorry to say that I doubt if there is a judge in Massachusetts who is prepared to resign his office, and get his living innocently, whenever it is required of him to pass sentence under a law which is merely contrary to the law of God. I am compelled to see that they put themselves, or rather are by character, in this respect, exactly on a level with the marine who discharges his musket in any direction he is ordered to. They are just as much tools, and as little men. Certainly, they are not the more to be respected, because their master enslaves their understandings and consciences, instead of their bodies.

The judges and lawyers,—simply as such, I mean,—and all men of expediency, try this case by a very low and incompetent standard. They consider, not whether the Fugitive Slave Law is right, but whether it is what they call *constitutional*. Is virtue constitutional, or vice? Is equity constitutional, or iniquity? In important moral and vital questions, like this, it is just as impertinent to ask whether a law is constitutional or not, as to ask whether it is profitable or not. They persist in being the servants of the worst of men, and not the servants of humanity. The question is, not whether you or your grandfather, seventy years ago, did not enter into an agreement to serve the devil, and that service is not accordingly now due; but whether you will not now, for once and at last, serve God,—in spite of your own past recreancy, or that of your ancestor,—by obeying that eternal and only just CONSTITUTION, which He, and not any Jefferson or Adams, has written in your being.

The amount of it is, if the majority vote the devil to be God, the minority will live and behave accordingly, and obey the successful candidate, trusting that, some time or other, by some speaker's casting-vote, perhaps, they may reinstate God. This is the highest principle I can get out or invent for my neighbors. These men act as if they believed that they could safely slide down a hill a little way,—or a good way,—and would surely come to a place, by and by, where they could begin to slide up again. This is expediency, or choosing that course which offers the slightest obstacles to the feet, that is, a down-hill one. But there is no such thing as accomplishing a righteous reform by the use of "expediency." There is no such thing as sliding up-hill. In morals the only sliders are backsliders.

Thus we steadily worship Mammon, both school and state and church, and on the seventh day curse God with a tintamar from one end of the Union to the other.

Will mankind never learn that policy is not morality,—that it never secures any moral right, but considers merely what is expedient? chooses the available candidate,—who is invariably the devil,—and what right have his constituents to he surprised, because the devil does not behave like an angel of light? What is wanted is men, not of policy, but of probity,—who recognize a higher law than the Constitution, or the decision of the majority. The fate of the country does not depend on how you vote at the polls,—the worst man is as strong as the best at that game; it does not depend on what kind of paper you drop into the ballot-box once a year, but on what kind of man you drop from your chamber into the street every morning.

What should concern Massachusetts is not the Nebraska Bill, nor the Fugitive Slave Bill, but her own slaveholding and servility. Let the State dissolve her union with the slaveholder. She may wriggle and hesitate, and ask leave to read the Constitution once more; but she can find no respectable law or precedent which sanctions the continuance of such a union for an instant.

Let each inhabitant of the State dissolve his union with her, as long as she delays to do her duty.

The events of the past month teach me to distrust Fame. I see that she does not finely discriminate, but coarsely hurrahs. She considers not the simple heroism of an action, but only as it is connected with its apparent consequences. She praises till she is hoarse the easy exploit of the Boston tea-party, but will be comparatively silent about the braver and more disinterestedly heroic attack on the Boston Court-House, simply because it was unsuccessful!

Covered with disgrace, the State has sat down coolly to try for their lives and liberties the men who attempted to do its duty for it. And this is called *justice!* They who have shown that they can behave particularly well may perchance be put under bonds for *their good behavior.* They whom truth requires at present to plead guilty are, of all the inhabitants of the State, preëminently innocent. While the Governor, and the Mayor, and countless officers of the Commonwealth are at large, the champions of liberty are imprisoned.

Only they are guiltless who commit the crime of contempt of such a court. It behooves every man to see that his influence is on the side of justice, and let the courts make their own characters. My sympathies in this case are wholly with the accused, and wholly against their accusers and judges. Justice is sweet and musical; but injustice is harsh and discordant. The judge still sits grinding at his organ, but it yields no music, and we hear only the sound of the handle. He believes that all the music resides in the handle, and the crowd toss him their coppers the same as before.

Do you suppose that that Massachusetts which is now doing these things,—which hesitates to crown these men, some of whose lawyers, and even judges, perchance, may be driven to take refuge in some poor quibble, that they may not wholly outrage their instinctive sense of justice,—do you suppose that she is anything but base and servile? that she is the champion of liberty?

Show me a free state, and a court truly of justice, and I will fight for them, if need be; but show me Massachusetts, and I refuse her my allegiance, and express contempt for her courts.

The effect of a good government is to make life more valuable; of a bad one, to make it less valuable. We can afford that railroad and all merely material stock should lose some of its value, for that only compels us to live more simply and economically; but suppose that the value of life itself should be diminished! How can we make a less demand on man and nature, how live more economically in respect to virtue and all noble qualities, than we do? I have lived for the last month— and I think that every man in Massachusetts capable of the sentiment of patriotism must have had a similar experience—with the sense of having suffered a vast and indefinite loss. I did not know at first what ailed me. At last it occurred to me that what I had lost was a country. I had never respected the government near to which I lived, but I had foolishly thought that I might mange to live here, minding my private affairs, and forget it. For my part, my old and worthiest pursuits have lost I cannot say how much of their attraction, and I feel that my investment in life here is worth many per cent. less since Massachusetts last deliberately sent back an innocent man, Anthony Burns, to slavery. I dwelt before, perhaps, in the illusion that my life passed somewhere only *between* heaven and hell, but now I cannot persuade myself that I do not dwell *wholly within* hell. The site of that political organization called Massachusetts is to me morally covered with volcanic scoriæ and cinders, such as Milton describes in the infernal regions. If there is any hell more unprincipled than our rulers, and we, the ruled, I feel curious to see it. Life itself being worth less, all things with it, which minister to it, are worth less. Suppose you have a small library, with pictures to adorn the walls,—a garden laid out around,—and contemplate scientific and literary pursuits, and discover all at once that your villa, with all its contents, is located in hell, and that the justice of the peace has a cloven foot and a forked tail,— do not these things suddenly lose their value in your eyes?

I feel that, to some extent, the State has fatally interfered with my lawful business. It has not only interrupted me in my passage through Court Street on errands of trade, but it has interrupted me and every man on his onward and upward path, on which he had trusted soon to leave Court Street far behind. What right had it to remind me of Court Street? I have found that hollow which even I had relied on for solid.

I am surprised to see men going about their business as if nothing had happened. I say to myself, "Unfortunates! they have not heard the news." I am surprised that the man whom I just met on horseback should be so earnest to overtake his newly bought cows running away,—since all property is insecure, and if they do not run away again, they may be taken away from him when he gets them. Fool! does he not know that his seed-corn is worth less this year,—that all beneficent harvests fail as you approach the empire of hell? No prudent man will build a stone house under these circumstances, or engage in any peaceful enterprise which it requires a long time to accomplish. Art is as long as ever, but life is more interrupted and less available for a man's proper pursuits. It is not an era of repose. We have used up all our inherited freedom. If we would save our lives, we must fight for them.

I walk toward one of our ponds; but what signifies the beauty of nature when men are base? We walk to lakes to see our serenity reflected in them; when we are not serene, we go not to them. Who can be serene in a country where both the rulers and the ruled are without principle? The remembrance of my country spoils my walk. My thoughts are murder to the State, and involuntarily go plotting against her.

But it chanced the other day that I scented a white water-lily, and a season I had waited for had arrived. It is the emblem of purity. It bursts up so pure and fair to the eye, and so sweet to the scent, as if to show us what purity and sweetness reside in, and can be extracted from, the slime and muck of earth. I think I have plucked the first one that has opened for a mile. What confirmation of our hopes is in the fragrance of this flower! I shall not so soon despair of the world for it, notwithstanding slavery, and the cowardice and want of principle of Northern men. It suggests what kind of laws have prevailed longest and widest, and still prevail, and that the time may come when man's deeds will smell as sweet. Such is the odor which the plant emits. If Nature can compound this fragrance still annually, I shall believe her still young and full of vigor, her integrity and genius unimpaired, and that there is virtue even in man, too, who is fitted to perceive and love it. It reminds me that Nature has been partner to no Missouri Compromise. I scent no compromise in the fragrance of the water-lily. It is not a *Nymphœa* DOUGLASII. In it, the sweet, and pure, and innocent are wholly sundered from the obscene and baleful. I do not scent in this the time-serving irresolution of a Massachusetts Governor, nor of a Boston Mayor. So behave that the odor of your actions may enhance the general sweetness of the atmosphere, that when we hold or scent a flower, we may not be reminded how inconsistent your deeds are with it; for all odor is but one form of advertisement of a moral quality, and if fair actions had not been performed, the lily would not smell sweet. The foul slime stands for the sloth and vice of man, the decay of humanity; the fragrant flower that springs from it, for the purity and courage which are immortal.

Slavery and servility have produced no sweet-scented flower annually, to charm the senses of men, for they have no real life: they are merely a decaying and a death, offensive to all healthy nostrils. We do not complain that they *live*, but that they do not *get buried*. Let the living bury them; even they are good for manure.

A PLEA FOR CAPTAIN JOHN BROWN
1860

I trust that you will pardon me for being here. I do not wish to force my thoughts upon you, but I feel forced myself. Little as I know of Captain Brown, I would fain do my part to correct the tone and the statements of the newspapers, and of my countrymen generally, respecting his character and actions. It costs us nothing to be just. We can at least express our sympathy with, and admiration of, him and his companions, and that is what I now propose to do.

First, as to his history. I will endeavor to omit, as much as possible, what you have already read. I need not describe his person to you, for probably most of you have seen and will not soon forget him. I am told that his grandfather, John Brown, was an officer in the Revolution; that he himself was born in Connecticut about the beginning of this century, but early went with his father to Ohio. I heard him say that his father was a contractor who furnished beef to the army there, in the War of 1812; that he accompanied him to the camp, and assisted him in that employment, seeing a good deal of military life,—more, perhaps, than if he had been a soldier; for he was often present at the councils of the officers. Especially, he learned by experience how armies are supplied and maintained in the field,—a work which, he observed, requires at least as much experience and skill as to lead them in battle. He said that few persons had any conception of the cost, even the pecuniary cost, of firing a single bullet in war. He saw enough, at any rate, to disgust him with a military life; indeed, to excite in him a great abhorrence of it; so much so, that though he was tempted by the offer of some petty office in the army, when he was about eighteen, he not only declined that, but he also refused to train when warned, and was

fined for it. He then resolved that he would never have anything to do with any war, unless it were a war for liberty.

When the troubles in Kansas began, he sent several of his
sons thither to strengthen the party of the Free State men, fitting
them out with such weapons as he had; telling them that if the
troubles should increase, and there should be need of him, he
would follow, to assist them with his hand and counsel. This, as
you all know, he soon after did; and it was through his agency,
far more than any other's, that Kansas was made free.

For a part of his life he was a surveyor, and at one time he
was engaged in wool-growing, and he went to Europe as an
agent about that business. There, as everywhere, he had his eyes
about him, and made many original observations. He said, for
instance, that he saw why the soil of England was so rich, and
that of Germany (I think it was) so poor, and he thought of writing to some of the crowned heads about it. It was because in England the peasantry live on the soil which they cultivate, but in
Germany they are gathered into villages at night. It is a pity that
he did not make a book of his observations.

I should say that he was an old-fashioned man in his respect for the Constitution, and his faith in the permanence of
this Union. Slavery he deemed to be wholly opposed to these,
and he was its determined foe.

He was by descent and birth a New England farmer, a man
of great common sense, deliberate and practical as that class is,
and tenfold more so. He was like the best of those who stood at
Concord Bridge once, on Lexington Common, and on Bunker
Hill, only he was firmer and higher-principled than any that I
have chanced to hear of as there. It was no abolition lecturer
that converted him. Ethan Allen and Stark, with whom he may
in some respects be compared, were rangers in a lower and less
important field. They could bravely face their country's foes, but
he had the courage to face his country herself when she was in
the wrong. A Western writer says, to account for his escape from
so many perils, that he was concealed under a "rural exterior"; as
if, in that prairie land, a hero should, by good rights, wear a citizen's dress only.

He did not go to the college called Harvard, good old
Alma Mater as she is. He was not fed on the pap that is there
furnished. As he phrased it, "I know no more of grammar than
one of your calves." But he went to the great university of the
West, where he sedulously pursued the study of Liberty, for

which he had early betrayed a fondness, and having taken many degrees, he finally commenced the public practice of Humanity in Kansas, as you all know. Such were *his humanities*, and not any study of grammar. He would have left a Greek accent slanting the wrong way, and righted up a falling man.

He was one of that class of whom we hear a great deal, but, for the most part, see nothing at all,—the Puritans. It would be in vain to kill him. He died lately in the time of Cromwell, but he reappeared here. Why should he not? Some of the Puritan stock are said to have come over and settled in New England. They were a class that did something else than celebrate their forefathers' day, and eat parched corn in remembrance of that time. They were neither Democrats nor Republicans, but men of simple habits, straightforward, prayerful; not thinking much of rulers who did not fear God, not making many compromises, nor seeking after available candidates.

"In his camp," as one has recently written, and as I have myself heard him state, "he permitted no profanity; no man of loose morals was suffered to remain there, unless, indeed, as a prisoner of war. 'I would rather,' said he, 'have the small-pox, yellow fever, and cholera, all together in my camp, than a man without principle. . . . It is a mistake, sir, that our people make, when they think that bullies are the best fighters, or that they are the fit men to oppose these Southerners. Give me men of good principles,—God-fearing men,—men who respect themselves, and with a dozen of them I will oppose any hundred such men as these Buford ruffians.'" He said that if one offered himself to be a soldier under him, who was forward to tell what he could or would do if he could only get sight of the enemy, he had but little confidence in him.

He was never able to find more than a score or so of recruits whom he would accept, and only about a dozen, among them his sons, in whom he had perfect faith. When he was here, some years ago, he showed to a few a little manuscript book,—his "orderly book" I think he called it,—containing the names of his company in Kansas, and the rules by which they bound themselves; and he stated that several of them had already sealed the contract with their blood. When some one remarked that, with the addition of a chaplain, it would have been a perfect Cromwellian troop, he observed that he would have been glad to add a chaplain to the list, if he could have found one who could fill that office worthily. It is easy enough to find one for the United States Army. I believe that he had prayers in his camp morning and evening, nevertheless.

He was a man of Spartan habits, and at sixty was scrupulous about his diet at your table, excusing himself by saying that he must eat sparingly and fare hard, as became a soldier, or one who was fitting himself for difficult enterprises, a life of exposure.

A man of rare common sense and directness of speech, as of action; a transcendentalist above all, a man of ideas and principles,—that was what distinguished him. Not yielding to a whim or transient impulse, but carrying out the purpose of a life. I noticed that he did not overstate anything, but spoke within bounds. I remember, particularly, how, in his speech here, he referred to what his family had suffered in Kansas, without ever giving the least vent to his pent-up fire. It was a volcano with an ordinary chimney-flue. Also referring to the deeds of certain Border Ruffians, he said, rapidly paring away his speech, like an experienced soldier, keeping a reserve of force and meaning, "They had a perfect right to be hung." He was not in the least a rhetorician, was not talking to Buncombe or his constituents anywhere, had no need to invent anything but to tell the simple truth, and communicate his own resolution; therefore he appeared incomparably strong, and eloquence in Congress and elsewhere seemed to me at a discount. It was like the speeches of Cromwell compared with those of an ordinary king.

As for his tact and prudence, I will merely say, that at a time when scarcely a man from the Free States was able to reach Kansas by any direct route, at least without having his arms taken from him, he, carrying what imperfect guns and other weapons he could collect, openly and slowly drove an ox-cart through Missouri, apparently in the capacity of a surveyor, with his surveying compass exposed in it, and so passed unsuspected, and had ample opportunity to learn the designs of the enemy. For some time after his arrival he still followed the same profession. When, for instance, he saw a knot of the ruffians on the prairie, discussing, of course, the single topic which then occupied their minds, he would, perhaps, take his compass and one of his sons, and proceed to run an imaginary line right through the very spot on which that conclave had assembled, and when he came up to them, he would naturally pause and have some talk with them, learning their news, and, at last, all their plans perfectly; and having thus completed his real survey he would resume his imaginary one, and run on his line till he was out of sight.

When I expressed surprise that he could live in Kansas at all, with a price set upon his head, and so large a number, including the authorities, exasperated against him, he accounted for it by saying, "It is perfectly well understood that I will not be taken." Much of the time for some years he has had to skulk in swamps, suffering from poverty, and from sickness which was the consequence of exposure, befriended only by Indians and a few whites. But though it might be known that he was lurking in a particular swamp, his foes commonly did not care to go in after him. He could even come out into a town where there were more Border Ruffians than Free State men, and transact some business, without delaying long, and yet not be molested; for, said he, "no little handful of men were willing to undertake it, and a large body could not be got together in season."

As for his recent failure, we do not know the facts about it. It was evidently far from being a wild and desperate attempt. His enemy Mr. Vallandigham is compelled to say that "it was among the best planned and executed conspiracies that ever failed."

Not to mention his other successes, was it a failure, or did it show a want of good management, to deliver from bondage a dozen human beings, and walk off with them by broad daylight, for weeks if not months, at a leisurely pace, through one State after another, for half the length of the North, conspicuous to all parties, with a price set upon his head, going into a courtroom on his way and telling what he had done, thus convincing Missouri that it was not profitable to try to hold slaves in his neighborhood?—and this, not because the government menials were lenient, but because they were afraid of him.

Yet he did not attribute his success, foolishly, to "his star," or to any magic. He said, truly, that the reason why such greatly superior numbers quailed before him was, as one of his prisoners confessed, because they *lacked a cause,*—a kind of armor which he and his party never lacked. When the time came, few men were found willing to lay down their lives in defense of what they knew to be wrong; they did not like that this should be their last act in this world.

But to make haste to *his* last act, and its effects.

The newspapers seem to ignore, or perhaps are really ignorant, of the fact that there are at least as many as two or three individuals to a town throughout the North who think much as the present speaker does about him and his enterprise. I do not hesitate to say that they are an important and growing party. We aspire to be something more than stupid and timid chattels, pretending to read history and our Bibles, but desecrating every house and every day we breathe in. Perhaps anxious politicians may prove that only seventeen white men and five negroes were concerned in the late enterprise; but their very anxiety to prove this might suggest to themselves that all is not told. Why do they still dodge the truth? They are so anxious because of a dim consciousness of the fact, which they do not distinctly face, that at least a million of the free inhabitants of the United States would have rejoiced if it had succeeded. They at most only criticise the tactics. Though we wear no crape, the thought of that man's position and probable fate is spoiling many a man's day here at the North for other thinking. If any one who has seen him here can pursue successfully any other train of thought, I do not know what he is made of. If there is any such who gets his usual allowance of sleep, I will warrant him to fatten easily under any circumstances which do not touch his body or purse. I put a piece of paper and a pencil under my pillow, and when I could not sleep I wrote in the dark.

On the whole, my respect for my fellow-men, except as one may outweigh a million, is not being increased these days. I have noticed the cold-blooded way in which newspaper writers and men generally speak of this event, as if an ordinary malefactor, though one of unusual "pluck,"—as the Governor of Virginia is reported to have said, using the language of the cock-pit, "the gamest man he ever saw,"—had been caught, and were about to be hung. He was not dreaming of his foes when the governor thought he looked so brave. It turns what sweetness I have to gall, to hear, or hear of, the remarks of some of my neighbors. When we heard at first that he was dead, one of my townsmen observed that "he died as the fool dieth"; which, pardon me, for an instant suggested a likeness in him dying to my neighbor living. Others, craven-hearted, said disparagingly, that "he threw his life away," because he resisted the government. Which way have they thrown *their* lives, pray?—such as would praise a man for attacking singly an ordinary band of thieves or murderers. I hear another ask, Yankee-like, "What will he gain by it?" as if he expected to fill his pockets by this enterprise. Such a one has no idea of gain but in this worldly sense. If it does not lead to a "surprise" party, if he does not get a new pair of boots, or a vote of thanks, it must be a failure. "But he won't gain anything by it." Well, no, I don't suppose he could get four-and-six-pence a day for being hung, take the year round; but then he stands a chance to save a considerable part of his soul,—and *such* a soul!—when *you* do not. No doubt you can get more in your market for a quart of milk than for a quart of blood, but that is not the market that heroes carry their blood to.

Such do not know that like the seed is the fruit, and that, in the moral world, when good seed is planted, good fruit is inevitable, and does not depend on our watering and cultivating; that when you plant, or bury, a hero in his field, a crop of heroes is sure to spring up. This is a seed of such force and vitality, that it does not ask our leave to germinate.

The momentary charge at Balaklava, in obedience to a blundering command, proving what a perfect machine the soldier is, has, properly enough, been celebrated by a poet laureate; but the steady, and for the most part successful, charge of this man, for some years, against the legions of Slavery, in obedience to an infinitely higher command, is as much more memorable than that as an intelligent and conscientious man is superior to a machine. Do you think that that will go unsung?

"Served him right,"—"A dangerous man,"—"He is undoubtedly insane." So they proceed to live their sane, and wise, and altogether admirable lives, reading their Plutarch a little, but chiefly pausing at that feat of Putnam, who was let down into a wolf's den; and in this wise they nourish themselves for brave and patriotic deeds some time or other. The Tract Society could afford to print that story of Putnam. You might open the district schools with the reading of it, for there is nothing about Slavery or the Church in it; unless it occurs to the reader that some pastors are *wolves* in sheep's clothing. "The American Board of Commissioners for Foreign Missions," even, might dare to protest against *that* wolf. I have heard of boards, and of American boards, but it chances that I never heard of this particular lumber till lately. And yet I hear of Northern men, and women, and children, by families, buying a "life-membership" in such societies as these. A life-membership in the grave! You can get buried cheaper than that.

Our foes are in our midst and all about us. There is hardly a house but is divided against itself, for our foe is the all but universal woodenness of both head and heart, the want of vitality in man, which is the effect of our vice; and hence are begotten fear, superstition, bigotry, persecution, and slavery of all kinds. We are mere figure-heads upon a hulk, with livers in the place of hearts. The curse is the worship of idols, which at length changes the worshiper into a stone image himself; and the New Englander is just as much an idolater as the Hindoo. This man was an exception, for he did not set up even a political graven image between him and his God.

A church that can never have done with excommunicating Christ while it exists! Away with your broad and flat churches, and your narrow and tall churches! Take a step forward, and invent a new style of out-houses. Invent a salt that will save you, and defend our nostrils.

The modern Christian is a man who has consented to say all the prayers in the liturgy, provided you will let him go straight to bed and sleep quietly afterward. All his prayers begin with "Now I lay me down to sleep," and he is forever looking forward to the time when he shall go to his "*long* rest." He has consented to perform certain old-established charities, too, after a fashion, but he does not wish to hear of any new-fangled ones; he doesn't wish to have any supplementary articles added to the contract, to fit it to the present time. He shows the whites of his eyes on the Sabbath, and the blacks all the rest of the week. The evil is not merely a stagnation of blood, but a stagnation of spirit. Many, no doubt, are well disposed, but sluggish by constitution and by habit, and they cannot conceive of a man who is actuated by higher motives than they are. Accordingly they pronounce this man insane, for they know that *they* could never act as he does, as long as they are themselves.

We dream of foreign countries, of other times and races of men, placing them at a distance in history or space; but let some significant event like the present occur in our midst, and we discover, often, this distance and this strangeness between us and our nearest neighbors. *They* are our Austrias, and Chinas, and South Sea Islands. Our crowded society becomes well spaced all at once, clean and handsome to the eye,—a city of magnificent distances. We discover why it was that we never got beyond compliments and surfaces with them before; we become aware of as many vents between us and them as there are between a wandering Tartar and a Chinese town. The thoughtful man becomes a hermit in the thoroughfares of the market-place. Impassable seas suddenly find their level between us, or dumb steppes stretch themselves out there. It is the difference of constitution, of intelligence, and faith, and not streams and mountains, that make the true and impassable boundaries between individuals and between states. None but the like-minded can come plenipotentiary to our court.

I read all the newspapers I could get within a week after this event, and I do not remember in them a single expression of sympathy for these men. I have since seen one noble statement, in a Boston paper, not editorial. Some voluminous sheets decided not to print the full report of Brown's words to the exclusion of other matter. It was as if a publisher should reject the manuscript of the New Testament, and print Wilson's last speech. The same journal which contained this pregnant news was chiefly filled, in parallel columns, with the reports of the political conventions that were being held. But the descent to them was too steep. They should have been spared this contrast,—been printed in an extra, at least. To turn from the voices and deeds of earnest men to the *cackling* of political conventions! Office-seekers and speech-makers, who do not so much as lay an honest egg, but wear their breasts bare upon an egg of chalk! Their great game is the game of straws, or rather that universal aboriginal game of the platter, at which the Indians cried *hub, bub*! Exclude the reports of religious and political conventions, and publish the words of a living man.

But I object not so much to what they have omitted as to what they have inserted. Even the *Liberator* called it "a misguided, wild, and apparently insane—effort." As for the herd of newspapers and magazines, I do not chance to know an editor in the country who will deliberately print anything which he knows will ultimately and permanently reduce the number of his subscribers. They do not believe that it would be expedient. How then can they print truth? If we do not say pleasant things, they argue, nobody will attend to us. And so they do like some traveling auctioneers, who sing an obscene song, in order to draw a crowd around them. Republican editors, obliged to get their sentences ready for the morning edition, and accustomed to look at everything by the twilight of politics, express no admiration, nor true sorrow even, but call these men "deluded fanatics,"—"mistaken men,"—"insane," or "crazed." It suggests what a *sane* set of editors we are blessed with, *not* "mistaken men"; who know very well on which side their bread is buttered, at least.

A man does a brave and humane deed, and at once, on all sides, we hear people and parties declaring, "I didn't do it, nor countenance *him* to do it, in any conceivable way. It can't be fairly inferred from my past career." I, for one, am not interested to hear you define your position. I don't know that I ever was or ever shall be. I think it is mere egotism, or impertinent at this time. Ye needn't take so much pains to wash your skirts of him. No intelligent man will ever be convinced that he was any creature of yours. He went and came, as he himself informs us, "under the auspices of John Brown and nobody else." The Republican Party does not perceive how many his *failure* will make to vote more correctly than they would have them. They have counted the votes of Pennsylvania & Co., but they have not correctly counted Captain Brown's vote. He has taken the wind out of their sails,—the little wind they had,—and they may as well lie to and repair.

What though he did not belong to your clique! Though you may not approve of his method or his principles, recognize his magnanimity. Would you not like to claim kindredship with him in that, though in no other thing he is like, or likely, to you? Do you think that you would lose your reputation so? What you lost at the spile, you would gain at the bung.

If they do not mean all this, then they do not speak the truth, and say what they mean. They are simply at their old tricks still.

"It was always conceded to him," *says one who calls him crazy,* "that he was a conscientious man, very modest in his demeanor, apparently inoffensive, until the subject of Slavery was introduced, when he would exhibit a feeling of indignation unparalleled."

The slave-ship is on her way, crowded with its dying victims; new cargoes are being added in mid-ocean; a small crew of slaveholders, countenanced by a large body of passengers, is smothering four millions under the hatches, and yet the politician asserts that the only proper way by which deliverance is to be obtained is by "the quiet diffusion of the sentiments of humanity," without any "outbreak." As if the sentiments of humanity were ever found unaccompanied by its deeds, and you could disperse them, all finished to order, the pure article, as easily as water with a watering-pot, and so lay the dust. What is that that I hear cast overboard? The bodies of the dead that have found deliverance. That is the way we are "diffusing" humanity, and its sentiments with it.

Prominent and influential editors, accustomed to deal with politicians, men of an infinitely lower grade, say, in their ignorance, that he acted "on the principle of revenge." They do not know the man. They must enlarge themselves to conceive of him. I have no doubt that the time will come when they will begin to see him as he was. They have got to conceive of a man of faith and of religious principle, and not a politician or an Indian; of a man who did not wait till he was personally interfered with or thwarted in some harmless business before he gave his life to the cause of the oppressed.

If Walker may be considered the representative of the South, I wish I could say that Brown was the representative of the North. He was a superior man. He did not value his bodily life in comparison with ideal things. He did not recognize unjust human laws, but resisted them as he was bid. For once we are lifted out of the trivialness and dust of politics into the region of truth and manhood. No man in America has ever stood up so persistently and effectively for the dignity of human nature, knowing himself for a man, and the equal of any and all governments. In that sense he was the most American of us all. He needed no babbling lawyer, making false issues, to defend him. He was more than a match for all the judges that American voters, or office-holders of whatever grade, can create. He could not have been tried by a jury of his peers, because his peers did not exist. When a man stands up serenely against the condemnation and vengeance of mankind, rising above them literally *by a whole body*,—even though he were of late the vilest murderer, who has settled that matter with himself,—the spectacle is a sublime one,—didn't ye know it, ye *Liberators*, ye *Tribunes*, ye *Republicans*?—and we become criminal in comparison. Do yourselves the honor to recognize him. He needs none of your respect.

As for the Democratic journals, they are not human enough to affect me at all. I do not feel indignation at anything they may say.

I am aware that I anticipate a little,—that he was still, at the last accounts, alive in the hands of his foes; but that being the case, I have all along found myself thinking and speaking of him as physically dead.

I do not believe in erecting statues to those who still live in our hearts, whose bones have not yet crumbled in the earth around us, but I would rather see the statue of Captain Brown in the Massachusetts State-House yard than that of any other man whom I know. I rejoice that I live in this age, that I am his contemporary.

What a contrast, when we turn to that political party which is so anxiously shuffling him and his plot out of its way, and looking around for some available slaveholder, perhaps, to he its candidate, at least for one who will execute the Fugitive Slave Law, and all those other unjust laws which he took up arms to annul!

Insane! A father and six sons, and one son-in-law, and several more men besides,—as many at least as twelve disciples,—all struck with inanity at once; while the sane tyrant holds with a firmer gripe than ever his four millions of slaves, and a thousand sane editors, his abettors, are saving their country and their bacon! Just as insane were his efforts in Kansas. Ask the tyrant who is his most dangerous foe, the sane man or the insane? Do the thousands who know him best, who have rejoiced at his deeds in Kansas, and have afforded him material aid there, think him insane? Such a use of this word is a mere trope with most who persist in using it, and I have no doubt that many of the rest have already in silence retracted their-words.

Read his admirable answers to Mason and others. How they are dwarfed and defeated by the contrast! On the one side, half-brutish, half-timid questioning; on the other, truth, clear as lightning, crashing into their obscene temples. They are made to stand with Pilate, and Gessler, and the Inquisition. How ineffectual their speech and action! and what a void their silence! They are but helpless tools in this great work. It was no human power that gathered them about this preacher.

What have Massachusetts and the North sent a few sane representatives to Congress for, of late years?—to declare with effect what kind of sentiments? All their speeches put together and boiled down—and probably they themselves will confess it—do not match for manly directness and force, and for simple truth, the few casual remarks of crazy John Brown on the floor of the Harper's Ferry engine-house,—that man whom you are about to hang, to send to the other world, though not to represent *you* there. No, he was not our representative in any sense. He was too fair a specimen of a man to represent the like of us.

Who, then, *were* his constituents? If you read his words under-
standingly you will find out. In his case there is no idle eloquence, no made, nor maiden speech, no compliments to the
oppressor. Truth is his inspirer, and earnestness the polisher of
his sentences. He could afford to lose his Sharp's rifles, while he
retained his faculty of speech,—a Sharp's rifle of infinitely surer
and longer range.

And the New York *Herald* reports the conversation *verba-
tim*! It does not know of what undying words it is made the vehicle.

I have no respect for the penetration of any man who can
read the report of that conversation and still call the principal in
it insane. It has the ring of a saner sanity than an ordinary disci-
pline and habits of life, than an ordinary organization, secure.
Take any sentence of it,—"Any questions that I can honorably
answer, I will; not otherwise. So far as I am myself concerned, I
have told everything truthfully. I value my word, sir." The few
who talk about his vindictive spirit, while they really admire his
heroism, have no test by which to detect a noble man, no amal-
gam to combine with his pure gold. They mix their own dross
with it.

It is a relief to turn from these slanders to the testimony of
his more truthful, but frightened jailers and hangmen. Governor Wise speaks far more justly and appreciatingly of him than
any Northern editor, or politician, or public personage, that I
chance to have heard from. I know that you can afford to hear
him again on this subject. He says: "They are themselves mistaken who take him to be a madman. . . . He is cool, collected,
and indomitable, and it is but just to him to say that he was humane to his prisoners. . . . And he inspired me with great trust
in his integrity as a man of truth. He is a fanatic, vain and garrulous" (I leave that part to Mr. Wise), "but firm, truthful, and intelligent. His men, too, who survive, are like him. . . . Colonel
Washington says that he was the coolest and firmest man he
ever saw in defying danger and death. With one son dead by his
side, and another shot through, he felt the pulse of his dying son
with one hand, and held his rifle with the other, and commanded his men with the utmost composure, encouraging
them to be firm, and to sell their lives as dear as they could. Of
the three white prisoners, Brown, Stevens, and Coppoc, it was
hard to say which was most firm."

Almost the first Northern men whom the slaveholder has learned to respect!

The testimony of Mr. Vallandigham, though less valuable, is of the same purport, that "it is vain to underrate either the man or his conspiracy. . . . He is the farthest possible removed from the ordinary ruffian, fanatic, or madman."

"All is quiet at Harper's Ferry," say the journals. What is the character of that calm which follows when the law and the slaveholder prevail? I regard this event as a touchstone designed to bring out, with glaring distinctness, the character of this government. We needed to be thus assisted to see it by the light of history. It needed to see itself. When a government puts forth its strength on the side of injustice, as ours to maintain slavery and kill the liberators of the slave, it reveals itself a merely brute force, or worse, a demoniacal force. It is the head of the Plug-Uglies. It is more manifest than ever that tyranny rules. I see this government to be effectually allied with France and Austria in oppressing mankind. There sits a tyrant holding fettered four millions of slaves; here comes their heroic liberator. This most hypocritical and diabolical government looks up from its seat on the gasping four millions, and inquires with an assumption of innocence: "What do you assault me for? Am I not an honest man? Cease agitation on this subject, or I will make a slave of you, too, or else hang you."

We talk about a *representative* government; but what a monster of a government is that where the noblest faculties of the mind, and the *whole* heart, are not *represented*! A semi-human tiger or ox, stalking over the earth, with its heart taken out and the top of its brain shot away. Heroes have fought well on their stumps when their legs were shot off, but I never heard of any good done by such a government as that.

The only government that I recognize—and it matters not how few are at the head of it, or how small its army—is that power that establishes justice in the land, never that which establishes injustice. What shall we think of a government to which all the truly brave and just men in the land are enemies, standing between it and those whom it oppresses? A government that pretends to be Christian and crucifies a million Christs every day!

Treason! Where does such treason take its rise? I cannot help thinking of you as you deserve, ye governments. Can you dry up the fountains of thought? High treason, when it is resistance to tyranny here below, has its origin in, and is first committed by, the power that makes and forever re-creates man. When you have caught and hung all these human rebels, you have accomplished nothing but your own guilt, for you have not struck at the fountain-head. You presume to contend with a foe against whom West Point cadets and rifled cannon *point* not. Can all the art of the cannon-founder tempt matter to turn against its maker? Is the form in which the founder thinks he casts it more essential than the constitution of it and of himself?

The United States have a coffle of four millions of slaves. They are determined to keep them in this condition; and Massachusetts is one of the confederated overseers to prevent their escape. Such are not all the inhabitants of Massachusetts, but such are they who rule and are obeyed here. It was Massachusetts, as well as Virginia, that put down this insurrection at Harper's Ferry. She sent the marines there, and she will have *to pay the penalty of her sin*.

Suppose that there is a society in this State that out of its own purse and magnanimity saves all the fugitive slaves that run to us, and protects our colored fellow-citizens, and leaves the other work to the government, so called. Is not that government fast losing its occupation, and becoming contemptible to mankind? If private men are obliged to perform the offices of government, to protect the weak and dispense justice, then the government becomes only a hired man, or clerk, to perform menial or indifferent services. Of course, that is but the shadow of a government whose existence necessitates a Vigilant Committee. What should we think of the Oriental Cadi even, behind whom worked in secret a Vigilant Committee? But such is the character of our Northern States generally; each has its Vigilant Committee. And, to a certain extent, these crazy governments recognize and accept this relation. They say, virtually, "We'll be glad to work for you on these terms, only don't make a noise about it." And thus the government, its salary being insured, withdraws into the back shop, taking the Constitution with it, and bestows most of its labor on repairing that. When I hear it at work sometimes, as I go by, it reminds me, at best, of those farmers who in winter contrive to turn a penny by following the coopering business. And what kind of spirit is their barrel made to hold? They speculate in stocks, and bore holes in mountains, but they are not competent to lay out even a decent highway. The only *free* road, the Underground Railroad, is owned and managed by the Vigilant Committee. *They* have tunneled under the whole breadth of the land. Such a government is losing its power and respectability as surely as water runs out of a leaky vessel, and is held by one that can contain it.

I hear many condemn these men because they were so few. When were the good and the brave ever in a majority? Would you have had him wait till that time came?—till you and I came over to him? The very fact that he had no rabble or troop of hirelings about him would alone distinguish him from ordinary heroes. His company was small indeed, because few could he found worthy to pass muster. Each one who there laid down his life for the poor and oppressed was a picked man, culled out of many thousands, if not millions; apparently a man of principle, of rare courage, and devoted humanity; ready to sacrifice his life at any moment for the benefit of his fellow-man. It may be doubted if there were as many more their equals in these respects in all the country,—I speak of his followers only, for their leader, no doubt, scoured the land far and wide, seeking to swell his troop. These alone were ready to step between the oppressor and the oppressed. Surely they were the very best men you could select to be hung. That was the greatest compliment which this country could pay them. They were ripe for her gallows. She has tried a long time, she has hung a good many, but never found the right one before.

When I think of him, and his six sons, and his son-in-law, not to enumerate the others, enlisted for this fight, proceeding coolly, reverently, humanely to work, for months if not years, sleeping and waking upon it, summering and wintering the thought, without expecting any reward but a good conscience, while almost all America stood ranked on the other side,—I say again that it affects me as a sublime spectacle. If he had had any journal advocating "*his cause*," any organ, as the phrase is, monotonously and wearisomely playing the same old tune, and then passing round the hat, it would have been fatal to his efficiency. If he had acted in any way so as to be let alone by the government, he might have been suspected. It was the fact that the tyrant must give place to him, or he to the tyrant, that distinguished him from all the reformers of the day that I know.

It was his peculiar doctrine that a man has a perfect right to interfere by force with the slaveholder, in order to rescue the slave. I agree with him. They who are continually shocked by slavery have some right to be shocked by the violent death of the slaveholder, but no others. Such will be more shocked by his life than by his death. I shall not be forward to think him mistaken in his method who quickest succeeds to liberate the slave. I speak for the slave when I say that I prefer the philanthropy of Captain Brown to that philanthropy which neither shoots me nor liberates me. At any rate, I do not think it is quite sane for one to spend his whole life in talking or writing about this matter, unless he is continuously inspired, and I have not done so. A man may have other affairs to attend to. I do not wish to kill nor to be killed, but I can foresee circumstances in which both these things would be by me unavoidable. We preserve the so-called peace of our community by deeds of petty violence every day. Look at the policeman's billy and handcuffs! Look at the jail! Look at the gallows! Look at the chaplain of the regiment! We are hoping only to live safely on the outskirts of *this* provisional army. So we defend ourselves and our hen-roosts, and maintain slavery. I know that the mass of my countrymen think that the only righteous use that can be made of Sharp's rifles and revolvers is to fight duels with them, when we are insulted by other nations, or to hunt Indians, or shoot fugitive slaves with them, or the like. I think that for once the Sharp's rifles and the revolvers were employed in a righteous cause. The tools were in the hands of one who could use them.

The same indignation that is said to have cleared the temple once will clear it again. The question is not about the weapon, but the spirit in which you use it. No man has appeared in America, as yet, who loved his fellow-man so well, and treated him so tenderly. He lived for him. He took up his life and he laid it down for him. What sort of violence is that which is encouraged, not by soldiers, but by peaceable citizens, not so much by laymen as by ministers of the Gospel, not so much by the fighting sects as by the Quakers, and not so much by Quaker men as by Quaker women?

This event advertises me that there is such a fact as death,—the possibility of a man's dying. It seems as if no man had ever died in America before; for in order to die you must first have lived. I don't believe in the hearses, and palls, and funerals that they have had. There was no death in the case, because there had been no life; they merely rotted or sloughed off, pretty much as they had rotted or sloughed along. No temple's veil was rent, only a hole dug somewhere. Let the dead bury their dead. The best of them fairly ran down like a clock.

Franklin,—Washington,—they were let off without dying; they were merely missing one day. I hear a good many pretend that they are going to die; or that they have died, for aught that I know. Nonsense! I'll defy them to do it. They haven't got life enough in them. They'll deliquesce like fungi, and keep a hundred eulogists mopping the spot where they left off. Only half a dozen or so have died since the world began. Do you think that you are going to die, sir? No! there's no hope of you. You haven't got your lesson yet. You've got to stay after school. We make a needless ado about capital punishment,—taking lives, when there is no life to take. *Memento mori!* We don't understand that sublime sentence which some worthy got sculptured on his gravestone once. We've interpreted it in a groveling and sniveling sense; we've wholly forgotten how to die.

But be sure you do die nevertheless. Do your work, and finish it. If you know how to begin, you will know when to end.

These men, in teaching us how to die, have at the same time taught us how to live. If this man's acts and words do not create a revival, it will be the severest possible satire on the acts and words that do. It is the best news that America has ever heard. It has already quickened the feeble pulse of the North, and infused more and more generous blood into her veins and heart than any number of years of what is called commercial and political prosperity could. How many a man who was lately contemplating suicide has now something to live for!

One writer says that Brown's peculiar monomania made him to be "dreaded by the Missourians as a supernatural being." Sure enough, a hero in the midst of us cowards is always so dreaded. He is just that thing. He shows himself superior to nature. He has a spark of divinity in him.

> "Unless above himself he can
> Erect himself, how poor a thing is man!"

Newspaper editors argue also that it is a proof of his *insanity* that he thought he was appointed to do this work which he did,—that he did not suspect himself for a moment! They talk as if it were impossible that a man could be "divinely appointed" in these days to do any work whatever; as if vows and religion were out of date as connected with any man's daily work; as if the agent to abolish slavery could only be somebody appointed by the President, or by some political party. They talk as if a man's death were a failure, and his continued life, be it of whatever character, were a success.

When I reflect to what a cause this man devoted himself, and how religiously, and then reflect to what cause his judges and all who condemn him so angrily and fluently devote themselves, I see that they are as far apart as the heavens and earth are asunder.

The amount of it is, our "*leading men*" are a harmless kind of folk, and they know *well enough* that *they* were not divinely appointed, but elected by the votes of their party.

Who is it whose safety requires that Captain Brown be hung? Is it indispensable to any Northern man? Is there no resource but to cast this man also to the Minotaur? If you do not wish it, say so distinctly. While these things are being done, beauty stands veiled and music is a screeching lie. Think of him,—of his rare qualities!—such a man as it takes ages to make, and ages to understand; no mock hero, nor the representative of any party. A man such as the sun may not rise upon again in this benighted land. To whose making went the costliest material, the finest adamant; sent to be the redeemer of those in captivity; and the only use to which you can put him is to hang him at the end of a rope! You who pretend to care for Christ crucified, consider what you are about to do to him who offered himself to be the saviour of four millions of men.

Any man knows when he is justified, and all the wits in the world cannot enlighten him on that point. The murderer always knows that he is justly punished; but when a government takes the life of a man without the consent of his conscience, it is an audacious government, and is taking a step towards its own dissolution. Is it not possible that an individual may he right and a government wrong? Are laws to be enforced simply because they were made? or declared by any number of men to he good, if they are *not* good? Is there any necessity for a man's being a tool to perform a deed of which his better nature disapproves? Is it the intention of law-makers that *good* men shall be hung ever? Are judges to interpret the law according to the letter, and not the spirit? What right have *you* to enter into a compact with yourself that you *will* do thus or so, against the light within you? Is it for *you* to *make up* your mind,—to form any resolution whatever,—and not accept the convictions that are forced upon you, and which ever pass your understanding? I do not believe in lawyers, in that mode of attacking or defending

a man, because you descend to meet the judge on his own
ground, and, in cases of the highest importance, it is of no consequence whether a man breaks a human law or not. Let lawyers
decide trivial cases. Business men may arrange that among
themselves. If they were the interpreters of the everlasting laws
which rightfully bind man, that would be another thing. A
counterfeiting law-factory, standing half in a slave land and half
in a free! What kind of laws for free men can you expect from
that?

I am here to plead his cause with you. I plead not for his
life, but for his character,—his immortal life; and so it becomes
your cause wholly, and is not his in the least. Some eighteen
hundred years ago Christ was crucified; this morning, perchance,
Captain Brown was hung. These are the two ends of a chain
which is not without its links. He is not Old Brown any longer;
he is an angel of light.

I see now that it was necessary that the bravest and hu-
manest man in all the country should be hung. Perhaps he saw
it himself. I *almost fear* that I may yet hear of his deliverance,
doubting if a prolonged life, if *any* life, can do as much good as
his death.

"Misguided!" "Garrulous!" "Insane!" "Vindictive!" So ye
write in your easy-chairs, and thus he wounded responds from
the floor of the armory, clear as a cloudless sky, true as the voice
of nature is: "No man sent me here; it was my own prompting
and that of my Maker. I acknowledge no master in human
form."

And in what a sweet and noble strain he proceeds, ad-
dressing his captors, who stand over him: "I think, my friends,
you are guilty of a great wrong against God and humanity, and it
would be perfectly right for any one to interfere with you, so far
as to free those you willfully and wickedly hold in bondage."

And, referring to his movement: "It is, in my opinion, the
greatest service a man can render to God."

"I pity the poor in bondage that have none to help them;
that is why I am here; not to gratify any personal animosity, revenge, or vindictive spirit. It is my sympathy with the oppressed
and the wronged, that are as good as you, and as precious in the
sight of God."

You don't know your testament when you see it. "I want
you to understand that I respect the rights of the poorest and

weakest of colored people, oppressed by the slave power, just as much as I do those of the most wealthy and powerful."

"I wish to say, furthermore, that you had better, all you people at the South, prepare yourselves for a settlement of that question, that must come up for settlement sooner than you are prepared for it. The sooner you are prepared the better. You may dispose of me very easily. I am nearly disposed of now; but this question is still to be settled,—this negro question, I mean; the end of that is not yet."

I foresee the time when the painter will paint that scene, no longer going to Rome for a subject; the poet will sing it; the historian record it; and, with the Landing of the Pilgrims and the Declaration of Independence, it will be the ornament of some future national gallery, when at least the present form of slavery shall be no more here. We shall then be at liberty to weep for Captain Brown. Then, and not till then, we will take our revenge.

THE LAST DAYS OF JOHN BROWN
1860

John Brown's career for the last six weeks of his life was meteor-like, flashing through the darkness in which we live. I know of nothing so miraculous in our history.

If any person, in a lecture or conversation at that time, cited any ancient example of heroism, such as Cato or Tell or Winkelried, passing over the recent deeds and words of Brown, it was felt by any intelligent audience of Northern men to be tame and inexcusably far-fetched.

For my own part, I commonly attend more to nature than to man, but any affecting human event may blind our eyes to natural objects. I was so absorbed in him as to be surprised whenever I detected the routine of the natural world surviving still, or met persons going about their affairs indifferent. It appeared strange to me that the "little dipper" should be still diving quietly in the river, as of yore; and it suggested that this bird might continue to dive here when Concord should be no more.

I felt that he, a prisoner in the midst of his enemies and under sentence of death, if consulted as to his next step or resource, could answer more wisely than all his countrymen beside. He best understood his position; he contemplated it most calmly. Comparatively, all other men, North and South, were beside themselves. Our thoughts could not revert to any greater or wiser or better man with whom to contrast him, for he, then and there, was above them all. The man this country was about to hang appeared the greatest and best in it.

Years were not required for a revolution of public opinion; days, nay hours, produced marked changes in this case. Fifty who were ready to say, on going into our meeting in honor of him in Concord, that he ought to be hung, would not say it when they came out. They heard his words read; they saw the earnest faces of the congregation; and perhaps they joined at last in singing the hymn in his praise.

The order of instructors was reversed. I heard that one preacher, who at first was shocked and stood aloof, felt obliged at last, after he was hung, to make him the subject of a sermon, in which, to some extent, he eulogized the man, but said that his act was a failure. An influential class-teacher thought it necessary, after the services, to tell his grown-up pupils that at first he thought as the preacher did then, but now he thought that John Brown was right. But it was understood that his pupils were as much ahead of the teacher as he was ahead of the priest; and I know for a certainty that very little boys at home had already asked their parents, in a tone of surprise, why God did not interfere to save him. In each case, the constituted teachers were only half conscious that they were not *leading*, but being *dragged*, with some loss of time and power.

The more conscientious preachers, the Bible men, they who talk about principle, and doing to others as you would that they should do unto you, how could they fail to recognize him, by far the greatest preacher of them all, with the Bible in his life and in his acts, the embodiment of principle, who actually carried the golden rule? All whose moral sense had been aroused, who had a calling from on high to preach, sided with him. What confessions he extracted from the cold and conservative! It is remarkable, but on the whole it is well, that it did not prove the occasion for a new sect of *Brownites* being formed in our midst.

They, whether within the Church or out of it, who adhere to the spirit and let go the letter, and are accordingly called infidel, were as usual foremost to recognize him. Men have been hung in the South before for attempting to rescue slaves, and the North was not much stirred by it. Whence, then, this wonderful difference? We were not so sure of *their* devotion to principle. We made a subtle distinction, forgot human laws, and did homage to an idea. The North, I mean the *living* North, was suddenly all transcendental. It went behind the human law, it went behind the apparent failure, and recognized eternal justice and glory. Commonly, men live according to a formula, and are satisfied if the order of law is observed, but in this they, to some extent, returned to original perceptions, and there was a slight revival of old religion. They saw that what was called order was confusion, what was called justice, injustice, and that the best was deemed the worst. This attitude suggested a more intelligent and generous spirit than that which actuated our forefathers, and the possibility, in the course of ages, of a revolution in behalf of another and an oppressed people.

Most Northern men, and a few Southern ones, were wonderfully stirred by Brown's behavior and words. They saw and felt that they were heroic and noble, and that there had been nothing quite equal to them in their kind in this country, or in the recent history of the world. But the minority were unmoved by them. They were only surprised and provoked by the attitude of their neighbors. They saw that Brown was brave, and that he believed that he had done right, but they did not detect any further peculiarity in him. Not being accustomed to make fine distinctions, or to appreciate magnanimity, they read his letters and speeches as if they read them not. They were not aware when they approached a heroic statement,—they did not know when they *burned*. They did not feel that he spoke with authority, and hence they only remembered that the law must he executed. They remembered the old formula, but did not hear the new revelation. The man who does not recognize in Brown's words a wisdom and nobleness, and therefore an authority, superior to our laws, is a modern Democrat. This is the test by which to discover him. He is not willfully but constitutionally blind on this side, and he is consistent with himself. Such has been his past life; no doubt of it. In like manner he has read history and his Bible, and he accepts, or seems to accept, the last only as an established formula, and not because he has been convicted by it. You will not find kindred sentiments in his commonplace-book, if he has one.

When a noble deed is done, who is likely to appreciate it? They who are noble themselves. I was not surprised that certain of my neighbors spoke of John Brown as an ordinary felon, for who are they? They have either much flesh, or much office, or much coarseness of some kind. They are not ethereal natures in any sense. The dark qualities predominate in them. Several of them are decidedly pachydermatous. I say it in sorrow, not in anger. How can a man behold the light who has no answering inward light? They are true to their *sight*, but when they look this way they *see* nothing, they are blind. For the children of the light to contend with them is as if there should be a contest between eagles and owls. Show me a man who feels bitterly to-

ward John Brown, and let me hear what noble verse he can repeat. He'll be as dumb as if his lips were stone.

It is not every man who can be a Christian, even in a very
moderate sense, whatever education you give him. It is a matter
of constitution and temperament, after all. He may have to be
born again many times. I have known many a man who pretended to be a Christian, in whom it was ridiculous, for he had
no genius for it. It is not every man who can be a free man,
even.

Editors persevered for a good while in saying that Brown
was crazy; but at last they said only that it was "a crazy scheme,"
and the only evidence brought to prove it was that it cost him
his life. I have no doubt that if he had gone with five thousand
men, liberated a thousand slaves, killed a hundred or two slaveholders, and had as many more killed on his own side, but not
lost his own life, these same editors would have called it by a
more respectable name. Yet he has been far more successful
than that. He has liberated many thousands of slaves, both
North and South. They seem to have known nothing about living or dying for a principle. They all called him crazy then; who
calls him crazy now?

All through the excitement occasioned by his remarkable
attempt and subsequent behavior the Massachusetts legislature,
not taking any steps for the defense of her citizens who were
likely to be carried to Virginia as witnesses and exposed to the
violence of a slaveholding mob, was wholly absorbed in a liquor-
agency question, and indulging in poor jokes on the word "extension." Bad spirits occupied their thoughts. I am sure that no
statesman up to the occasion could have attended to that question at all at that time,—a very vulgar question to attend to at
any time!

When I looked into a liturgy of the Church of England,
printed near the end of the last century, in order to find a service
applicable to the case of Brown, I found that the only martyr recognized and provided for by it was King Charles the First, an eminent scamp. Of all the inhabitants of England and of the world,
he was the only one, according to this authority, whom that
church had made a martyr and saint of; and for more than a century it had celebrated his martyrdom, so called, by an annual
service. What a satire on the Church is that!

Look not to legislatures and churches for your guidance, nor to any soulless *incorporated* bodies, but to *inspirited* or inspired ones.

What avail all your scholarly accomplishments and learning, compared with wisdom and manhood? To omit his other behavior, see what a work this comparatively unread and unlettered man wrote within six weeks. Where is our professor of *belles-lettres*, or of logic and rhetoric, who can write so well? He wrote in prison, not a History of the World, like Raleigh, but an American book which I think will live longer than that. I do not know of such words, uttered under such circumstances, and so copiously withal, in Roman or English or any history. What a variety of themes he touched on in that short space! There are words in that letter to his wife, respecting the education of his daughters, which deserve to be framed and hung over every mantelpiece in the land. Compare this earnest wisdom with that of Poor Richard.

The death of Irving, which at any other time would have attracted universal attention, having occurred while these things were transpiring, went almost unobserved. I shall have to read of it in the biography of authors.

Literary gentlemen, editors, and critics think that they know how to write, because they have studied grammar and rhetoric; but they are egregiously mistaken. The art of composition is as simple as the discharge of a bullet from a rifle, and its masterpieces imply an infinitely greater force behind them. This unlettered man's speaking and writing are standard English. Some words and phrases deemed vulgarisms and Americanisms before, he has made standard American; such as "*It will pay.*" It suggests that the one great rule of composition—and if I were a professor of rhetoric I should insist on this—is, to *speak the truth*. This first, this second, this third; pebbles in your mouth or not. This demands earnestness and manhood chiefly.

We seem to have forgotten that the expression "a *liberal* education" originally meant among the Romans one worthy of *free* men; while the learning of trades and professions by which to get your livelihood merely was considered worthy of *slaves* only. But taking a hint from the word, I would go a step further, and say that it is not the man of wealth and leisure simply, though devoted to art, or science, or literature, who, in a true sense, is *liberally* educated, but only the earnest and *free* man. In a slaveholding country like this, there can be no such thing as a *liberal* education tolerated by the State; and those scholars of Austria and France who, however learned they may he, are contented under their tyrannies have received only a *servile* education.

Nothing could his enemies do but it redounded to his infinite advantage,—that is, to the advantage of his cause. They did not hang him at once, but reserved him to preach to them. And then there was another great blunder. They did not hang his four followers with him; that scene was still postponed; and so his victory was prolonged and completed. No theatrical manager could have arranged things so wisely to give effect to his behavior and words. And who, think you, *was* the manager? *Who* placed the slave-woman and her child, whom he stooped to kiss for a symbol, between his prison and the gallows?

We soon saw, as he saw, that he was not to be pardoned or rescued by men. That would have been to disarm him, to restore to him a material weapon, a Sharp's rifle, when he had taken up the sword of the spirit,—the sword with which he has really won his greatest and most memorable victories. Now he has not laid aside the sword of the spirit, for he is pure spirit himself, and his sword is pure spirit also.

> "He nothing common did or mean
> Upon that memorable scene, . . .
> Nor called the gods with vulgar spite,
> To vindicate his helpless right;
> But bowed his comely head
> Down, as upon a bed."

What a transit was that of his horizontal body alone, but just cut down from the gallows-tree! We read that at such a time it passed through Philadelphia, and by Saturday night had reached New York. Thus like a meteor it shot through the Union from the Southern regions toward the North! No such freight had the cars borne since they carried him southward alive.

On the day of his translation, I heard, to be sure, that he was *hung*, but I did not know what that meant; I felt no sorrow on that account; but not for a day or two did I even *hear* that he was *dead*, and not after any number of days shall I believe it. Of all the men who were said to be my contemporaries, it seemed to me that John Brown was the only one who *had not died*. I never hear of a man named Brown now,—and I hear of them pretty often,—I never hear of any particularly brave and earnest man, but my first thought is of John Brown, and what relation he may be to him. I meet him at every turn. He is more alive than ever he was. He has earned immortality. He is not confined to North Elba nor to Kansas. He is no longer working in secret. He works in public, and in the clearest light that shines on this land.

AFTER THE DEATH OF JOHN BROWN
1860

At the services held in Concord, Massachusetts, December 2, 1859, in commemoration of John Brown, executed that day, Mr. Thoreau said: So universal and widely related is any transcendent moral greatness. and so nearly identical with greatness everywhere and in every age,—as a pyramid contracts the nearer you approach its apex,—that, when I now look over my commonplace-book of poetry, I find that the best of it is oftenest applicable, in part or wholly, to the case of Captain Brown. Only what is true, and strong, and solemnly earnest will recommend itself to our mood at this time. Almost any noble verse may be read, either as his elegy or eulogy, or be made the text of an oration on him. Indeed, such are now discovered to be the parts of a universal liturgy, applicable to those rare cases of heroes and martyrs for which the ritual of no church has provided. This is the formula established on high,—their burial service,—to which every great genius has contributed its stanza or line. As Marvell wrote:—

> "When the sword glitters o'er the judge's head.
> And far has coward churchmen silencèd,
> Then is the poet's time; 't is then he draws,
> And single fights forsaken virtue's cause;
> He, when the wheel of empire whirleth back,
> And though the world's disjointed axle crack,
> Sings still of ancient rights and better times,
> Seeks suffering good, arraigns successful crimes."

The sense of grand poetry, read by the light of this event, is brought out distinctly like an invisible writing held to the fire:—

"All heads must come
To the cold tomb,—
Only the actions of the just
Smell sweet and blossom in the dust."

We have heard that the Boston lady who recently visited our hero in prison found him wearing still the clothes, all cut and torn by sabres and by bayonet-thrusts, in which he had been taken prisoner; and thus he had gone to his trial; and without a hat. She spent her time in prison mending those clothes, and, for a memento, brought home a pin covered with blood.

What are the clothes that endure?

"The garments lasting evermore
Are works of mercy to the poor;
And neither tetter, time, nor moth
Shall fray that silk or fret this cloth."

The well-known verses called "The Soul's Errand," supposed, by some, to have been written by Sir Walter Raleigh when he was expecting to be executed the following day, are at least worthy of such an origin, and are equally applicable to the present case. [Mr. Thoreau then read these verses, as well as a number of poetical passages selected by another citizen of Concord, and closed with the following translation front Tacitus made by himself.]

"You, Agricola, are fortunate, not only because your life was glorious, but because your death was timely. As they tell us who heard your last words, unchanged and willing you accepted your fate; as if, as far as in your power, you would make the emperor appear innocent. But, besides the bitterness of having lost a parent, it adds to our grief, that it was not permitted us to minister to your health, . . . to gaze on your countenance, and receive your last embrace; surely, we might have caught some words and commands which we would have treasured in the inmost part of our souls. This is our pain, this our wound. . . . You were buried with the fewer tears, and in your last earthly light your eyes looked around for something which they did not see.

"If there is any abode for the spirits of the pious, if, as wise men suppose, great souls are not extinguished with the body, may you rest placidly, and call your family from weak regrets and womanly laments to the contemplation of your virtues, which must not be lamented, either silently or aloud. Let us honor you by our admiration rather than by short-lived praises, and, if nature aid us, by our emulation of you. That is true honor, that the piety of whoever is most akin to you. This also I would teach your family, so to venerate your memory as to call to mind all your actions and words, and embrace your character and the form of your soul rather than of your body; not because I think that statues which are made of marble or brass are to be condemned, but as the features of men, so images of the features are frail and perishable. The form of the soul is eternal; and this we can retain and express, not by a foreign material and art, but by our own lives. Whatever of Agricola we have loved, whatever we have admired, remains, and will remain, in the minds of men and the records of history, through the eternity of ages. For oblivion will overtake many of the ancients, as if they were inglorious and ignoble: Agricola, described and transmitted to posterity, will survive."

LIFE WITHOUT PRINCIPLE
1863

At a lyceum, not long since, I felt that the lecturer had chosen a theme too foreign to himself, and so failed to interest me as much as he might have done. He described things not in or near to his heart, but toward his extremities and superficies. There was, in this sense, no truly central or centralizing thought in the lecture. I would have had him deal with his privatest experience, as the poet does. The greatest compliment that was ever paid me was when one asked me what I *thought*, and attended to my answer. I am surprised, as well as delighted, when this happens, it is such a rare use he would make of me, as if he were acquainted with the tool. Commonly, if men want anything of me, it is only to know how many acres I make of their land,— since I am a surveyor,—or, at most, what trivial news I have burdened myself with. They never will go to law for my meat; they prefer the shell. A man once came a considerable distance to ask me to lecture on Slavery; but on conversing with him, I found that he and his clique expected seven eighths of the lecture to be theirs, and only one eighth mine; so I declined. I take it for granted, when I am invited to lecture anywhere,—for I have had a little experience in that business,—that there is a desire to hear what I *think* on some subject, though I may be the greatest fool in the country,—and not that I should say pleasant things merely, or such as the audience will assent to; and I resolve, accordingly, that I will give them a strong dose of myself. They have sent for me, and engaged to pay for me, and I am determined that they shall have me, though I bore them beyond all precedent.

So now I would say something similar to you, my readers. Since *you* are my readers, and I have not been much of a traveler, I will not talk about people a thousand miles off, but come

as near home as I can. As the time is short, I will leave out all
the flattery, and retain all the criticism.

Let us consider the way in which we spend our lives. This
world is a place of business. What an infinite bustle! I am
awaked almost every night by the panting of the locomotive. It
interrupts my dreams, There is no sabbath. It would be glorious
to see mankind at leisure for once. It is nothing but work, work,
work. I cannot easily buy a blank-book to write thoughts in; they
are commonly ruled for dollars and cents. An Irishman, seeing
me making a minute in the fields, took it for granted that I was
calculating my wages. If a man was tossed out of a window
when an infant, and so made a cripple for life, or scared out of
his wits by the Indians, it is regretted chiefly because he was thus
incapacitated for—business! I think that there is nothing, not
even crime, more opposed to poetry, to philosophy, ay, to life itself, than this incessant business.

There is a coarse and boisterous money-making fellow in
the outskirts of our town, who is going to build a bank-wall under the hill along the edge of his meadow. The powers have put
this into his head to keep him out of mischief, and he wishes me
to spend three weeks digging there with him. The result will be
that be will perhaps get some more money to hoard, and leave
for his heirs to spend foolishly. If I do this, most will commend
me as an industrious and hard-working man; but if I choose to
devote myself to certain labors which yield more real profit,
though but little money, they may be inclined to look on me as
an idler. Nevertheless, as I do not need the police of
meaningless labor to regulate me, and do not see anything absolutely praiseworthy in this fellow's undertaking any more than
in many an enterprise of our own or foreign governments,
however amusing it may be to him or them, I prefer to finish
my education at a different school.

If a man walk in the woods for love of them half of each
day, he is in danger of being regarded as a loafer; but if he spends
his whole day as a speculator, shearing off those woods and making earth bald before her time, he is esteemed an industrious and
enterprising citizen. As if a town had no interest in its forests
but to cut them down!

Most men would feel insulted if it were proposed to employ them in throwing stones over a wall, and then in throwing
them back, merely that they might earn their wages. But many
are no more worthily employed now. For instance: just after

sunrise, one summer morning, I noticed one of my neighbors walking beside his team, which was slowly drawing a heavy hewn stone swung under the axle, surrounded by an atmosphere of industry,—his day's work begun,—his brow commenced to sweat,—a reproach to all sluggards and idlers,—pausing abreast the shoulders of his oxen, and half turning round with a flourish of his merciful whip, while they gained their length on him.   And I thought, Such is the labor which the American Congress exists to protect,—honest, manly toil,—honest as the day is long,—that makes his bread taste sweet, and keeps society sweet,—which all men respect and have consecrated; one of the sacred band, doing the needful but irksome drudgery. Indeed, I felt a slight reproach, because I observed this from a window, and was not abroad and stirring about a similar business. The day went by, and at evening I passed the yard of another neighbor, who keeps many servants, and spends much money foolishly, while he adds nothing to the common stock, and there I saw the stone of the morning lying beside a whimsical structure intended to adorn this Lord Timothy Dexter's premises, and the dignity forthwith departed from the teamster's labor, in my eyes. In my opinion, the sun was made to light worthier toil than this. I may add that his employer has since run off, in debt to a good part of the town, and, after passing through Chancery, has settled somewhere else, there to become once more a patron of the arts.

The ways by which you may get money almost without exception lead downward. To have done anything by which you earned money *merely* is to have been truly idle or worse. If the laborer gets no more than the wages which his employer pays him, he is cheated, he cheats himself. If you would get money as a writer or lecturer, you must be popular, which is to go down perpendicularly. Those services which the community will most readily pay for, it is most disagreeable to render. You are paid for being something less than a man. The state does not commonly reward a genius any more wisely. Even the poet laureate would rather not have to celebrate the accidents of royalty. He must be bribed with a pipe of wine; and perhaps another poet is called away from his muse to gauge that very pipe. As for my own business, even that kind of surveying which I could do with most satisfaction my employers do not want. They would prefer that I should do my work coarsely and not too well, ay, not well enough. When I observe that there are different ways of surveying, my employer commonly asks which will give him the most land, not which is most correct. I once invented a rule for measuring cord-wood, and tried to introduce it in Boston; but the measurer there told me that the sellers did not wish to have their wood measured correctly,—that he was already too accurate for them, and therefore they commonly got their wood measured in Charlestown before crossing the bridge.

The aim of the laborer should be, not to get his living, to get "a good job," but to perform well a certain work; and, even in a pecuniary sense, it would be economy for a town to pay its laborers so well that they would not feel that they were working for low ends, as for a livelihood merely, but for scientific, or even moral ends. Do not hire a man who does your work for money, but him who does it for love of it.

It is remarkable that there are few men so well employed, so much to their minds, but that a little money or fame would commonly buy them off from their present pursuit. I see advertisements for *active* young men, as if activity were the whole of a young man's capital. Yet I have been surprised when one has with confidence proposed to me, a grown man, to embark in some enterprise of his, as if I had absolutely nothing to do, my life having been a complete failure hitherto. What a doubtful compliment this to pay me! As if he had met me half-way across the ocean beating up against the wind, but bound nowhere, and proposed to me to go along with him! If I did, what do you think the underwriters would say? No, no! I am not without employment at this stage of the voyage. To tell the truth, I saw an advertisement for able-bodied seamen, when I was a boy, sauntering in my native port, and as soon as I came of age I embarked.

The community has no bribe that will tempt a wise man. You may raise money enough to tunnel a mountain, but you cannot raise money enough to hire a man who is minding *his own* business. An efficient and valuable man does what he can, whether the community pay him for it or not. The inefficient offer their inefficiency to the highest bidder, and are forever expecting to be put into office. One would suppose that they were rarely disappointed.

Perhaps I am more than usually jealous with respect to my freedom. I feel that my connection with and obligation to society are still very slight and transient. Those slight labors which afford me a livelihood, and by which it is allowed that I am to some extent serviceable to my contemporaries, are as yet commonly a pleasure to me, and I am not often reminded that they are a necessity. So far I am successful. But I foresee that if my wants should be much increased, the labor required to supply them would become a drudgery. If I should sell both my forenoons and afternoons to society, as most appear to do, I am sure that for me there would be nothing left worth living for. I trust that I shall never thus sell my birthright for a mess of pottage. I wish to suggest that a man may be very industrious, and yet not spend his time well. There is no more fatal blunderer than he who consumes the greater part of his life getting his living. All great enterprises are self-supporting. The poet, for instance, must sustain his body by his poetry, as a steam planing-mill feeds its boilers with the shavings it makes. You must get your living by loving. But as it is said of the merchants that ninety-seven in a hundred fail, so the life of men generally, tried by this standard, is a failure, and bankruptcy may be surely prophesied.

Merely to come into the world the heir of a fortune is not to be born, but to be still-born, rather. To be supported by the charity of friends, or a government pension,—provided you continue to breathe,—by whatever fine synonyms you describe these relations, is to go into the almshouse. On Sundays the poor debtor goes to church to take an account of stock, and finds, of course, that his outgoes have been greater than his income. In the Catholic Church, especially, they go into chancery, make a clean confession, give up all, and think to start again. Thus men will lie on their backs, talking about the fall of man, and never make an effort to get up.

As for the comparative demand which men make on life, it is an important difference between two, that the one is satisfied with a level success, that his marks can all be hit by point-blank shots, but the other, however low and unsuccessful his life may be, constantly elevates his aim, though at a very slight angle to the horizon. I should much rather be the last man,—though, as the Orientals say, "Greatness doth not approach him who is forever looking down; and all those who are looking high are growing poor."

It is remarkable that there is little or nothing to be remembered written on the subject of getting a living; how to make getting a living not merely honest and honorable, but altogether inviting and glorious; for if *getting* a living is not so, then living is not. One would think, from looking at literature, that this question had never disturbed a solitary individual's musings. Is it that men are too much disgusted with their experience to speak of it? The lesson of value which money teaches, which the Author of the Universe has taken so much pains to teach us, we are inclined to skip altogether. As for the means of living, it is wonderful how indifferent men of all classes are about it, even reformers, so called,—whether they inherit, or earn, or steal it. I think that Society has done nothing for us in this respect, or at least has undone what she has done. Cold and hunger seem more friendly to my nature than those methods which men have adopted and advise to ward them off.

The title *wise* is, for the most part, falsely applied. How can one be a wise man, if he does not know any better how to live than other men?—if he is only more cunning and intellectually subtle? Does Wisdom work in a tread-mill? or does she teach how to succeed by *her example*? Is there any such thing as wisdom not applied to life? Is she merely the miller who grinds the finest logic? It is pertinent to ask if Plato got his *living* in a better way or more successfully than his contemporaries,—or did he succumb to the difficulties of life like other men? Did he seem to prevail over some of them merely by indifference, or by assuming grand airs? or find it easier to live, because his aunt remembered him in her will? The ways in which most men get their living, that is, live, are mere makeshifts, and a shirking of the real business of life,—chiefly because they do not know, but partly because they do not mean, any better.

The rush to California, for instance, and the attitude, not merely of merchants, but of philosophers and prophets, so called, in relation to it, reflect the greatest disgrace on mankind. That so many are ready to live by luck, and so get the means of commanding the labor of others less lucky, without contributing any value to society! And that is called enterprise! I know of no more startling development of the immorality of trade, and all the common modes of getting a living. The philosophy and poetry and religion of such a mankind are not worth the dust of a puff ball. The hog that gets his living by rooting, stirring up the soil so, would be ashamed of such company. If I could command the wealth of all the worlds by lifting my finger, I would not pay *such* a price for it. Even Mahomet knew that God did not make this world in jest. It makes God to be a moneyed gentleman who scatters a handful of pennies in order to see mankind scramble

for them. The world's raffle! A subsistence in the domains of
Nature a thing to be raffled for! What a comment, what a satire,
on our institutions! The conclusion will be, that mankind will
hang itself upon a tree. And have all the precepts in all the
Bibles taught men only this? and is the last and most admirable
invention of the human race only an improved muck-rake? Is
this the ground on which Orientals and Occidentals meet? Did
God direct us so to get our living, digging where we never
planted,—and He would, perchance, reward us with lumps of
gold?

God gave the righteous man a certificate entitling him to
food and raiment, but the unrighteous man found a facsimile of
the same in God's coffers, and appropriated it, and obtained food
and raiment like the former. It is one of the most extensive systems of counterfeiting that the world has seen. I did not know
that mankind was suffering for want of gold. I have seen a little
of it. I know that it is very malleable, but not so malleable as wit.
A grain of gold will gild a great surface, but not so much as a
grain of wisdom.

The gold-digger in the ravines of the mountains is as
much a gambler as his fellow in the saloons of San Francisco.
What difference does it make whether you shake dirt or shake
dice? If you win, society is the loser. The gold-digger is the enemy of the honest laborer, whatever checks and compensations
there may be. It is not enough to tell me that you worked hard
to get your gold. So does the Devil work hard. The way of
transgressors may be hard in many respects. The humblest
observer who goes to the mines sees and says that gold-digging is
of the character of a lottery; the gold thus obtained is not the
same thing with the wages of honest toil. But, practically, he
forgets what he has seen, for he has seen only the fact, not the
principle, and goes into trade there, that is, buys a ticket in what
commonly proves another lottery, where the fact is not so obvious.

After reading Howitt's account of the Australian gold-dig-
gings one evening, I had in my mind's eye, all night, the numerous valleys, with their streams, all cut up with foul pits,
from ten to one hundred feet deep, and half a dozen feet across,
as close as they can be dug, and partly filled with water,—the locality to which men furiously rush to probe for their fortunes,—
uncertain where they shall break ground,—not knowing but the
gold is under their camp itself,—sometimes digging one hun-

dred and sixty feet before they strike the vein, or then missing it by a foot,—turned into demons, and regardless of each others' rights, in their thirst for riches,—whole valleys, for thirty miles, suddenly honeycombed by the pits of the miners, so that even hundreds are drowned in them,—standing in water, and covered with mud and clay, they work night and day, dying of exposure and disease. Having read this, and partly forgotten it, I was thinking, accidentally, of my own unsatisfactory life, doing as others do; and with that vision of the diggings still before me, I asked myself why *I* might not be washing some gold daily, though it were only the finest particles,—why *I* might not sink a shaft down to the gold within me, and work that mine. *There* is a Ballarat, a Bendigo for you,—what though it were a sulky-gully? At any rate, I might pursue some path, however solitary and narrow and crooked, in which I could walk with love and reverence. Wherever a man separates from the multitude, and goes his own way in this mood, there indeed is a fork in the road, though ordinary travelers may see only a gap in the paling. His solitary path across lots will turn out the *higher way* of the two.

Men rush to California and Australia as if the true gold were to be found in that direction; but that is to go to the very opposite extreme to where it lies. They go prospecting farther and farther away from the true lead, and are most unfortunate when they think themselves most successful. Is not our *native* soil auriferous? Does not a stream from the golden mountains flow through our native valley? and has not this for more than geologic ages been bringing down the shining particles and forming the nuggets for us? Yet, strange to tell, if a digger steal away, prospecting for this true gold, into the unexplored solitudes around us, there is no danger that any will dog his steps, and endeavor to supplant him. He may claim and undermine the whole valley even, both the cultivated and the uncultivated portions, his whole life long in peace, for no one will ever dispute his claim. They will not mind his cradles or his toms. He is not confined to a claim twelve feet square, as at Ballarat, but may mine anywhere, and wash the whole wide world in his tom.

Howitt says of the man who found the great nugget which weighed twenty-eight pounds, at the Bendigo diggings in Australia: "He soon began to drink; got a home, and rode all about, generally at full gallop, and, when he met people, called out to inquire if they knew who he was, and then kindly informed

them that he was 'the bloody wretch that had found the nugget.'
At last he rode full speed against a tree, and nearly knocked his
brains out." I think, however, there was no danger of that, for
he had already knocked his brains out against the nugget.
Howitt adds, "He is a hopelessly ruined man." But he is a type of
the class. They are all fast men. Hear some of the names of the
places where they dig: "Jackass Flat,"—"Sheep's-Head Gully,"—
"Murderer's Bar," etc. Is there no satire in these names? Let
them carry their ill-gotten wealth where they will, I am thinking
it will still be "Jackass Flat," if not "Murderer's Bar," where they
live.

   The last resource of our energy has been the robbing of
graveyards on the Isthmus of Darien, an enterprise which appears to be but in its infancy; for, according to late accounts, an
act has passed its second reading in the legislature of New
Granada, regulating this kind of mining; and a correspondent of
the "Tribune" writes: "In the dry season, when the weather will
permit of the country being properly prospected, no doubt other
rich *guacas* [that is, graveyards] will be found." To emigrants he
says: "Do not come before December; take the Isthmus route in
preference to the Boca del Toro one; bring no useless baggage,
and do not cumber yourself with a tent; but a good pair of blan-
kets will he necessary; a pick, shovel, and axe of good material
will be almost all that is required:" advice which might have
been taken from the "Burker's Guide." And he concludes with
this line in Italics and small capitals: "*If you are doing well at
home*, STAY THERE," which may fairly be interpreted to mean, "If
you are getting a good living by robbing graveyards at home, stay
there."

   But why go to California for a text? She is the child of
New England, bred at her own school and church.

   It is remarkable that among all the preachers there are so
few moral teachers. The prophets are employed in excusing the
ways of men. Most reverend seniors, the *illuminati* of the age,
tell me, with a gracious, reminiscent smile, betwixt an aspiration
and a shudder, not to be too tender about these things,—to lump
all that, that is, make a lump of gold of it. The highest advice I
have heard on these subjects was groveling. The burden of it
was,—It is not worth your while to undertake to reform the
world in this particular. Do not ask how your bread is buttered;
it will make you sick, if you do,—and the like. A man had better
starve at once than lose his innocence in the process of getting

his bread. If within the sophisticated man there is not an unsophisticated one, then he is but one of the devil's angels. As we grow old, we live more coarsely, we relax a little in our disciplines, and, to some extent, cease to obey our finest instincts. But we should be fastidious to the extreme of sanity, disregarding the gibes of those who are more unfortunate than ourselves.

In our science and philosophy, even, there is commonly no true and absolute account of things. The spirit of sect and bigotry has planted its hoof amid the stars. You have only to discuss the problem, whether the stars are inhabited or not, in order to discover it. Why must we daub the heavens as well as the earth? It was an unfortunate discovery that Dr. Kane was a Mason, and that Sir John Franklin was another. But it was a more cruel suggestion that possibly that was the reason why the former went in search of the latter. There is not a popular magazine in this country that would dare to print a child's thought on important subjects without comment. It must be submitted to the D.D.'s. I would it were the chickadee-dees.

You come from attending the funeral of mankind to attend to a natural phenomenon. A little thought is sexton to all the world.

I hardly know an *intellectual* man, even, who is so broad and truly liberal that you can think aloud in his society. Most with whom you endeavor to talk soon come to a stand against some institution in which they appear to hold stock,—that is, some particular, not universal, way of viewing things. They will continually thrust their own low roof, with its narrow skylight, between you and the sky, when it is the unobstructed heavens you would view. Get out of the way with your cobwebs; wash your windows, I say! In some lyceums they tell me that they have voted to exclude the subject of religion. But how do I know what their religion is, and when I am near to or far from it? I have walked into such an arena and done my best to make a clean breast of what religion I have experienced, and the audience never suspected what I was about. The lecture was as harmless as moonshine to them. Whereas, if I had read to them the biography of the greatest scamps in history, they might have thought that I had written the lives of the deacons of their church. Ordinarily, the inquiry is, Where did you come from? or, Where are you going? That was a more pertinent question which I overheard one of my auditors put to another once,— "What does he lecture for?" It made me quake in my shoes.

To speak impartially, the best men that I know are not serene, a world in themselves. For the most part, they dwell in forms, and flatter and study effect only more finely than the rest. We select granite for the underpinning of our houses and barns; we build fences of stone; but we do not ourselves rest on an underpinning of granitic truth, the lowest primitive rock. Our sills are rotten. What stuff is the man made of who is not coexistent in our thought with the purest and subtlest truth? I often accuse my finest acquaintances of an immense frivolity; for, while there are manners and compliments we do not meet, we do not teach one another the lessons of honesty and sincerity that the brutes do, or of steadiness and solidity that the rocks do. The fault is commonly mutual, however; for we do not habitually demand any more of each other.

That excitement about Kossuth, consider how characteristic, but superficial, it was!—only another kind of politics or dancing. Men were making speeches to him all over the country, but each expressed only the thought, or the want of thought, of the multitude. No man stood on truth. They were merely banded together, as usual one leaning on another, and all together on nothing; as the Hindoos made the world rest on an elephant, the elephant on a tortoise, and the tortoise on a serpent, and had nothing to put under the serpent. For all fruit of that stir we have the Kossuth hat.

Just so hollow and ineffectual, for the most part, is our ordinary conversation. Surface meets surface. When our life ceases to be inward and private, conversation degenerates into mere gossip. We rarely meet a man who can tell us any news which he has not read in a newspaper, or been told by his neighbor; and, for the most part, the only difference between us and our fellow is that he has seen the newspaper, or been out to tea, and we have not. In proportion as our inward life fails, we go more constantly and desperately to the post-office. You may depend on it, that the poor fellow who walks away with the greatest number of letters, proud of his extensive correspondence, has not heard from himself this long while.

I do not know but it is too much to read one newspaper a week. I have tried it recently, and for so long it seems to me that I have not dwelt in my native region. The sun, the clouds, the snow, the trees say not so much to me. You cannot serve two masters. It requires more than a day's devotion to know and to possess the wealth of a day.

We may well be ashamed to tell what things we have read or heard in our day. I do not know why my news should be so trivial,—considering what one's dreams and expectations are, why the developments should be so paltry. The news we hear, for the most part, is not news to our genius. It is the stalest repetition. You are often tempted to ask why such stress is laid on a particular experience which you have had,—that, after twenty-five years, you should meet Hobbins, Registrar of Deeds, again on the sidewalk. Have you not budged an inch, then? Such is the daily news. Its facts appear to float in the atmosphere, insignificant as the sporules of fungi, and impinge on some neglected *thallus,* or surface of our minds, which affords a basis for them, and hence a parasitic growth. We should wash ourselves clean of such news. Of what consequence, though our planet explode, if there is no character involved in the explosion? In health we have not the least curiosity about such events. We do not live for idle amusement. I would not run round a corner to see the world blow up.

All summer, and far into the autumn, perchance, you unconsciously went by the newspapers and the news, and now you find it was because the morning and the evening were full of news to you. Your walks were full of incidents. You attended, not to the affairs of Europe, but to your own affairs in Massachusetts fields. If you chance to live and move and have your being in that thin stratum in which the events that make the news transpire,—thinner than the paper on which it is printed,—then these things will fill the world for you; but if you soar above or dive below that plane, you cannot remember nor be reminded of them. Really to see the sun rise or go down every day, so to relate ourselves to a universal fact, would preserve us sane forever. Nations! What are nations? Tartars, and Huns, and Chinamen! Like insects, they swarm. The historian strives in vain to make them memorable. It is for want of a man that there are so many men. It is individuals that populate the world. Any man thinking may say with the Spirit of Lodin,—

"I look down from my height on nations,
And they become ashes before me;—
Calm is my dwelling in the clouds;
Pleasant are the great fields of my rest."

Pray, let us live without being drawn by dogs, Esquimaux-fashion, tearing over hill and dale, and biting each other's ears.

Not without a slight shudder at the danger, I often perceive how near I had come to admitting into my mind the details of some trivial affair,—the news of the street; and I am astonished to observe how willing men are to lumber their minds with such rubbish,—to permit idle rumors and incidents of the most insignificant kind to intrude on ground which should be sacred to thought. Shall the mind be a public arena, where the affairs of the street and the gossip of the tea-table chiefly are discussed? Or shall it be a quarter of heaven itself,—an hypæthral temple, consecrated to the service of the gods? I find it so difficult to dispose of the few facts which to me are significant, that I hesitate to burden my attention with those which are insignificant, which only a divine mind could illustrate. Such is, for the most part, the news in newspapers and conversation. It is important to preserve the mind's chastity in this respect. Think of admitting the details of a single case of the criminal court into our thoughts, to stalk profanely through their very *sanctum sanctorum* for an hour, ay, for many hours! to make a very barroom of the mind's inmost apartment, as if for so long the dust of the street had occupied us,—the very street itself, with all its travel, its bustle, and filth, had passed through our thoughts' shrine! Would it not be an intellectual and moral suicide? When I have been compelled to sit spectator and auditor in a court-room for some hours, and have seen my neighbors, who were not compelled, stealing in from time to time, and tiptoeing about with washed hands and faces, it has appeared to my mind's eye, that, when they took off their hats, their ears suddenly expanded into vast hoppers for sound, between which even their narrow heads were crowded. Like the vanes of windmills, they caught the broad but shallow stream of sound, which, after a few titillating gyrations in their coggy brains, passed out the other side. I wondered if, when they got home, they were as careful to wash their ears as before their hands and faces. It has seemed to me, at such a time, that the auditors and the witnesses, the jury and the counsel, the judge and the criminal at the bar,—if I may presume him guilty before he is convicted,—were all equally criminal, and a thunderbolt might be expected to descend and consume them all together.

By all kinds of traps and signboards, threatening the extreme penalty of the divine law, exclude such trespassers from the only ground which can be sacred to you. It is so hard to forget what it is worse than useless to remember! If I am to be a thoroughfare, I prefer that it be of the mountain brooks, the Parnassian streams, and not the town sewers. There is inspiration, that gossip which comes to the ear of the attentive mind from the courts of heaven. There is the profane and stale revelation of the barroom and the police court. The same ear is fitted to receive both communications. Only the character of the hearer determines to which it shall be open, and to which closed. I believe that the mind can be permanently profaned by the habit of attending to trivial things, so that all our thoughts shall be tinged with triviality. Our very intellect shall be macadamized, as it were,—its foundation broken into fragments for the wheels of travel to roll over; and if you would know what will make the most durable pavement, surpassing rolled stones, spruce blocks, and asphaltum, you have only to look into some of our minds which have been subjected to this treatment so long.

If we have thus desecrated ourselves,—as who has not?—the remedy will be by wariness and devotion to reconsecrate ourselves, and make once more a fane of the mind. We should treat our minds, that is, ourselves, as innocent and ingenuous children, whose guardians we are, and be careful what objects and what subjects we thrust on their attention. Read not the Times. Read the Eternities. Conventionalities are at length as bad as impurities. Even the facts of science may dust the mind by their dryness, unless they are in a sense effaced each morning, or rather rendered fertile by the dews of fresh and living truth. Knowledge does not come to us by details, but in flashes of light from heaven. Yes, every thought that passes through the mind helps to wear and tear it, and to deepen the ruts, which, as in the streets of Pompeii, evince how much it has been used. How many things there are concerning which we might well deliberate whether we had better know them,—had better let their peddling-carts be driven, even at the slowest trot or walk, over that bridge of glorious span by which we trust to pass at last from the farthest brink of time to the nearest shore of eternity! Have we no culture, no refinement,—but skill only to live coarsely and serve the Devil?—to acquire a little worldly wealth, or fame, or liberty, and make a false show with it, as if we were all husk and shell, with no tender and living kernel to us? Shall our institutions be like those chestnut burs which contain abortive nuts, perfect only to prick the fingers?

America is said to be the arena on which the battle of freedom is to be fought; but surely it cannot be freedom in a merely political sense that is meant. Even if we grant that the American has freed himself from a political tyrant, he is still the slave of an economical and moral tyrant. Now that the republic—the *res-publica*—has been settled, it is time to look after the *res-privata,*—the private state,—to see, as the Roman senate charged its consuls, "*ne quid res*-PRIVATA *detrimenti caperet,*" that the *private* state receive no detriment.

Do we call this the land of the free? What is it to be free from King George and continue the slaves of King Prejudice? What is it to be born free and not to live free? What is the value of any political freedom, but as a means to moral freedom? Is it a freedom to be slaves, or a freedom to be free, of which we boast? We are a nation of politicians, concerned about the outmost defenses only of freedom. It is our children's children who may perchance be really free. We tax ourselves unjustly. There is a part of us which is not represented. It is taxation without representation. We quarter troops, we quarter fools and cattle of all sorts upon ourselves. We quarter our gross bodies on our poor souls, till the former eat up all the latter's substance.

With respect to a true culture and manhood, we are essentially provincial still, not metropolitan,—mere Jonathan's. We are provincial, because we do not find at home our standards; because we do not worship truth, but the reflection of truth; because we are warped and narrowed by an exclusive devotion to trade and commerce and manufactures and agriculture and the like, which are but means, and not the end.

So is the English Parliament provincial. Mere country bumpkins, they betray themselves, when any more important question arises for them to settle, the Irish question, for instance,—the English question why did I not say? Their natures are subdued to what they work in. Their "good breeding" respects only secondary objects. The finest manners in the world are awkwardness and fatuity when contrasted with a finer intelligence. They appear but as the fashions of past days,—mere courtliness, knee-buckles and small clothes, out of date. It is the vice, but not the excellence of manners, that they are continually being deserted by the character; they are cast-off clothes or shells, claiming the respect which belonged to the living creature. You are presented with the shells instead of the meat, and it is no excuse generally, that, in the case of some fishes, the shells are of more worth than the meat. The man who thrusts his manners upon me does as if he were to insist on introducing me to his cabinet of curiosities, when I wished to see himself. It was not in this sense that the poet Decker called Christ "the first true gentleman that ever breathed." I repeat that in this sense the most splendid court in Christendom is provincial, having authority to consult about Transalpine interests only, and not the affairs of Rome. A prætor or proconsul would suffice to settle the questions which absorb the attention of the English Parliament and the American Congress.

Government and legislation! these I thought were respectable professions. We have heard of heaven-born Numas, Lycurguses, and Solons, in the history of the world, whose *names* at least may stand for ideal legislators; but think of legislating to *regulate* the breeding of slaves, or the exportation of tobacco! What have divine legislators to do with the exportation or the importation of tobacco? what humane ones with the breeding of slaves? Suppose you were to submit the question to any son of God,—and has He no children in the Nineteenth Century? is it a family which is extinct?—in what condition would you get it again? What shall a State like Virginia say for itself at the last day, in which these have been the principal, the staple productions? What ground is there for patriotism in such a State? I derive my facts from statistical tables which the States themselves have published.

A commerce that whitens every sea in quest of nuts and raisins, and makes slaves of its sailors for this purpose! I saw, the other day, a vessel which had been wrecked, and many lives lost, and her cargo of rags, juniper berries, and bitter almonds were strewn along the shore. It seemed hardly worth the while to tempt the dangers of the sea between Leghorn and New York for the sake of a cargo of juniper berries and bitter almonds. America sending to the Old World for her bitters! Is not the sea-brine, is not shipwreck, bitter enough to make the cup of life go down here? Yet such, to a great extent, is our boasted commerce; and there are those who style themselves statesmen and philosophers who are so blind as to think that progress and civilization depend on precisely this kind of interchange and activity,—the activity of flies about a molasses-hogshead. Very well, observes one, if men were oysters. And very well, answer I, if men were mosquitoes.

Lieutenant Herndon, whom our government sent to explore the Amazon, and, it is said, to extend the area of slavery, observed that there was wanting there "an industrious and active population, who know what the comforts of life are, and who have artificial wants to draw out the great resources of the country." But what are the "artificial wants" to be encouraged? Not the love of luxuries, like the tobacco and slaves of, I believe, his native Virginia, nor the ice and granite and other material wealth of our native New England; nor are "the great resources of a country" that fertility or barrenness of soil which produces these. The chief want, in every State that I have been into, was a high and earnest purpose in its inhabitants. This alone draws out "the great resources" of Nature, and at last taxes her beyond her resources; for man naturally dies out of her. When we want culture more than potatoes, and illumination more than sugar-plums, then the great resources of a world are taxed and drawn out, and the result, or staple production, is, not slaves, nor oper-atives, but men—those rare fruits called heroes, saints, poets, philosophers, and redeemers.

In short, as a snow-drift is formed where there is a lull in the wind, so, one would say, where there is a lull of truth, an in-stitution springs up. But the truth blows right on over it, never-theless, and at length blows it down.

What is called politics is comparatively something so su-perficial and inhuman, that practically I have never fairly recog-nized that it concerns me at all. The newspapers, I perceive, de-vote some of their columns specially to politics or government without charge; and this, one would say, is all that saves it; but as I love literature and to some extent the truth also, I never read those columns at any rate. I do not wish to blunt my sense of right so much. I have not got to answer for having read a single President's Message. A strange age of the world this, when em-pires, kingdoms, and republics come a-begging to a private man's door, and utter their complaints at his elbow! I cannot take up a newspaper but I find that some wretched government or other, hard pushed and on its last legs, is interceding with me, the reader, to vote for it,—more importunate than an Italian beggar; and if I have a mind to look at its certificate, made, per-chance, by some benevolent merchant's clerk, or the skipper that brought it over, for it cannot speak a word of English itself, I shall probably read of the eruption of some Vesuvius, or the overflowing of some Po, true or forged, which brought it into this condition. I do not hesitate, in such a case, to suggest work, or the almshouse; or why not keep its castle in silence, as I do commonly? The poor President, what with preserving his popularity and doing his duty, is completely bewildered. The newspapers are the ruling power. Any other government is reduced to a few marines at Fort Independence. If a man neglects to read the Daily Times, government will go down on its knees to him, for this is the only treason in these days.

Those things which now most engage the attention of men, as politics and the daily routine, are, it is true, vital functions of human society, but should be unconsciously performed, like the corresponding functions of the physical body. They are *infra*-human, a kind of vegetation. I sometimes awake to a half-consciousness of them going on about me, as a man may become conscious of some of the processes of digestion in a morbid state, and so have the dyspepsia, as it is called. It is as if a thinker submitted himself to be rasped by the great gizzard of creation. Politics is, as it were, the gizzard of society, full of grit and gravel, and the two political parties are its two opposite halves,—sometimes split into quarters, it may be, which grind on each other. Not only individuals, but states, have thus a confirmed dyspepsia, which expresses itself, you can imagine by what sort of eloquence. Thus our life is not altogether a forgetting, but also, alas! to a great extent, a remembering, of that which we should never have been conscious of, certainly not in our waking hours. Why should we not meet, not always as dyspeptics, to tell our bad dreams, but sometimes as *eu*peptics, to congratulate each other on the ever-glorious morning? I do not make an exorbitant demand, surely.

Section II

Informal Essays: Excursions

A WALK TO WACHUSETT
1843

Concord, July 19, 1842.
The needles of the pine
All to the west incline.

Summer and winter our eyes had rested on the dim outline of the mountains in our horizon, to which distance and in-
distinctness lent a grandeur not their own, so that they served
equally to interpret all the allusions of Poets and travelers;
whether with Homer, on a spring morning, we sat down on the
many-peaked Olympus, or with Virgil and his compeers roamed
the Etrurian and Thessalian hills, or with Humboldt measured
the more modern Andes and Teneriffe.   Thus we spoke our
mind to them, standing on the Concord cliffs:—

> With frontier strength ye stared your ground,
> With grand content ye circle round,
> Tumultuous silence for all sound,
> Ye distant nursery of rills,
> Monadnock, and the Peterboro' hills;
> Like some vast fleet,
> Sailing through rain and sleet,
> Through winter's cold and summer's heat;
> Still holding on, upon your high emprise,
> Until ye find a shore amid the skies;
> Not skulking close to land,
> With cargo contraband,
> For they who sent a venture out by ye
> Have set the sun to see
> Their honesty.
> Ships of the line, each one,
> Ye to the westward run,
> Always before the gale,
> Under a press of sail,

With weight of metal all untold.
I seem to feel ye, in my firm seat here,
Immeasurable depth of hold,
And breadth of beam, and length of running gear.

Methinks ye take luxurious pleasure
In your novel western leisure;
So cool your brows, and freshly blue,
As Time had sought for ye to do;
For ye lie at your length,
An unappropriated strength,
Unhewn primeval timber,
For knees so stiff, for masts so limber;
The stock of which new earths are made
One day to be our western trade,
Fit for the stanchions of a world
Which through the seas of space is hurled.

While we enjoy a lingering ray,
Ye still o'ertop the western day,
Reposing yonder on God's croft,
Like solid stacks of hay.
Edged with silver, and with gold,
The clouds hang o'er in damask fold,
And with such depth of amber light
The west is dight,
Where still a few rays slant,
That even haven seems extravagant.
On the earth's edge mountains and trees
Stand as they were on air graven,
Or as the vessels in a haven
Await the morning breeze.
I fancy even
Through your defiles windeth the way to heaven;
And yonder still, in spite of history's page,
Linger the golden and the silver age;
Upon the laboring gale
The news of future centuries is brought,
And of new dynasties of thought,
From your remotest vale.

But special I remember thee,
Wachusett, who like me
Standest alone without society.
Thy far blue eye,
A remnant of the sky,
Seen through the clearing or the gorge
Or from the windows of the forge,
Doth leaven all it passes by.

Nothing is true,
But stands 'tween me and you,
Thou western pioneer,
Who know'st not shame nor fear
By venturous spirit driven,
Under the eaves of heaven.
And canst expand thee there,
And breathe enough of air?
Upholding heaven, holding down earth,
They pastime from thy birth,
Not steadied by the one, nor leaning on the other;
May I approve myself thy worthy brother!

At length, like Rasselas, and other inhabitants of happy valleys, we resolved to scale the blue wall which bounded the western horizon, though not without misgivings that thereafter no visible fairyland would exist for us. But we will not leap at once to our journey's end, though near, but imitate Homer, who conducts his reader over the plain, and along the resounding sea, though it be but to the tent of Achilles. In the spaces of thought are the reaches of land and water, where men go and come. The landscape lies far and fair within, and the deepest thinker is the farthest traveled.

At a cool and early hour on a pleasant morning in July, my companion and I passed rapidly through Acton and Stow, stopping to rest and refresh us on the bank of a small stream, a tributary of the Assabet, in the latter town. As we traversed the cool woods of Acton, with stout staves in our hands, we were cheered by the song of the red-eye, the thrushes, the phœbe, and the cuckoo; and as we passed through the open country, we inhaled the fresh scent of every field, and all nature lay passive, to be viewed and traveled. Every rail, every farmhouse, seen dimly in the twilight, every tinkling sound told of peace and purity, and we moved happily along the dank roads, enjoying not such privacy as the day leaves when it withdraws, but such as it has not profaned. It was solitude with light; which is better than darkness. But anon, the sound of the mower's rifle was heard in the fields, and this, too, mingled with the lowing of kine.

This part of our route lay through the country of hops, which plant perhaps supplies the want of the vine in American scenery, and may remind the traveler of Italy and the South of France, whether he traverses the country when the hop-fields, as then, present solid and regular masses of verdure, hanging in graceful festoons from pole to pole, the cool coverts where lurk

the gales which refresh the wayfarer; or in September, when the
women and children, and the neighbors from far and near, are
gathered to pick the hops into long troughs; or later still, when
the poles stand piled in vast pyramids in the yards, or lie in
heaps by the roadside.

The culture of the hop, with the processes of picking, dry-
ing in the kiln, and packing for the market, as well as the uses to
which it is applied, so analogous to the culture and uses of the
grape, may afford a theme for future poets.

The mower in the adjacent meadow could not tell us the
name of the brook on whose banks we had rested, or whether it
had any, but his younger companion, perhaps his brother, knew
that it was Great Brook. Though they stood very near together
in the field, the things they knew were very far apart; nor did
they suspect each other's reserved knowledge, till the stranger
came by. In Bolton, while we rested on the rails of a cottage
fence, the strains of music which issued from within, probably in
compliment to us, sojourners, reminded us that thus far men
were fed by the accustomed pleasures. So soon did we, wayfar-
ers, begin to learn that man's life is rounded with the same few
facts, the same simple relations everywhere, and it is vain to
travel to find it new. The flowers grow more various ways than
he. But coming soon to higher land, which afforded a prospect
of the mountains, we thought we had not traveled in vain, if it
were only to hear a truer and wilder pronunciation of their
names from the lips of the inhabitants; not *Way*-tatic, *Way*-
chusett, but *Wor*-tatic, *Wor*-chusett. It made us ashamed of our
tame and civil pronunciation, and we looked upon them as born
and bred farther west than we. Their tongues had a more generous accent than ours, as if breath was cheaper where they
wagged. A countryman, who speaks but seldom, talks copiously,
as it were, as his wife sets cream and cheese before you without
stint. Before noon we had reached the highlands overlooking
the valley of Lancaster (affording the first fair and open prospect
into the west), and there, on the top of a hill, in the shade of
some oaks, near to where a spring bubbled out from a leaden
pipe, we rested during the heat of the day, reading Virgil and enjoying the scenery. It was such a place as one feels to be on the
outside of the earth; for from it we could, in some measure, see
the form and structure of the globe. There lay Wachusett, the
object of our journey, lowering upon us with unchanged proportions, though with a less ethereal aspect than had greeted our

morning gaze, while further north, in successive order, slumbered its sister mountains along the horizon.

We could get no further into the Æneid than

> —atque altae moenia Romae,
> —and the wall of high Rome,

before we were constrained to reflect by what myriad tests a work of genius has to be tried; that Virgil, away in Rome, two thousand years off, should have to unfold his meaning, the inspiration of Italian vales, to the pilgrim on New England hills. This life so raw and modern, that so civil and ancient; and yet we read Virgil mainly to be reminded of the identity of human nature in all ages, and, by the poet's own account, we are both the children of a late age, and live equally under the reign of Jupiter.

> "He shook honey from the leaves, and removed fire,
> And stayed the wine, everywhere flowing in rivers;
> That experience, by meditating, might invent various arts
> By degrees, and seek the blade of corn in furrows,
> And strike out hidden fire from the veins of the flint."

The old world sands serenely behind the new, as one mountain yonder towers behind another, more dim and distant. Rome imposes her story still upon this late generation. The very children in the school we had that morning passed had gone through her wars, and recited her alarms, ere they had heard of the wars of neighboring Lancaster. The roving eye still rests inevitably on her hills, and she still holds up the skirts of the sky on that side, and makes the past remote.

The lay of the land hereabouts is well worthy the attention of the traveler. The hill on which we were resting made part of an extensive range, running from southwest to northeast, across the country, and separating the waters of the Nashua from those of the Concord, whose banks we had left in the morning, and by beating in mind this fact, we could easily determine whither each brook was bound that crossed our path. Parallel to this, and fifteen miles further west, beyond the deep and broad valley in which lie Groton, Shirley, Lancaster, and Boylston, runs the Wachusett range, in the same general direction. The descent into the valley on the Nashua side is by far the most sudden; and a couple of miles brought us to the southern branch of the Nashua, a shallow but rapid stream, flowing between high and gravelly banks. But we soon learned that these were no *gel-idae valles* into which we had descended, and, missing the coolness of the morning air, feared it had become the sun's turn to try his power upon us.

> "The sultry sun had gained the middle sky,
> And not a tree, and not an herb was nigh,"

and with melancholy pleasure we echoed the melodious plaint of our fellow-traveler, Hassan, in the desert,—

> "Sad was the hour, and luckless was the day,
> When first from Schiraz' walls I bent my way."

The air lay lifeless between the hills, as in a seething caldron, with no leaf stirring, and instead of the fresh odor of grass and clover, with which we had before been regaled, the dry scent of every herb seemed merely medicinal. Yielding, therefore, to the heat, we strolled into the woods, and aiming the course of a rivulet, on whose banks we loitered, observing at our leisure the products of these new fields. He who traverses the woodland paths, at this season, will have occasion to remember the small, drooping, bell-like flowers and slender red stem of the dogsbane, and the coarser stem and berry of the poke, which are both common in remoter and wilder scenes; and if "the sun casts such a reflecting heat from the sweet-fern" as makes him faint, when he is climbing the bare hills, as they complained who first penetrated into these parts, the cool fragrance of the swamp-pink restores him again, when traversing the valleys between.

As we went on our way late in the afternoon, we refreshed ourselves by bathing our feet in every rill that crossed the road, and anon, as we were able to walk in the shadows of the hills, recovered our morning elasticity. Passing through Sterling, we reached the banks of the Stillwater, in the western part of the town, at evening, where is a small village collected. We fancied that there was already a certain western look about this place, a smell of pines and roar of water, recently confined by dams, belying its name, which were exceedingly grateful. When the first inroad has been made, a few acres leveled, and a few houses erected, the forest looks wilder than ever. Left to herself, nature is always more or less civilized, and delights in a certain refinement; but where the axe has encroached upon the edge of the forest, the dead and unsightly limbs of the pine, which she had concealed with green banks of verdure, are exposed to sight. This village had, as yet, no post-office, nor any settled name. In the small villages which we entered, the villagers gazed after us, with a complacent, almost compassionate look, as if we were just making our *début* in the world at a late hour. "Nevertheless," did they seem to say, "come and study us, and learn men and manners." So is each one's world but a clearing in the forest, so much open and inclosed ground. The landlord had not yet returned from the field with his men, and the cows had yet to be milked. But we remembered the inscription on the wall of the Swedish inn, "You will find at Trolhate excellent bread, meat, and wine, provided you bring them with you," and were contented. But I must confess it did somewhat disturb our pleasure, in this withdrawn spot, to have our own village newspaper handed us by our host, as if the greatest charm the country offered to the traveler was the facility of communication with the town. Let it recline on its own everlasting hills, and not be looking out from their summits for some petty Boston or New York in the horizon.

At intervals we heard the murmuring of water, and the slumberous breathing of crickets, throughout the night; and left the inn the next morning in the gray twilight, after it had been hallowed by the night air, and when only the innocent cows were stirring, with a kind of regret. It was only four miles to the base of the mountain, and the scenery was already more picturesque. Our road lay along the course of the Stillwater, which was brawling at the bottom of a deep ravine, filled with pines and rocks, tumbling fresh from the mountains, so soon, alas! to commence its career of usefulness. At first, a cloud hung between us and the summit, but it was soon blown away. As we gathered the raspberries, which grew abundantly by the roadside, we fancied that that action was consistent with a lofty prudence; as if the traveler who ascends into a mountainous region should fortify himself by eating of such light ambrosial fruits as grow there, and drinking of the springs which gush out from the mountain-sides, as he gradually inhales the subtler and purer atmosphere of those elevated places, thus propitiating the mountain gods by a sacrifice of their own fruits. The gross products of the plains and valleys are for such as dwell therein; but it seemed to us that the juices of this berry had relation to the thin air of the mountain-tops.

In due time we began to ascend the mountain, passing, first, through a grand sugar maple wood, which bore the marks of the auger, then a denser forest, which gradually became dwarfed, till there were no trees whatever. We at length pitched our tent on the summit. It is but nineteen hundred feet above the village of Princeton, and three thousand above the level of the sea; but by this slight elevation it is infinitely removed from the plain, and when we reached it we felt a sense of remoteness, as if we had traveled into distant regions, to Arabia Petræa, or the farthest East. A robin upon a staff was the highest object in sight. Swallows were flying about us, and the chewink and cuckoo were heard near at hand. The summit consists of a few acres, destitute of trees, covered with bare rocks, interspersed with blueberry bushes, raspberries, gooseberries, strawberries, moss, and a fine, wiry grass. The common yellow lily and dwarf cornel grow abundantly in the crevices of the rocks. This clear space, which is gently rounded, is bounded a few feet lower by a thick shrubbery of oaks, with maples, aspens, beeches, cherries, and occasionally a mountain-ash intermingled, among which we found the bright blueberries of the Solomon's-seal, and the fruit of the pyrola. From the foundation of a wooden observatory, which was formerly erected on the highest point, forming a rude, hollow structure of stone, a dozen feet in diameter, and five or six in height, we could see Monadnock, in simple grandeur, in the northwest, rising nearly a thousand feet higher, still the "far blue mountain," though with an altered profile. The first day the weather was so hazy that it was in vain we endeavored to unravel the obscurity. It was like looking into the sky again, and the patches of forest here and there seemed to flit like clouds over a lower heaven. As to voyagers of an aerial Polynesia, the earth seemed like a larger island in the ether; on every side, even as low as we, the sky shutting down, like an unfathomable deep, around it, a blue Pacific island, where who knows what islanders inhabit? and as we sail near its shores we see the waving of trees and hear the lowing of kine.

We read Virgil and Wordsworth in our tent, with new pleasure there, while waiting for a clearer atmosphere, nor did the weather prevent our appreciating the simple truth and beauty of Peter Bell:—

> "And he had lain beside his asses,
> On lofty Cheviot Hills:

"And he had trudged through Yorkshire dales,
Among the rocks and winding *scars*;
Where deep and low the hamlets lie
Beneath their little patch of sky
And little lot of stars."

Who knows but this hill may one day be a Helvellyn, or even a Parnassus, and the Muses haunt here, and other Homers frequent the neighboring plains?

Not unconcerned Wachusett rears his head
Above the field, so late from nature won,
With patient brow reserved, as one who read
New annals in the history of man.

The blueberries which the mountain afforded, added to the milk we had brought, made our frugal supper, while for entertainment the even-song of the wood thrush rang along the ridge. Our eyes rested on no painted ceiling nor carpeted hall, but on skies of Nature's painting, and hills and forests of her embroidery. Before sunset, we rambled along the ridge to the north, while a hawk soared still above us. It was a place where gods might wander, so solemn and solitary, and removed from all contagion with the plain. As the evening came on, the haze was condensed in vapor, and the landscape became more distinctly visible, and numerous sheets of water were brought to light.

"Et jam summa procul villarum culmina fumant,
Majoresque cadunt altis de montibus umbrae."

And now the tops of the villas smoke afar off,
And the shadows fall longer from the high mountains.

As we stood on the stone tower while the sun was setting, we saw the shades of night creep gradually over the valleys of the east; and the inhabitants went into their houses, and shut their doors, while the moon silently rose up, and took possession of that part. And then the same scene was repeated on the west side, as far as the Connecticut and the Green Mountains, and the sun's rays fell on us two alone, of all New England men.

It was the night but one before the full of the moon, so bright that we could see to read distinctly by moonlight, and in the evening strolled over the summit without danger. There was, by chance, a fire blazing on Monadnock that night, which lighted up the whole western horizon, and, by making us aware of a community of mountains, made our position seem less solitary. But at length the wind drove us to the shelter of our tent, and we closed its door for the night, and fell asleep.

It was thrilling to hear the wind roar over the rocks, at intervals when we waked, for it had grown quite cold and windy. The night was, in its elements, simple even to majesty in that bleak place,—a bright moonlight and a piercing wind. It was at no time darker than twilight within the tent, and we could easily see the moon through its transparent roof as we lay; for there was the moon still above us, with Jupiter and Saturn on either hand, looking down on Wachusett, and it was a satisfaction to know that they were our fellow-travelers still, as high and out of our reach as our own destiny. Truly the stars were given for a consolation to man. We should not know but our life were fated to be always groveling, but it is permitted to behold them, and surely they are deserving of a fair destiny. We see laws which never fail, of whose failure we never conceived; and their lamps burn all the night, too, as well as all day,—so rich and lavish is that nature which can afford this superfluity of light.

The morning twilight began as soon as the moon had set, and we arose and kindled our fire, whose blaze might have been seen for thirty miles around. As the daylight increased, it was remarkable how rapidly the wind went down. There was no dew on the summit, but coldness supplied its place. When the dawn had reached its prime, we enjoyed the view of a distinct horizon line, and could fancy ourselves at sea, and the distant hills the waves in the horizon, as seen from the deck of a vessel. The cherry-birds flitted around us, the nuthatch and flicker were heard among the bushes, the titmouse perched within a few feet, and the song of the wood thrush again rang along the ridge. At length we saw the run rise up out of the sea, and shine on Massachusetts; and from this moment the atmosphere grew more and more transparent till the time of our departure, and we began to realize the extent of the view, and how the earth, in some degree, answered to the heavens in breadth, the white villages to the constellations in the sky. There was little of the sublimity and grandeur which belong to mountain scenery, but an immense landscape to ponder on a summer's day. We could see how ample and roomy is nature. As far as the eye could reach there was little life in the landscape; the few birds that flitted past did not crowd. The travelers on the remote highways, which intersect the country on every side, had no fellow-travelers for miles, before or behind. On every side, the eye ranged over successive circles of towns, rising one above another, like the terraces of a vineyard, till they were lost in the horizon. Wachusett is, in fact, the observatory of the State. There lay Massachusetts, spread out before us in its length and breadth, like a map. There was the level horizon which told of the sea on the east and south, the well-known hills of New Hampshire on the north, and the misty summits of the Hoosac and Green Mountains, first made visible to us the evening before, blue and unsubstantial, like some bank of clouds which the morning wind would dissipate, on the northwest and west. These last distant ranges, on which the eye rests unwearied, commence with an abrupt boulder in the north, beyond the Connecticut, and travel southward, with three or four peaks dimly seen. But Monadnock, rearing its masculine front in the northwest, is the grandest feature. As we beheld it, we knew that it was the height of land between the two rivers, on this side the valley of the Merrimack, on that of the Connecticut, fluctuating with their blue seas of air,— these rival vales, already teeming with Yankee men along their respective streams, born to what destiny who shall tell? Watatic and the neighboring hills, in this State and in New Hampshire, are a continuation of the same elevated range on which we were standing. But that New Hampshire bluff,—that promontory of a State,— lowering day and night on this our State of Massachusetts, will longest haunt our dreams.

We could at length realize the place mountains occupy on the land, and how they come into the general scheme of the universe. When first we climb their summits and observe their lesser irregularities, we do not give credit to the comprehensive intelligence which shaped them; but when afterward we behold their outlines in the horizon, we confess that the hand which moulded their opposite slopes, making one to balance the other, worked round a deep centre, and was privy to the plan of the universe. So is the least part of nature in its bearings referred to all space. These lesser mountain ranges, as well as the Alleghanies, run from northeast to southwest, and parallel with these mountain streams are the more fluent rivers, answering to the general direction of the coast, the bank of the great ocean stream itself. Even the clouds, with their thin bars, fall into the same direction by preference, and such even is the course of the prevailing winds, and the migration of men and birds. A mountain chain determines many things for the statesman and philosopher. The improvements of civilization rather creep along its sides than cross its summit. How often is it a barrier to prejudice and fanaticism! In passing over these heights of land, through their thin atmosphere, the follies of the plain are refined and purified; and as many species of plants do not scale their summits, so many species of folly, no doubt, do not cross the Alleghanies; it is only the hardy mountain-plant that creeps quite over the ridge, and descends into the valley beyond.

We get a dim notion of the flight of birds, especially of such as fly high in the air, by having ascended a mountain. We can now see what landmarks mountains are to their migrations; how the Catskills and Highlands have hardly sunk to them, when Wachusett and Monadnock open a passage to the northeast; how they are guided, too, in their course by the river and valleys; and who knows but by the stars, as well as the mountain ranges, and not by the petty landmarks which we use. The bird whose eye takes in the Green Mountains on the one side, and the ocean on the other, need not be at a loss to find its way.

At noon we descended the mountain, and, having returned to the abodes of men, turned our faces to the east again; measuring our progress, from time to time, by the more ethereal hues which the mountain assumed. Passing swiftly through Stillwater and Sterling, as with a downward impetus, we found ourselves almost at home again in the green meadows of Lancaster, so like our own Concord, for both are watered by two streams which unite near their centres, and have many other features in common. There is an unexpected refinement about this scenery; level prairies of great extent, interspersed with elms and hop-fields and groves of trees, give it almost a classic appearance. This, it will be remembered, was the scene of Mrs. Rowlandson's capture, and of other events in the indian wars, but from this July afternoon, and under that mild exterior, those times seemed as remote as the irruption of the Goths. They were the dark age of New England. On beholding a picture of a New England village as it then appeared, with a fair open prospect, and a light on trees and river, as if it were broad noon, we find we had not thought the sun shone in those days, or that men lived in broad daylight then. We do not imagine the sun shining on hill and valley during Philip's war, nor on the warpath of Paugus, or Standish, or Church, or Lovell, with serene summer weather, but a dim twilight or night did those events transpire in. They must have fought in the shade of their own dusky deeds.

At length, as we plodded along the dusty roads, our thoughts became as dusty as they; all thought indeed stopped, thinking broke down, or proceeded only passively in a sort of rhythmical cadence of the confused material of thought, and we found ourselves mechanically repeating some familiar measure which timed with our tread; some verse of the Robin Hood ballads, for instance, which one can recommend to travel by:—

> "Sweavens are swift, sayd lyttle John,
>   As the wind blows over the hill;
> For if it be never so loud this night,
>   To-morrow it may he still."

And so it went, up-hill and down, till a stone interrupted the line, when a new verse was chosen:—

> "His shoote it was but loosely shott,
>   Yet flewe not the arrowe in vaine,
> For it mett one of the sheriffe's men,
>   And William a Trent was slaine."

There is, however, this consolation to the most way-worn traveler, upon the dustiest road, that the path his feet describe is so perfectly symbolical of human life,—now climbing the hills, now descending into the vales. From the summits he beholds the heavens and the horizon, from the vales he looks up to the heights again. He is treading his old lessons still, and though he may be very weary and travel-worn, it is yet sincere experience.

Leaving the Nashua, we changed our route a little, and arrived at Stillriver Village, in the western part of Harvard, just as the sun was setting. From this place, which lies to the northward, upon the western slope of the same range of hills on which we had spent the noon before, in the adjacent town, the prospect is beautiful, and the grandeur of the mountain outlines unsurpassed. There was such a repose and quiet here at this hour, as if the very hillsides were enjoying the scene; and as we passed slowly along, looking back over the country we had traversed, and listening to the evening song of the robin, we could not help contrasting the equanimity of Nature with the bustle and impatience of man. His words and actions presume always a crisis near at hand, but she is forever silent and unpretending.

And now that we have returned to the desultory life of the plain, let us endeavor to import a little of that mountain grandeur into it. We will remember within what walls we lie, and understand that this level life too has its summit, and why from the mountain-top the deepest valleys have a tinge of blue; that there is elevation in every hour, as no part of the earth is so low that the heavens may not be seen from, and we have only to stand on the summit of our hour to command an uninterrupted horizon.

We rested that night at Harvard, and the next morning, while one bent his steps to the nearer village of Groton, the other took his separate and solitary way to the peaceful meadows of Concord; but let him not forget to record the brave hospitality of a farmer and his wife, who generously entertained him at their board, though the poor wayfarer could only congratulate the one on the continuance of hay weather, and silently accept the kindness of the other. Refreshed by this instance of generosity, no less than by the substantial viands set before him, he pushed forward with new vigor, and ached the banks of the Concord before the sun had climbed many degrees into the heavens.

A WINTER WALK
1843

The wind has gently murmured through the blinds, or puffed with feathery softness against the windows, and occasionally sighed like a summer zephyr lifting the leaves along, the livelong night. The meadow mouse has slept in his snug gallery in the sod, the owl has sat in a hollow tree in the depth of the swamp, the rabbit, the squirrel, and the fox have all been housed. The watch-dog has lain quiet on the hearth, and the cattle have stood silent in their stalls. The earth itself has slept, as it were its first, not its last sleep, save when some street-sign or wood-house door has faintly creaked upon its hinge, cheering forlorn nature at her midnight work,—the only sound awake 'twixt Venus and Mars,—advertising us of a remote inward warmth, a divine cheer and fellowship, where gods are met together, but where it is very bleak for men to stand. But while the earth has slumbered, all the air has been alive with feathery flakes descending as if some northern Ceres reigned, showering her silvery grain over all the fields.

We sleep, and at length awake to the still reality of a winter morning. The snow lies warm as cotton or down upon the window-sill; the broadened sash and frosted panes admit a dim and private light, which enhances the snug cheer within. The stillness of the morning is impressive. The floor creaks under our feet as we move toward the window to look abroad through some clear space over the fields. We see the roofs stand under their snow burden. From the caves and fences hang stalactites of snow, and in the yard stand stalagmites covering some concealed core. The trees and shrubs rear white arms to the sky on every side; and where were walls and fences, we see fantastic forms stretching in frolic gambols across the dusky landscape, as if Nature had strewn her fresh designs over the fields by night as models for man's art.

Silently we unlatch the door, letting the drift fall in, and step abroad to face the cutting air. Already the stars have lost some of their sparkle, and a dull, leaden mist skirts the horizon. A lurid brazen light in the east proclaims the approach of day, while the western landscape is dim and spectral still, and clothed in a sombre Tartarean light, like the shadowy realms. They are Infernal sounds only that you hear,—the crowing of cocks, the barking of dogs, the chopping of wood, the lowing of kine, all seem to come from Pluto's barnyard and beyond the Styx,—not for any melancholy they suggest, but their twilight bustle is too solemn and mysterious for earth. The recent tracks of the fox or otter, in the yard, remind us that each hour of the night is crowded with events, and the primeval nature is still working and making tracks in the snow. Opening the gate, we tread briskly along the lone country road, crunching the dry and crisped snow under our feet, or aroused by the sharp, clear creak of the wood-sled, just starting for the distant market, from the early farmer's door, where it has lain the summer long, dreaming amid the chips and stubble; while far through the drifts and powdered windows we see the farmer's early candle, like a paled star, emitting a lonely beam, as if some severe virtue were at its matins there. And one by one the smokes begin to ascend from the chimneys amid the trees and snows.

> The sluggish smoke curls up from some deep dell,
> The stiffened air exploring in the dawn,
> And making slow acquaintance with the day
> Delaying now upon its heavenward course,
> In wreathèd loiterings dallying with itself,
> With as uncertain purpose and slow deed
> As its half-wakened master by the hearth,
> Whose mind still slumbering and sluggish thoughts
> Have not yet swept into the onward current
> Of the new day;—and now it streams afar,
> The while the chopper goes with step direct,
> And mind intent to swing the early axe.
> First in the dusky dawn he sends abroad
> His early scout, his emissary, smoke,
> The earliest, latest pilgrim from the roof,
> To feel the frosty air, inform the day;
> And while he crouches still beside the hearth,
> Nor musters courage to unbar the door,
> It has gone down the glen with the light wind,

And o'er the plain unfurled its venturous wreath,
Draped the tree-tops, loitered upon the hill,
And warmed the pinions of the early bird;
And now, perchance, high in the crispy air,
Has caught sight of the day o'er the earth's edge,
And greets its master's eye at his low door,
As some refulgent cloud in the upper sky.

We hear the sound of wood-chopping at the farmers' doors, far over the frozen earth, the baying of the house-dog, and the distant clarion of the cock,—though the thin and frosty air conveys only the finer particles of sound to our ears, with short and sweet vibrations, as the waves subside soonest on the purest and lightest liquids, in which gross substances sink to the bottom. They come clear and bell-like, and from a greater distance in the horizon, as if there were fewer impediments than in summer to make them faint and ragged. The ground is sonorous, like seasoned wood, and even the ordinary rural sounds are melodious, and the jingling of the ice on the trees is sweet and liquid. There is the least possible moisture in the atmosphere, all being dried up or congealed, and it is of such extreme tenuity and elasticity that it becomes a source of delight. The withdrawn and tense sky seems groined like the aisles of a cathedral, and the polished air sparkles a if there were crystals of ice floating in it. As they who have resided in Greenland tell us that when it freezes "the sea smokes like burning turf-land, and a fog or mist arises, called frost-smoke," which "cutting smoke frequently raises blisters on the face and hands, and is very pernicious to the health." But this pure, stinging cold is an elixir to the lungs, and not so much a frozen mist as a crystallized midsummer haze, refined and purified by cold.

The sun at length rises through the distant woods, as if with the faint clashing, swinging sound of cymbals, melting the air with his beams, and with such rapid steps the morning travels, that already his rays are gilding the distant western mountains. Meanwhile we step hastily along through the powdery snow, warmed by an inward heat, enjoying an Indian summer still, in the increased glow of thought and feeling. Probably if our lives were more conformed to nature, we should not need to defend ourselves against her heats and colds, but find her our constant nurse and friend, as do plants and quadrupeds. If our bodies were fed with pure and simple elements, and not with a stimulating and heating diet, they would afford no more pasture for cold than a leafless twig, but thrive like the trees, which find even winter genial to their expansion.

The wonderful purity of nature at this season is a most pleasing fact. Every decayed stump and moss-grown stone and rail, and the dead leaves of autumn, are concealed by a clean napkin of snow. In the bare fields and tinkling woods, see what virtue survives. In the coldest and bleakest places, the warmest charities still maintain a foothold. A cold and searching wind drives away all contagion, and nothing can withstand it but what has a virtue in it, and accordingly, whatever we meet with in cold and bleak places, as the tops of mountains, we respect for a sort of sturdy innocence, a Puritan toughness. All things beside seem to be called in for shelter, and what stays out must be part of the original frame of the universe, and of such valor as God himself. It is invigorating to breathe the cleansed air. Its greater fineness and purity are visible to the eye, and we would fain stay out long and late, that the gales may sigh through us, too, as through the leafless trees, and fit us for the winter,—as if we hoped so to borrow some pure and steadfast virtue, which will stead us in all seasons.

There is a slumbering subterranean fire in nature which never goes out, and which no cold can chill. It finally melts the great snow, and in January or July is only buried under a thicker or thinner covering. In the coldest day it flows somewhere, and the snow melts around every tree. This field of winter rye, which sprouted late in the fall, and now speedily dissolves the snow, is where the fire is thinly covered. We feel warmed by it. In the winter, warmth stands for all virtue, and we resort in thought to a trickling rill, with its bare stones shining in the sun, and to warm springs in the woods, with as much eagerness as rabbits and robins. The steam which rises from swamps and pools is as dear and domestic as that of our own kettle. What fire could ever equal the sunshine of a winter's day, when the meadow mice come out by the wall-sides, and the chickadee lisps in the defiles of the wood? The warmth comes directly from the sun, and is not radiated from the earth, as in summer; and when we feel his beams on our backs as we are treading some snowy dell, we are grateful as for a special kindness, and bless the sun which has followed us into that by-place.

This subterranean fire has its altar in each man's breast; for in the coldest day, and on the bleakest hill, the traveler cherishes a warmer fire within the folds of his cloak than is kindled on any hearth. A healthy man, indeed, is the complement of the seasons, and in winter, summer is in his heart. There is the south. Thither have all birds and insects migrated, and around the warm springs in his breast are gathered the robin and the lark.

At length, having reached the edge of the woods, and shut out the gadding town, we enter within their covert as we go under the roof of a cottage, and cross its threshold, all ceiled and banked up with snow. They are glad and warm still, and as genial and cheery in winter as in summer. As we stand in the midst of the pines in the flickering and checkered light which straggles but little way into their maze, we wonder if the towns have ever heard their simple story. It seems to us that no traveler has ever explored them, and notwithstanding the wonders which science is elsewhere revealing every day, who would not like to bear their annals? Our humble villages in the plain are their contribution. We borrow from the forest the boards which shelter and the sticks which warm us. How important is their evergreen to the winter, that portion of the summer which does not fade, the permanent year, the unwithered grass! Thus simply, and with little expense of altitude, is the surface of the earth diversified. What would human life he without forests, those natural cities? From the tops of mountains they appear like smooth-shaven lawns, yet whither shall we walk but in this taller grass?

In this glade covered with bushes of a year's growth, see how the silvery dust lies on every seared leaf and twig, deposited in such infinite and luxurious forms as by their very variety atone for the absence of color. Observe the tiny tracks of mice around every stem, and the triangular tracks of the rabbit. A pure elastic heaven hangs over all, as if the impurities of the summer sky, refined and shrunk by the chaste winter's cold, had been winnowed from the heavens upon the earth.

Nature confounds her summer distinctions at this season. The heavens seem to be nearer the earth. The elements are less reserved and distinct. Water turns to ice, rain to snow. The day is but a Scandinavian night. The winter is an arctic summer.

How much more living is the life that is in nature, the furred life which still survives the stinging nights, and, from amidst fields and woods covered with frost and snow, sees the sun rise!

"The foodless wilds
Pour forth their brown inhabitants."

The gray squirrel and rabbit are brisk and playful in the remote glens, even on the morning of the cold Friday. Here is our Lapland and Labrador, and for our Esquimaux and Knistenaux, Dog-ribbed Indians, Novazemblaites, and Spitzbergeners, are there not the ice-cutter and wood-chopper, the fox, muskrat, and mink?

Still, in the midst of the arctic day, we may trace the summer to its retreats, and sympathize with some contemporary life. Stretched over the brooks, in the midst of the frost-bound meadows, we may observe the submarine cottages of the caddis-worms, the larvæ of the Plicipennes; their small cylindrical cases built around themselves, composed of flags, sticks, grass, and withered leaves, shells, and pebbles, in form and color like the wrecks which strew the bottom,—now drifting along over the pebbly bottom, now whirling in tiny eddies and dashing down steep falls, or sweeping rapidly along with the current, or else swaying to and fro at the end of some grass-blade or root. Anon they will leave their sunken habitations, and, crawling up the stems of plants, or to the surface, like gnats, as perfect insects henceforth, flutter over the surface of the water, or sacrifice their short lives in the flame of our candles at evening. Down yonder little glen the shrubs are drooping under their burden, and the red elder-berries contrast with the white ground. Here are the marks of a myriad feet which have already been abroad. The sun rises as proudly over such a glen as over the valley of the Seine or the Tiber, and it seems the residence of a pure and self-subsistent valor, such as they never witnessed,—which never knew defeat nor fear. Here reign the simplicity and purity of a primitive age, and a health and hope far remote from towns and cities. Standing quite alone, far in the forest, while the wind is shaking down snow from the trees, and leaving the only human tracks behind us, we find our reflections of a richer variety than the life of cities. The chickadee and nuthatch are more inspiring society than statesmen and philosophers, and we shall return to these last as to more vulgar companions. In this lonely glen, with its brook draining the slopes, its creased ice and crystals of all hues, where the spruces and hemlocks stand up on either side, and the rush and sere wild oats in the rivulet itself, our lives are more serene and worthy to contemplate.

As the day advances, the heat of the sun is reflected by the hillsides, and we hear a faint but sweet music, where flows the rill released from its fetters, and the icicles are melting on the trees; and the nuthatch and partridge are heard and seen. The south wind melts the snow at noon, and the bare ground appears with its withered grass and leaves, and we are invigorated by the perfume which exhales from it, as by the scent of strong meats.

Let us go into this deserted woodsman's hut, and see how he has passed the long winter nights and the short and stormy days. For here man has lived under this south hillside, and it seems a civilized and public spot. We have such associations as when the traveler stands by the ruins of Palmyra or Hecatompolis. Singing birds and flowers perchance have begun to appear here, for flowers as well as weeds follow in the footsteps of man. These hemlocks whispered over his head, these hickory logs were his fuel, and these pitch pine roots kindled his fire; yonder fuming rill in the hollow, whose thin and airy vapor still ascends as busily as ever, though he is far off now, was his well. These hemlock boughs, and the straw upon this raised platform, were his bed, and this broken dish held his drink. But he has not been here this season, for the phœbes built their nest upon this shelf last summer. I find some embers left as if he had but just gone out, where he baked his pot of beans; and while at evening he smoked his pipe, whose stemless bowl lies in the ashes, chatted with his only companion, if perchance he had any, about the depth of the snow on the morrow, already falling fast and thick without, or disputed whether the last sound was the screech of an owl, or the creak of a bough, or imagination only; and through his broad chimney-throat, in the late winter evening, ere he stretched himself upon the straw, he looked up to learn the progress of the storm, and, seeing the bright stars of Cassiopeia's Chair shining brightly down upon him, fell contentedly asleep.

See how many traces from which we may learn the chopper's history! From this stump we may guess the sharpness of his axe, and from the slope of the stroke, on which side he stood, and whether he cut down the tree without going round it or changing hands; and, from the flexure of the splinters, we may know which way it fell. This one chip contains inscribed on it the whole history of the wood-chopper and of the world. On this scrap of paper, which held his sugar or salt, perchance, or was the wadding of his gun, sitting on a log in the forest, with what interest we read the tattle of cities, of those larger huts, empty and to let, like this, in High Streets and Broadways. The caves are dripping on the south side of this simple roof, while the titmouse lisps in the pine and the genial warmth of the sun around the door is somewhat kind and human.

After two seasons, this rude dwelling does not deform the scene. Already the birds resort to it, to build their nests, and you may track to its door the feet of many quadrupeds. Thus, for a long time, nature overlooks the encroachment and profanity of man. The wood still cheerfully and unsuspiciously echoes the strokes of the axe that fells it, and while they are few and seldom, they enhance its wildness, and all the elements strive to naturalize the sound.

Now our path begins to ascend gradually to the top of this high hill, from whose precipitous south side we can look over the broad country of forest and field and river, to the distant snowy mountains. See yonder thin column of smoke curling up through the woods from some invisible farmhouse, the standard raised over some rural homestead. There must be a warmer and more genial spot there below, as where we detect the vapor from a spring forming a cloud above the trees. What fine relations are established between the traveler who discovers this airy column from some eminence in the forest and him who sits below! Up goes the smoke as silently and naturally as the vapor exhales from the leaves, and as busy disposing itself in wreaths as the housewife on the hearth below. It is a hieroglyphic of man's life, and suggests more intimate and important things than the boiling of a pot. Where its fine column rises above the forest, like an ensign, some human life has planted itself,—and such is the beginning of Rome, the establishment of the arts, and the foundation of empires, whether on the prairies of America or the steppes of Asia.

And now we descend again, to the brink of this woodland lake, which lies in a hollow of the hills, as if it were their expressed juice, and that of the leaves which are annually steeped in it. Without outlet or inlet to the eye, it has still its history, in the lapse of its waves, in the rounded pebbles on its shore, and in the pines which grow down to its brink. It has not been idle, though sedentary, but, like Abu Musa, teaches that "sitting still at home is the heavenly way; the going out is the way of the world." Yet in its evaporation it travels as far as any. In summer it is the earth's liquid eye, a mirror in the breast of nature. The sins of the wood are washed out in it. See how the woods form an amphitheatre about it, and it is an arena for all the genialness of nature. All trees direct the traveler to its brink, all paths seek it out, birds fly to it, quadrupeds flee to it, and the very ground inclines toward it. It is nature's saloon, where she has sat down to her toilet. Consider her silent economy and tidiness; how the sun comes with his evaporation to sweep the dust from its surface each morning, and a fresh surface is constantly welling up; and annually, after whatever impurities have accumulated herein, its liquid transparency appears again in the spring. In summer a hushed music seems to sweep across its surface. But now a plain sheet of snow conceals it from our eyes, except where the wind has swept the ice bare, and the sere leaves are gliding from side to side, tacking and veering on their tiny voyages. Here is one just keeled up against a pebble on shore, a dry beech leaf, rocking still, as if it would start again. A skillful engineer, methinks, might project its course since it fell from the parent stem. Here are all the elements for such a calculation. Its present position, the direction of the wind, the level of the pond, and how much more is given. In its scarred edges and veins is its log rolled up.

We fancy ourselves in the interior of a larger house. The surface of the pond is our deal table or sanded floor, and the woods rise abruptly from its edge, like the walls of a cottage. The lines set to catch pickerel through the ice look like a larger culinary preparation, and the men stand about on the white ground like pieces of forest furniture. The actions of these men, at the distance of half a mile over the ice and snow, impress us as when we read the exploits of Alexander in history. They seem not unworthy of the scenery, and as momentous as the conquest of kingdoms.

Again we have wandered through the arches of the wood, until from its skirts we hear the distant booming of ice from yonder bay of the river, as if it were moved by some other and subtler tide than oceans know. To me it has a strange sound of home, thrilling as the voice of one's distant and noble kindred. A mild summer sun shines over forest and lake, and though there is but one green leaf for many rods, yet nature enjoys a serene health. Every sound is fraught with the same mysterious assurance of health, as well now the creaking of the boughs in January, as the soft sough of the wind in July.

When Winter fringes every bough
    With his fantastic wreath,
And puts the seal of silence now
    Upon the leaves beneath;

When every stream in its penthouse
    Goes gurgling on its way,
And in his gallery the mouse
    Nibbleth the meadow hay;

Methinks the summer still is nigh,
    And lurketh underneath,
As that same meadow mouse doth lie
    Snug in that last year's heath.

And if perchance the chickadee
    Lisp & faint note anon,
The snow is summer's canopy,
    Which she herself put on.

Fair blossoms deck the cheerful trees,
    And dazzling fruits depend;
The north wind sighs a summer breeze,
    The nipping frosts to fend,

Bringing glad tidings unto me.
    The while I stand all ear,
Of a serene eternity,
    Which need not winter fear.

Out on the silent pond straightway
    The restless ice doth crack,
And pond sprites merry gambols play
    Amid the deafening rack.

Eager I hasten to the vale;
    As if I heard brave news,
How nature held high festival,
    Which it were hard to lose.

I gambol with my neighbor ice,
    And sympathizing quake,
As each new crack darts in a trice
    Across the gladsome lake.

One with the cricket in the ground,
    And fagot on the hearth,
Resounds the rare domestic sound
    Along the forest path.

Before night we will take a journey on skates along the
course of this meandering river, as full of novelty to one who
sits by the cottage fire all the winter's day, as if it were over the
polar ice, with Captain Parry or Franklin; following the winding
of the stream, now flowing amid hills, now spreading out into
fair meadows, and forming a myriad coves and bays where the
pine and hemlock overarch. The river flows in the rear of the
towns, and we see all things from a new and wilder side. The
fields and gardens come down to it with a frankness, and freedom from pretension, which they do not wear on the highway.
It is the outside and edge of the earth. Our eyes are not offended
by violent contrasts. The last rail of the farmer's fence is some
swaying willow bough, which still preserves its freshness, and
here at length all fences stop, and we no longer cross any road.
We may go far up within the country now by the most retired
and level road, never climbing a hill, but by broad levels ascend-
ing to the upland meadows. It is a beautiful illustration of the
law of obedience, the flow of a river; the path for a sick man, a
highway down which an acorn cup may float secure with its
freight. Its slight occasional falls, whose precipices would not
diversify the landscape, are celebrated by mist and spray, and attract the traveler from far and near. From the remote interior,
its current conducts him by broad and easy steps, or by one gentler inclined plane, to the sea. Thus by an early and constant
yielding to the inequalities of the ground it secures itself the eas-
iest passage.

No domain of nature is quite closed to man at all times,
and now we draw near to the empire of the fishes. Our feet glide
swiftly over unfathomed depths, where in summer our line
tempted the pout and perch, and where the stately pickerel
lurked in the long corridors formed by the bulrushes. The deep,
impenetrable marsh, where the heron waded and bittern squatted, is made pervious to our swift shoes, as if a thousand railroads had been made into it. With one impulse we are carried to
the cabin of the muskrat, that earliest settler, and see him dart
away under the transparent ice, like a furred fish, to his hole in
the bank; and we glide rapidly over meadows where lately "the
mower whet his scythe," through beds of frozen cranberries
mixed with meadow-grass. We skate near to where the black-
bird, the pewee, and the kingbird hung their nests over the water, and the hornets builded from the maple in the swamp. How
many gay warblers, following the sun, have radiated from this

nest of silver birch and thistle-down! On the swamp's outer
edge was hung the supermarine village, where no foot penetrated. In this hollow tree the wood duck reared her brood, and
slid away each day to forage in yonder fen.

In winter, nature is a cabinet of curiosities, full of dried
specimens, in their natural order and position. The meadows
and forests are a *hortus siccus*. The leaves and grasses stand perfectly pressed by the air without screw or gum, and the birds'
nests are not hung on an artificial twig, but where they builded
them. We go about dryshod to inspect the summer's work in
the rank swamp, and see what a growth have got the alders, the
willows, and the maples; testifying to how many warm suns,
and fertilizing dews and showers. See what strides their boughs
took in the luxuriant summer,—and anon these dormant buds
will carry them onward and upward another span into the
heavens.

Occasionally we wade through fields of snow, under
whose depths the river is lost for many rods, to appear again to
the right or left, where we least expected; still holding on its way
underneath, with a faint, stertorous rumbling sound, as if, like
the bear and marmot, it too had hibernated, and we had followed its faint summer trail to where it earthed itself in snow
and ice. At first we should have thought that rivers would be
empty and dry in midwinter, or else frozen solid till the spring
thawed them; but their volume is not diminished even, for only
a superficial cold bridges their surfaces. The thousand springs
which feel the lakes and streams are flowing still. The issues of a
few surface springs only are closed, and they go to swell the deep
reservoirs. Nature's wells are below the frost. The summer
brooks are not filled with snow-water, nor does the mower
quench his thirst with that alone. The streams are swollen
when the snow melts in the spring, because nature's work has
been delayed, the water being turned into ice and snow, whose
particles are less smooth and round, and do not find their level
so soon.

Far over the ice, between the hemlock woods and snow-
clad hills, stands the pickerel-fisher, his lines set in some retired
cove, like a Finlander, with his arms thrust into the pouches of
his dreadnaught; with dull, snowy, fishy thoughts, himself a fin-
less fish, separated a few inches from his race; dumb, erect, and
made to be enveloped in clouds and snows, like the pines on
shore. In these wild scenes, men stand about in the scenery, or

move deliberately and heavily, having sacrificed the sprightliness and vivacity of towns to the dumb sobriety of nature. He does not make the scenery less wild, more than the jays and muskrats, but stands there as a part of it, as the natives are represented in the voyages of early navigators, at Nootka Sound, and on the Northwest coast, with their furs about them, before they were tempted to loquacity by a scrap of iron. He belongs to the natural family of man, and is planted deeper in nature and has more root than the inhabitants of towns. Go to him, ask what luck, and you will learn that he too is a worshiper of the unseen. Hear with what sincere deference and waving gesture in his tone he speaks of the lake pickerel, which he has never seen, his primitive and ideal race of pickerel. He is connected with the shore still, as by a fish-line, and yet remembers the season when he took fish through the ice on the pond, while the peas were up in his garden at home.

But now, while we have loitered, the clouds have gathered again, and a few straggling snowflakes are beginning to descend. Faster and faster they fall, shutting out the distant objects from sight. The snow falls on every wood and field, and no crevice is forgotten; by the river and the pond, on the hill and in the valley. Quadrupeds are confined to their coverts and the birds sit upon their perches this peaceful hour. There is not so much sound as in fair weather, but silently and gradually every slope, and the gray walls and fences, and the polished ice, and the sere leaves, which were not buried before, are concealed, and the tracks of men and beasts are lost. With so little effort does nature reassert her rule and blot out the traces of men. Hear how Homer has described the same: "The snowflakes fall thick and fast on a winter's day. The winds are lulled, and the snow falls incessant, covering the tops of the mountains, and the hills, and the plains where the lotus-tree grows, and the cultivated fields, and they are falling by the inlets and shores of the foaming sea, but are silently dissolved by the waves." The snow levels all things, and infolds them deeper in the bosom of nature, as, in the slow summer, vegetation creeps up to the entablature of the temple, and the turrets of the castle, and helps her to prevail over art.

The surly night-wind rustles through the wood, and warns us to retrace our steps, while the sun goes down behind the thickening storm, and birds seek their roosts, and cattle their stalls.

> "Drooping the lab'rer ox
> Stands covered o'er with snow, and now demands
> The fruit of all his toil."

Though winter is represented in the almanac as an old man, facing the wind and sleet, and drawing his cloak about him, we rather think of him as a merry wood-chopper, and warm-blooded youth, as blithe as summer. The unexplored grandeur of the storm keeps up the spirits of the traveler. It does not trifle with us, but has a sweet earnestness. In winter we lead a more inward life. Our hearts are warm and cheery, like cottages under drifts, whose windows and doors are half concealed, but from whose chimneys the smoke cheerfully ascends. The imprisoning drifts increase the sense of comfort which the house affords, and in the coldest days we are content to sit over the hearth and see the sky through the chimney-top, enjoying the quiet and serene life that may be had in a warm corner by the chimney-side, or feeling our pulse by listening to the low of cattle in the street, or the sound of the flail in distant barns all the long afternoon. No doubt a skillful physician could determine our health by observing how these simple and natural sounds affected us. We enjoy now, not an Oriental, but a Boreal leisure, around warm stoves and fireplaces, and watch the shadow of motes in the sunbeams.

Sometimes our fate grows too homely and familiarly serious ever to be cruel. Consider how for three months the human destiny is wrapped in furs. The good Hebrew Revelation takes no cognizance of all this cheerful snow. Is there no religion for the temperate and frigid zones? We know of no scripture which records the pure benignity of the gods on a New England winter night. Their praises have never been sung, only their wrath deprecated. The best scripture, after all, records but a meager faith. Its saints live reserved and austere. Let a brave, devout man spend the year in the woods of Maine or Labrador, and see if the Hebrew Scriptures speak adequately to his condition and experience, from the setting in of winter to the breaking up of the ice.

Now commences the long winter evening around the farmer's hearth, when the thoughts of the indwellers travel far abroad, and men are by nature and necessity charitable and liberal to all creatures. Now is the happy resistance to cold, when the farmer reaps his reward, and thinks of his preparedness for winter, and, through the glittering panes, sees with equanimity "the mansion of the northern bear," for now the storm is over,—

> "The full ethereal round,
> Infinite worlds disclosing to the view,
> Shines out intensely keen; and all one cope
> Of starry glitter glows from pole to pole."

WALKING
1862

I wish to speak a word for Nature, for absolute freedom and wildness, as contrasted with a freedom and culture merely civil,—to regard man as an inhabitant, or a part and parcel of Nature, rather than a member of society. I wish to make an extreme statement, if so I may make an emphatic one, for there are enough champions of civilization: the minister and the school committee and every one of you will take care of that.

I have met with but one or two persons in the course of my life who understood the art of Walking, that is, of taking walks,—who had a genius, so to speak, for *sauntering*, which word is beautifully derived "from idle people who roved about the country, in the Middle Ages, and asked charity, under pretense of going *à la Sainte Terre*," to the Holy Land, till the children exclaimed, "There goes a *Sainte-Terrer*," a Saunterer, a Holy-Lander. They who never go to the Holy Land in their walks, as they pretend, are indeed mere idlers and vagabonds; but they who do go there are saunterers in the good sense, such as I mean. Some, however, would derive the word from *sans terre*, without land or a home, which, therefore, in the good sense, will mean, having no particular home, but equally at home everywhere. For this is the secret of successful sauntering. He who sits still in a house all the time may be the greatest vagrant of all; but the saunterer, in the good sense, is no more vagrant than the meandering river, which is all the while sedulously seeking the shortest course to the sea. But I prefer the first, which, indeed, is the most probable derivation. For every walk is a sort of crusade, preached by some Peter the Hermit in us, to go forth and reconquer this Holy Land from the hands of the Infidels.

It is true, we are but faint-hearted crusaders, even the walkers, nowadays, who undertake no persevering, never-ending enterprises. Our expeditions are but tours, and come round again at evening to the old hearth-side from which we set out. Half the walk is but retracing our steps. We should go forth on the shortest walk, perchance, in the spirit of undying adventure, never to return,—prepared to send back our embalmed hearts only as relics to our desolate kingdoms. If you are ready to leave father and mother, and brother and sister, and wife and child and friends, and never see them again,—if you have paid your debts, and made your will, and settled all your affairs, and are a free man, then you are ready for a walk.

To come down to my own experience, my companion and I, for I sometimes have a companion, take pleasure in fancying ourselves knights of a new, or rather an old, order,—not Equestrians or Chevaliers, not Ritters or Riders, but Walkers, a still more ancient and honorable class, I trust. The chivalric and heroic spirit which once belonged to the Rider seems now to reside in, or perchance to have subsided into, the Walker,—not the Knight, but Walker, Errant. He is a sort of fourth estate, outside of Church and State and People.

We have felt that we almost alone hereabouts practiced this noble art; though, to tell the truth, at least if their own assertions are to be received, most of my townsmen would fain walk sometimes, as I do, but they cannot. No wealth can buy the requisite leisure, freedom, and independence which are the capital in this profession. It comes only by the grace of God. It requires a direct dispensation from Heaven to become a Walker. You must be born into the family of the Walkers. *Ambulator nascitur, non fit.* Some of my townsmen, it is true, can remember and have described to me some walks which they took ten years ago, in which they were so blessed as to lose themselves for half an hour in the woods; but I know very well that they have confined themselves to the highway ever since, whatever pretensions they may make to belong to this select class. No doubt they were elevated for a moment as by the reminiscence of a previous state of existence, when even they were foresters and outlaws.

"When he came to grene wode,
    In a mery mornynge,
There he herde the notes small
    Of byrdes mery syngynge.

"It is ferre gone, sayd Robyn,
    That I was last here;
Me lyste a lytell for to shote
    At the donne dere."

I think that I cannot preserve my health and spirits, un-less I spend four hours a day at least—and it is commonly more than that—sauntering through the woods and over the hills and fields, absolutely free from all worldly engagements. You may safely say, A penny for your thoughts, or a thousand pounds. When sometimes I am reminded that the mechanics and shop-keepers stay in their shops not only all the forenoon, but all the afternoon too, sitting with crossed legs, so many of them,—as if the legs were made to sit upon, and not to stand or walk upon,— I think that they deserve some credit for not having all commit-ted suicide long ego.

I, who cannot stay in my chamber for a single day without acquiring some rust, and when sometimes I have stolen forth for a walk at the eleventh hour, or four o'clock in the afternoon, too late to redeem the day, when the shades of night were al-ready beginning to be mingled with the daylight, have felt as if I had committed some sin to be atoned for,—I confess that I am astonished at the power of endurance, to say nothing of the moral insensibility, of my neighbors who confine themselves to shops and offices the whole day for weeks and months, aye, and years almost together. I know not what manner of stuff they are of,—sitting there now at three o'clock in the afternoon, as if it were three o'clock in the morning. Bonaparte may talk of the three-o'clock-in-the-morning courage, but it is nothing to the courage which can sit down cheerfully at this hour in the after-noon over against one's self whom you have known all the morning, to starve out a garrison to whom you are bound by such strong ties of sympathy. I wonder that about this time, or say between four and five o'clock in the afternoon, too late for the morning papers and too early for the evening ones, there is not a general explosion heard up and down the street, scattering a legion of antiquated and house-bred notions and whims to the four winds for an airing,—and so the evil cure itself.

How womankind, who are confined to the house still more than men, stand it I do not know; but I have ground to suspect that most of them do not *stand* it at all. When, early in a summer afternoon, we have been shaking the dust of the village from the skirts of our garments, making haste past those houses with purely Doric or Gothic fronts, which have such an air of repose about them, my companion whispers that probably about these times their occupants are all gone to bed. Then it is that I appreciate the beauty and the glory of architecture, which itself never turns in, but forever stands out and erect, keeping watch over the slumberers.

No doubt temperament, and, above all, age, have a good deal to do with it. As a man grows older, his ability to sit still and follow indoor occupations increases. He grows vespertinal in his habits as the evening of life approaches, till at last he comes forth only just before sundown, and gets all the walk that he requires in half an hour.

But the walking of which I speak has nothing in it akin to taking exercise, as it is called, as the sick take medicine at stated hours,—as the swinging of dumb-bells or chairs; but is itself the enterprise and adventure of the day. If you would get exercise, go in search of the springs of life. Think of a man's swinging dumb-bells for his health, when those springs are bubbling up in far-off pastures unsought by him!

Moreover, you must walk like a camel, which is said to be the only beast which ruminates when walking. When a traveler asked Wordsworth's servant to show him her master's study, she answered, "Here is his library, but his study is out of doors."

Living much out of doors, in the sun and wind, will no doubt produce a certain roughness of character,—will cause a thicker cuticle to grow over some of the finer qualifies of our nature, as on the face and hands, or as severe manual labor robs the hands of some of their delicacy of touch. So staying in the house, on the other hand, may produce a softness and smoothness, not to say thinness of skin, accompanied by an increased sensibility to certain impressions. Perhaps we should be more susceptible to some influences important to our intellectual and moral growth, if the sun had shone and the wind blown on us a little less; and no doubt it is a nice matter to proportion rightly the thick and thin skin. But methinks that is a scurf that will fall off fast enough,—that the natural remedy is to be found in the proportion which the night bears to the day, the winter to the summer, thought to experience. There will he so much the more air and sunshine in our thoughts. The callous palms of the laborer are conversant with finer tissues of self-respect and heroism, whose touch thrills the heart, than the languid fingers of idleness. That is mere sentimentality that lies abed by day and thinks itself white, far from the tan and callus of experience.

When we walk, we naturally go to the fields and woods: what would become of us, if we walked only in a garden or a mall? Even some sects of philosophers have felt the necessity of importing the woods to themselves, since they did not go to the woods. "They planted groves and walks of Platanes," where they took *subdiales ambulationes* in porticos open to the air. Of course it is of no use to direct our steps to the woods, if they do not carry us thither. I am alarmed when it happens that I have walked a mile into the woods bodily, without getting there in spirit. In my afternoon walk I would fain forget all my morning occupations and my obligations to society. But it sometimes happens that I cannot easily shake off the village. The thought of some work will run in my head and I am not where my body is,—I am out of my senses. In my walks I would fain return to my senses. What business have I in the woods, if I am thinking of something out of the woods? I suspect myself, and cannot help a shudder, when I find myself so implicated even in what are called good works,—for this may sometimes happen.

My vicinity affords many good walks; and though for so many years I have walked almost every day, and sometimes for several days together, I have not yet exhausted them. An absolutely new prospect is a great happiness, and I can still get this any afternoon. Two or three hours' walking will carry me to as strange a country as I expect ever to see. A single farmhouse, which I had not seen before is sometimes as good as the dominions of the King of Dahomey. There is in fact a sort of harmony discoverable between the capabilities of the landscape within a circle of ten miles' radius, or the limits of an afternoon walk, and the threescore years and ten of human life. It will never become quite familiar to you.

Nowadays almost all man's improvements, so called, as the building of houses and the cutting down of the forest and of all large trees, simply deform the landscape, and make it more and more tame and cheap. A people who would begin by burning the fences and let the forest stand! I saw the fences half consumed, their ends lost in the middle of the prairie, and some worldly miser with a surveyor looking after his bounds, while heaven had taken place around him, and he did not see the angels going to and fro, but was looking for an old post-hole in the midst of paradise. I looked again, and saw him standing in the middle of a boggy Stygian fen, surrounded by devils, and he had found his bounds without a doubt, three little stones, where a stake had been driven, and looking nearer, I saw that the Prince of Darkness was his surveyor.

I can easily walk ten, fifteen, twenty, any number of miles, commencing at my own door, without going by any house, without crossing a road except where the fox and the mink do: first along by the river, and then the brook, and then the meadow and the woodside. There are square miles in my vicinity which have no inhabitant. From many a hill I can see civilization and the abodes of man afar. The farmers and their works are scarcely more obvious than woodchucks and their burrows. Man and his affairs, church and state and school, trade and commerce, and manufactures and agriculture, even politics, the most alarming of them all,—I am pleased to see how little space they occupy in the landscape. Politics is but a narrow field, and that still narrower highway yonder leads to it. I sometimes direct the traveler thither. If you would go to the political world, follow the great road,—follow that market-man, keep his dust in your eyes, and it will lead you straight to it; for it, too, has its place merely, and does not occupy all space. I pass from it as from a bean-field into the forest, and it is forgotten. In one half-hour I can walk off to some portion of the earth's surface where a man does not stand from one year's end to another, and there, consequently politics are not, for they are but as the cigar-smoke of a man.

The village is the place to which the roads tend, a sort of expansion of the highway, as a lake of a river. It is the body of which roads are the arms and legs,—a trivial or quadrivial place, the thoroughfare and ordinary of travelers. The word is from the Latin *villa*, which together with *via*, a way, or more anciently *ved* and *vella*, Varro derives from *veho*, to carry, because the villa is the place to and from which things are carried. They who got their living by teaming were said *vellaturam facere*. Hence, too, the Latin word *vilis* and our vile, also *villain*. This suggests what kind of degeneracy villagers are liable to. They are wayworn by the travel that goes by and over them, without traveling themselves.

Some do not walk at all; others walk in the highways; a few walk across lots. Roads are made for horses and men of business. I do not travel in them much, comparatively, because I am not in a hurry to get to any tavern or grocery or livery-stable or depot to which they lead. I am a good horse to travel, but not from choice a roadster. The landscape-painter uses the figures of men to mark a road. He would not make that use of my figure. I walk out into a nature such as the old prophets and poets, Menu, Moses, Homer, Chaucer, walked in. You may name it America, but it is not America; neither Americus Vespucius, nor Columbus, nor the rest were the discoverers of it. There is a truer account of it in mythology than in any history of America, so called, that I have seen.

However, there are a few old roads that may be trodden with profit, as if they led somewhere now that they are nearly discontinued. There is the Old Marlborough Road, which does not go to Marlborough now, methinks, unless that is Marlborough where it carries me. I am the bolder to speak of it here, because I presume that there are one or two such roads in every town.

THE OLD MARLBOROUGH ROAD

Where they once dug for money,
But never found any;
Where sometimes Martial Miles
Singly files,
And Elijah Wood,
I fear for no good:
No other man,
Save Elisha Dugan,—
O man of wild habits,
Partridges and rabbits,
Who hast no cares
Only to set snares,
Who liv'st all alone,
Close to the bone,
And where life in sweetest
Constantly eatest.
When the spring stirs my blood
With the instinct to travel,
I can get enough gravel
On the Old Marlborough Road.
Nobody repairs it,
For nobody wears it;
It is a living way,

As the Christians say.
Not many there be
Who enter therein,
Only the guests of the
Irishman Quin.
What is it, what is it,
But a direction out there,
And the bare possibility
Of going somewhere?
Great guide-boards of stone,
But travelers none;
Cenotaphs of the towns
Named on their crowns
It is worth going to see
Where you *might* be.
What king
Did the thing,
I am still wondering;
Set up how or when,
By what selectmen,
Gourgas or Lee,
Clark or Darby?
They're a great endeavor
To be something forever;
Blank tablets of stone,
Where a traveler might groan,
And in one sentence
Grave all that is known;
Which another might read,
In his extreme need.
I know one or two
Lines that would do,
Literature that might stand
All over the land,
Which a man could remember
Till next December,
And read again in the spring,
After the thawing.
If with fancy unfurled
You leave your abode,
You may go round the world
By the Old Marlborough Road.

At present, in this vicinity, the best part of the land is not private property; the landscape is not owned, and the walker enjoys comparative freedom. But possibly the day will come when it will be partitioned off into so-called pleasure-grounds, in which a few will take a narrow and exclusive pleasure only,—

when fences shall be multiplied, and man-traps and other en-
gines invented to confine men to the *public* road, and walking
over the surface of God's earth shall be construed to mean tres-
passing on some gentleman's grounds. To enjoy a thing exclusively is commonly to exclude yourself from the true enjoyment
of it. Let us improve our opportunities, then, before the evil
days come.

   What is it that makes it so hard sometimes to determine
whither we will walk? I believe that there is a subtle magnetism
in Nature, which, if we unconsciously yield to it, will direct us
aright. It is not indifferent to us which way we walk. There is a
right way; but we are very liable from heedlessness and stupidity
to take the wrong one. We would fain take that walk, never yet
taken by us through this actual world, which is perfectly symbolical of the path which we love to travel in the interior and ideal
world; and sometimes, no doubt, we find it difficult to choose
our direction, because it does not yet exist distinctly in our idea.
   When I go out of the house for a walk, uncertain as yet
whither I will bend my steps, and submit myself to my instinct
to decide for me, I find, strange and whimsical as it may seem,
that I finally and inevitably settle southwest, toward some particular wood or meadow or deserted pasture or hill in that direction. My needle is slow to settle,—varies a few degrees, and does
not always point due southwest, it is true, and it has good authority for this variation, but it always settles between west and
south-southwest. The future lies that way to me, and the earth
seems more unexhausted and richer on that side. The outline
which would bound my walks would be, not a circle, but a
parabola, or rather like one of those cometary orbits which have
been thought to be non-returning curves, in this case opening
westward, in which my house occupies the place of the sun. I
turn round and round irresolute sometimes for a quarter of an
hour, until I decide, for a thousandth time, that I will walk into
the southwest or west. Eastward I go only force; but westward I
go free. Thither no business leads me. It is hard for me to believe that I shall find fair landscapes or sufficient wildness and
freedom behind the eastern horizon. I am not excited by the
prospect of a walk thither; but I believe that the forest which I see
in the western horizon stretches uninterruptedly toward the set-

ting sun, and there are no towns nor cities in it of enough consequence to disturb me. Let me live where I will, on this side is
the city, on that the wilderness, and ever I am leaving the city
more and more, and withdrawing into the wilderness. I should
not lay so much stress on this fact, if I did not believe that something like this is the prevailing tendency of my countrymen. I
must walk toward Oregon, and not toward Europe. And that
way the nation is moving, and I may say that mankind progress
from east to west. Within a few years we have witnessed the
phenomenon of a southeastward migration, in the settlement of
Australia; but this affects us as a retrograde movement, and,
judging from the moral and physical character of the first generation of Australians, has not yet proved a successful experiment.
The eastern Tartars think that there is nothing west beyond Thi-
bet. "The world ends there," say they; "beyond there is nothing
but a shoreless sea." It is unmitigated East where they live.

We go eastward to realize history and study the works of
art and literature, retracing the steps of the race; we go westward
as into the future, with a spirit of enterprise and adventure. The
Atlantic is a Lethean stream, in our passage over which we have
had an opportunity to forget the Old World and its institutions.
If we do not succeed this time, there is perhaps one more chance
for the race left before it arrives on the banks of the Styx; and that
is in the Lethe of the Pacific, which is three times as wide.

I know not how significant it is, or how far it is an evidence of singularity, that an individual should thus consent in
his pettiest walk with the general movement of the race; but I
know that something akin to the migratory instinct in birds and
quadrupeds,—which, in some instances, is known to have affected the squirrel tribe, impelling them to a general and mysterious movement, in which they were seen, say some, crossing
the broadest rivers, each on its particular chip, with its tall raised
for a sail, and bridging narrower streams with their dead,—that
something like the *juror* which affects the domestic cattle in the
spring, and which is referred to a worm in their tails, affects both
nations and individuals, either perennially or from time to
time. Not a flock of wild geese cackles over our town, but it to
some extent unsettles the value of real estate here, and, if I were
a broker, I should probably take that disturbance into account.

"Than longen folk to gon on pilgrimages,
And palmeres for to seken strange strondes."

Every sunset which I witness inspires me with the desire to go to a West as distant and as fair as that into which the sun goes down. He appears to migrate westward daily, and tempt us to follow him. He is the Great Western Pioneer whom the nations follow. We dream all night of those mountain-ridges in the horizon, though they may be of vapor only, which were last gilded by his rays. The island of Atlantis, and the islands and gardens of the Hesperides, a sort of terrestrial paradise, appear to have been the Great West of the ancients, enveloped in mystery and poetry. Who has not seen in imagination, when looking into the sunset sky, the gardens of the Hesperides, and the foundation of all those fables?

Columbus felt the westward tendency more strongly than any before. He obeyed it, and found a New World for Castile and Leon. The herd of men in those days scented fresh pastures from afar.

> "And now the sun had stretched out all the hills,
> And now was dropped into the western bay;
> At last *he* rose, and twitched his mantle blue;
> To-morrow to fresh woods and pastures new."

Where on the globe can there be found an area of equal extent with that occupied by the bulk of our States, so fertile and so rich and varied in its productions, and at the same time so habitable by the European, as this is? Michaux, who knew but part of them, says that "the species of large trees are much more numerous in North America than in Europe; in the United States there are more than one hundred and forty species that exceed thirty feet in height; in France there are but thirty that attain this size." Later botanists more than confirm his observations. Humboldt came to America to realize his youthful dreams of a tropical vegetation, and he beheld it in its greatest perfection in the primitive forests of the Amazon, the most gigantic wilderness on the earth, which he has so eloquently described. The geographer Guyot, himself a European, goes farther,—farther than I am ready to follow him; yet not when he says: "As the plant is made for the animal, as the vegetable world is made for the animal world, America is made for the man of the Old World. . . . The man of the Old World sets out upon his way. Leaving the highlands of Asia, he descends from station to station towards Europe. Each of his steps is marked by a new civilization superior to the preceding, by a greater power of development. Arrived at the Atlantic, he pauses on the shore of this unknown ocean, the bounds of which he knows not, and turns upon his footprints for an instant." When he has exhausted the rich soil of Europe, and reinvigorated himself, "then recommences his adventurous career westward as in the earliest ages." So far Guyot.

From this western impulse coming in contact with the barrier of the Atlantic sprang the commerce and enterprise of modern times. The younger Michaux, in his "Travels West of the Alleghanies in 1802," says that the common inquiry in the newly settled West was, "'From what part of the world have you come?' As if these vast and fertile regions would naturally be the place of meeting and common country of all the inhabitants of the globe."

To use an obsolete Latin word, I might say, *Ex Oriente lux; ex Occidente* FRUX. From the East light; from the West fruit.

Sir Francis Head, an English traveler and a Governor-General of Canada, tells us that "in both the northern and southern hemispheres of the New World, Nature has not only outlined her works on a larger scale, but has painted the whole picture with brighter and more costly colors than she used in delineating and in beautifying the Old World. . . . The heavens of America appear infinitely higher, the sky is bluer, the air is fresher, the cold is intenser, the moon looks larger, the stars are brighter, the thunder is louder, the lightning is vivider, the wind is stronger, the rain is heavier, the mountains are higher, the rivers longer, the forests bigger, the plains broader." This statement will do at least to set against Buffon's account of this part of the world and its productions.

Linnæus said long ago, "Nescio quae facies *laeta, glabra* plantis Americanis" (I know not what there is of joyous and smooth in the aspect of American plants); and I think that in this country there are no, or at most very few, *Africanae bestiae*, African beasts, as the Romans called them, and that in this respect also it is peculiarly fitted for the habitation of man. We are told that within three miles of the centre of the East-Indian city of Singapore, some of the inhabitants are annually carried off by tigers; but the traveler can lie down in the woods at night almost anywhere in North America without fear of wild beasts.

These are encouraging testimonies. If the moon looks larger here than in Europe, probably the sun looks larger also. If the heavens of America appear infinitely higher, and the stars brighter, I trust that these facts are symbolical of the height to which the philosophy and poetry and religion of her inhabitants may one day soar. At length, perchance, the immaterial heaven will appear as much higher to the American mind, and the intimations that star it as much brighter. For I believe that climate does thus react on man,—as there is something in the mountain air that feeds the spirit and inspires. Will not man grow to greater perfection intellectually as well as physically under these influences? Or is it unimportant how many foggy days there are in his life? I trust that we shall be more imaginative, that our thoughts will be clearer, fresher, and more ethereal, as our sky,— our understanding more comprehensive and broader, like our plains,—our intellect generally on a grander scale, like our thunder and lightning, our rivers and mountains and forests,— and our hearts shall even correspond in breadth and depth and grandeur to our inland seas. Perchance there will appear to the traveler something, he knows not what, of *laeta* and *glabra*, of joyous and serene, in our very faces. Else to what end does the world go on, and why was America discovered?

To Americans I hardly need to say,—

"Westward the star of empire takes its way."

As a true patriot, I should be ashamed to think that Adam in paradise was more favorably situated on the whole than the backwoodsman in this country.

Our sympathies in Massachusetts are not confined to New England; though we may be estranged from the South, we sympathize with the West. There is the home of the younger sons, as among the Scandinavians they took to the sea for their inheritance. It is too late to be studying Hebrew; it is more important to understand even the slang of to-day.

Some months ago I went to see a panorama of the Rhine. It was like a dream of the Middle Ages. I floated down its historic stream in something more than imagination, under bridges built by the Romans, and repaired by later heroes, past cities and castles whose very names were music to my ears, and each of which was the subject of a legend. There were Ehrenbreitstein and Rolandseck and Coblentz, which I knew only in history. They were ruins that interested me chiefly. There seemed to come up from its waters and its vine-clad hills and valleys a hushed music as of Crusaders departing for the Holy Land. I floated along under the spell of enchantment, as if I had been transported to an heroic age, and breathed an atmosphere of chivalry.

Soon after, I went to see a panorama of the Mississippi, and as I worked my way up the river in the light of to-day, and saw the steamboats wooding up, counted the rising cities, gazed on the fresh ruins of Nauvoo, beheld the Indians moving west across the stream, and, as before I had looked up the Moselle, now looked up the Ohio and the Missouri and heard the legends of Dubuque and of Wenona's Cliff,—still thinking more of the future than of the past or present,—I saw that this was a Rhine stream of a different kind; that the foundations of castles were yet to be laid, and the famous bridges were yet to be thrown over the river; and I felt that *this was the heroic age itself*, though we know it not, for the hero is commonly the simplest and obscurest of men.

The West of which I speak is but another name for the Wild; and what I have been preparing to say is, that in Wildness is the preservation of the World. Every tree sends its fibres forth in search of the Wild. The cities import it at any price. Men plow and sail for it. From the forest and wilderness come the tonics and barks which brace mankind. Our ancestors were savages. The story of Romulus and Remus being suckled by a wolf is not a meaningless fable. The founders of every state which has risen to eminence have drawn their nourishment and vigor from a similar wild source. It was because the children of the Empire were not suckled by the wolf that they were conquered and displaced by the children of the northern forests who were.

I believe in the forest, and in the meadow, and in the night in which the corn grows. We require an infusion of hemlock spruce or arbor-vitæ in our tea. There is a difference between eating and drinking for strength and from mere gluttony. The Hottentots eagerly devour the marrow of the koodoo and other antelopes raw, as a matter of course. Some of our northern Indians eat raw the marrow of the Arctic reindeer, as well as various other parts, including the summits of the antlers, as long as they are soft. And herein, perchance, they have stolen a march on the cooks of Paris. They get what usually goes to feed the fire. This is probably better than stall-fed beef and slaughterhouse pork to make a man of. Give me a wildness whose glance no civilization can endure,—as if we lived on the marrow of koodoos devoured raw.

There are some intervals which border the strain of the wood thrush, to which I would migrate,—wild lands where no settler has squatted; to which, methinks, I am already acclimated.

The African hunter Cumming tells us that the skin of the eland, as well as that of most other antelopes just killed, emits the most delicious perfume of trees and grass. I would have every man so much like a wild antelope, so much a part and parcel of nature that his very person should thus sweetly advertise our senses of his presence, and remind us of those parts of nature which he most haunts. I feel no disposition to be satirical, when the trapper's coat emits the odor of musquash even; it is a sweeter scent to me than that which commonly exhales from the merchant's or the scholar's garments. When I go into their wardrobes and handle their vestments, I am reminded of no grassy plains and flowery meads which they have frequented, but of dusty merchants' exchanges and libraries rather.

A tanned skin is something more than respectable, and perhaps olive is a fitter color than white for a man,—a denizen of the woods. "The pale white man!" I do not wonder that the African pitied him. Darwin the naturalist says, "A white man bathing by the side of a Tahitian was like a plant bleached by the gardener's art, compared with a fine, dark green one, growing vigorously in the open fields."

Ben Jonson exclaims,—

"How near to good is what is fair!"

So I would say,—

How near to good is what is *wild!*

Life consists with wildness. The most alive is the wildest. Not yet subdued to man, its presence refreshes him. One who pressed forward incessantly and never rested from his labors, who grew fast and made infinite demands on life, would always find himself in a new country or wilderness, and surrounded by the raw material of life. He would he climbing over the prostrate stems of primitive forest-trees.

Hope and the future for me are not in lawns and cultivated fields, not in towns and cities, but in the impervious and
quaking swamps. When, formerly, I have analyzed my partiality
for some farm which I had contemplated purchasing, I have frequently found that I was attracted solely by a few square rods of
impermeable and unfathomable bog,—a natural sink in one
corner of it. That was the jewel which dazzled me. I derive
more of my subsistence from the swamps which surround my
native town than from the cultivated gardens in the village.
There are no richer parterres to my eyes than the dense beds of
dwarf andromeda (*Cassandra calyculata*) which cover these tender places on the earth's surface. Botany cannot go farther than
tell me the names of the shrubs which grow there,—the high
blueberry, panicled andromeda, lamb-kill, azalea, and rhodora,—
all standing in the quaking sphagnum. I often think that I
should like to have my house front on this mass of dull red
bushes, omitting other flower plots and borders, transplanted
spruce and trim box, even graveled walks,—to have this fertile
spot under my windows, not a few imported barrowfuls of soil
only to cover the sand which was thrown out in digging the cellar. Why not put my house, my parlor, behind this plot, instead
of behind that meagre assemblage of curiosities, that poor apology for a Nature and Art, which I call my front yard? It is an effort to clear up and make a decent appearance when the carpenter and mason have departed, though done as much for the
passer-by as the dweller within. The most tasteful front-yard
fence was never an agreeable object of study to me; the most
elaborate ornaments, acorn tops, or what not, soon wearied and
disgusted me. Bring your sills up to the very edge of the swamp,
then (though it may not be the best place for a dry cellar), so that
there be no access on that side to citizens. Front yards are not
made to walk in, but, at most, through, and you could go in the
back way.

Yes, though you may think me perverse, if it were proposed to me to dwell in the neighborhood of the most beautiful
garden that ever human art contrived, or else of a Dismal
Swamp, I should certainly decide for the swamp. How vain,
then, have been all your labors, citizens, for me!

My spirits infallibly rise in proportion to the outward
dreariness. Give me the ocean, the desert, or the wilderness! In
the desert, pure air and solitude compensate for want of moisture and fertility. The traveler Burton says of it: "Your *morale*

improves; you become frank and cordial, hospitable and single-minded. . . . In the desert, spirituous liquors excite only disgust. There is a keen enjoyment in a mere animal existence." They who have been traveling long on the steppes of Tartary say, "On reëntering cultivated lands, the agitation, perplexity, and turmoil of civilization oppressed and suffocated us; the air seemed to fail us, and we felt every moment as if about to die of asphyxia." When I would recreate myself, I seek the darkest wood, the thickest and most interminable and, to the citizen, most dismal, swamp. I enter a swamp as a sacred place, a *sanctum sanctorum*. There is the strength, the marrow, of Nature. The wildwood covers the virgin mould, and the same soil is good for men and for trees. A man's health requires as many acres of meadow to his prospect as his farm does loads of muck. There are the strong meats on which he feeds. A town is saved, not more by the righteous men in it than by the woods and swamps that surround it. A township where one primitive forest waves above while another primitive forest rots below,—such a town is fitted to raise not only corn and potatoes, but poets and philosophers for the coming ages. In such a soil grew Homer and Confucius and the rest, and out of such a wilderness comes the Reformer eating locusts and wild honey.

To preserve wild animals implies generally the creation of a forest for them to dwell in or resort to. So it is with man. A hundred years ago they sold bark in our streets peeled from our own woods. In the very aspect of those primitive and rugged trees there was, methinks, a tanning principle which hardened and consolidated the fibres of men's thoughts. Ah! already I shudder for these comparatively degenerate days of my native village, when you cannot collect a load of bark of good thickness, and we no longer produce tar and turpentine.

The civilized nations—Greece, Rome, England—have been sustained by the primitive forests which anciently rotted where they stand. They survive as long as the soil is not exhausted. Alas for human culture! little is to be expected of a nation, when the vegetable mould is exhausted, and it is compelled to make manure of the bones of its fathers. There the poet sustains himself merely by his own superfluous fat, and the philosopher comes down on his marrow-bones.

It is said to be the task of the American "to work the virgin soil," and that "agriculture here already assumes proportions unknown everywhere else." I think that the farmer displaces the Indian even because he redeems the meadow, and so makes himself stronger and in some respects more natural. I was surveying for a man the other day a single straight line one hundred and thirty-two rods long, through a swamp at whose entrance might have been written the words which Dante read over the entrance to the infernal regions, "Leave all hope, ye that enter,"—that is, of ever getting out again; where at one time I saw my employer actually up to his neck and swimming for his life in his property, though it was still winter. He had another similar swamp which I could not survey at all, because it was completely under water, and nevertheless, with regard to a third swamp, which I did *survey* from a distance, he remarked to me, true to his instincts, that he would not part with it for any consideration, on account of the mud which it contained. And that man intends to put a girdling ditch round the whole in the course of forty months, and so redeem it by the magic of his spade. I refer to him only as the type of a class.

The weapons with which we have gained our most important victories, which should be handed down as heirlooms from father to son, are not the sword and the lance, but the bushwhack, the turf-cutter, the spade, and the bog hoe, rusted with the blood of many a meadow, and begrimed with the dust of many a hard-fought fight. The very winds blew the Indian's cornfield into the meadow, and pointed out the way which he had not the skill to follow. He had no better implement with which to intrench himself in the land than a clamshell. But the farmer is armed with plow and spade.

In literature it is only the wild that attracts us. Dullness is but another name for tameness. It is the uncivilized free and wild thinking in Hamlet and the Iliad, in all the scriptures and mythologies, not learned in the schools, that delights us. As the wild duck is more swift and beautiful than the tame, so is the wild—the mallard—thought, which 'mid falling dews wings its way above the fens. A truly good book is something as natural, and as unexpectedly and unaccountably fair and perfect, as a wild-flower discovered on the prairies of the West or in the jungles of the East. Genius is a light which makes the darkness visible, like the lightning's flash, which perchance shatters the temple of knowledge itself,—and not a taper lighted at the hearthstone of the race, which pales before the light of common day.

English literature, from the days of the minstrels to the Lake Poets,—Chaucer and Spenser and Milton, and even Shakespeare, included,—breathes no quite fresh and, in this sense, wild strain. It is an essentially tame and civilized literature, reflecting Greece and Rome. Her wilderness is a greenwood, her wild man a Robin Hood. There is plenty of genial love of Nature, but not so much of Nature herself. Her chronicles inform us when her wild animals, but not when the wild man in her, became extinct.

The science of Humboldt is one thing, poetry is other thing. The poet to-day, notwithstanding all the discoveries of science, and the accumulated learning of mankind, enjoys no advantage over Homer.

Where is the literature which gives expression to Nature? He would be a poet who could impress the winds and streams into his service, to speak for him; who nailed words to their primitive senses, as farmers drive down stakes in the spring, which the frost has heaved; who derived his words as often as he used them,—transplanted them to his page with earth adhering to their roots; whose words were so true and fresh and natural that they would appear to expand like the buds at the approach of spring, though they lay half smothered between two musty leaves in a library,—aye, to bloom and bear fruit there, after their kind, annually, for the faithful reader, in sympathy with surrounding Nature.

I do not know of any poetry to quote which adequately expresses this yearning for the Wild. Approached from this side, the best poetry is tame. I do not know where to find in any literature, ancient or modern, any account which contents me of that Nature with which even I am acquainted. You will perceive that I demand something which no Augustan nor Elizabethan age, which no *culture*, in short, can give. Mythology comes nearer to it than anything. How much more fertile a Nature, at least, has Grecian mythology its root in than English literature! Mythology is the crop which the Old World bore before its soil was exhausted, before the fancy and imagination were affected with blight; and which it still bears, wherever its pristine vigor is unabated. All other literatures endure only as the elms which overshadow our houses; but this is like the great dragon-tree of the Western Isles, as old as mankind, and, whether that does or not, will endure as long; for the decay of other literatures makes the soil in which it thrives.

The West is preparing to add its fables to those of the East. The valleys of the Ganges, the Nile, and the Rhine having yielded their crop, it remains to be seen what the valleys of the Amazon, the Plate, the Orinoco, the St. Lawrence, and the Mississippi will produce. Perchance, when, in the course of ages, American liberty has become a fiction of the past,—as it is to some extent a fiction of the present,—the poets of the world will be inspired by American mythology.

The wildest dreams of wild men, even, are not the less true, though they may not recommend themselves to the sense which is most common among Englishmen and Americans today. It is not every truth that recommends itself to the common sense. Nature has a place for the wild clematis as well as for the cabbage. Some expressions of truth are reminiscent,—others merely *sensible*, as the phrase is,—others prophetic. Some forms of disease, even, may prophesy forms of health. The geologist has discovered that the figures of serpents, griffins, flying dragons, and other fanciful embellishments of heraldry, have their prototypes in the forms of fossil species which were extinct before man was created, and hence "indicate a faint and shadowy knowledge of a previous state of organic existence." The Hindoos dreamed that the earth rested on an elephant, and the elephant on a tortoise, and the tortoise on a serpent; and though it may be an unimportant coincidence, it will not be out of place here to state, that a fossil tortoise has lately been discovered in Asia large enough to support an elephant. I confess that I am partial to these wild fancies, which transcend the order of time and development. They are the sublimest recreation of the intellect. The partridge loves peas, but not those that go with her into the pot.

In short, all good things are wild and free. There is something in a strain of music, whether produced by an instrument or by the human voice,—take the sound of a bugle in a summer night, for instance,—which by its wildness, to speak without satire, reminds me of the cries emitted by wild beasts in their native forests. It is so much of their wildness as I can understand. Give me for my friends and neighbors wild men, not tame ones. The wildness of the savage is but a faint symbol of the awful ferity with which good men and lovers meet.

I love even to see the domestic animals reassert their native rights,—any evidence that they have not wholly lost their original wild habits and vigor; as when my neighbor's cow breaks out of her pasture early in the spring and boldly swims the river, a cold, gray tide, twenty-five or thirty rods wide, swollen by the melted snow. It is the buffalo crossing the Mississippi. This exploit confers some dignity on the herd in my eyes,—already dignified. The seeds of instinct are preserved under the thick hides of cattle and horses, like seeds in the bowels of the earth, an indefinite period.

Any sportiveness in cattle is unexpected. I saw one day a herd of a dozen bullocks and cows running about and frisking in unwieldy sport, like huge rats, even like kittens. They shook their heads, raised their tails, and rushed up and down a hill, and I perceived by their horns, as well as by their activity, their relation to the deer tribe. But, alas! a sudden loud *Whoa!* would have damped their ardor at once, reduced them from venison to beef, and stiffened their sides and sinews like the locomotive. Who but the Evil One has cried "Whoa!" to mankind? Indeed, the life of cattle, like that of many men, is but a sort of locomotiveness; they move a side at a time, and man, by his machinery, is meeting the horse and the ox half-way. Whatever part the whip has touched is thenceforth palsied. Who would ever think of a *side* of any of the supple cat tribe, as we speak of a *side* of beef?

I rejoice that horses and steers have to be broken before they can be made the slaves of men, and that men themselves have some wild oats still left to sow before they become submissive members of society. Undoubtedly, all men are not equally fit subjects for civilization; and because the majority, like dogs and sheep, are tame by inherited disposition, this is no reason why the others should have their natures broken that they may be reduced to the same level. Men are in the main alike, but they were made several in order that they might be various. If a low use is to be served, one man will do nearly or quite as well as another; if a high one, individual excellence is to be regarded. Any man can stop a hole to keep the wind away, but no other man could serve so rare a use as the author of this illustration did. Confucius says, "The skins of the tiger and the leopard, when they are tanned, are as the skins of the dog and the sheep tanned." But it is not the part of a true culture to tame tigers, any more than it is to make sheep ferocious; and tanning their skins for shoes is not the best use to which they can be put.

When looking over a list of men's names in a foreign language, as of military officers, or of authors who have written on a particular subject, I am reminded once more that there is nothing in a name. The name Menschikoff, for instance, has nothing in it to my ears more human than a whisker, and it may belong to a rat. As the names of the Poles and Russians are to us, so are ours to them. It is as if they had been named by the child's rigmarole, *Iery wiery ichery van, tittle-tol-tan*. I see in my mind a herd of wild creatures swarming over the earth, and to each the herdsman has affixed some barbarous sound in his own dialect. The names of men are, of course, as cheap and meaningless as *Bose* and *Tray*, the names of dogs.

Methinks it would be some advantage to philosophy if men were named merely in the gross, as they are known. It would be necessary only to know the genus and perhaps the race or variety, to know the individual. We are not prepared to believe that every private soldier in a Roman army had a name of his own,—because we have not supposed that he had a character of his own.

At present our only true names are nicknames. I knew a boy who, from his peculiar energy, was called "Buster" by his playmates, and this rightly supplanted his Christian name. Some travelers tell us that an Indian had no name given him at first, but earned it, and his name was his fame; and among some tribes he acquired a new name with every new exploit. It is pitiful when a man bears a name for convenience merely, who has earned neither name nor fame.

I will not allow mere names to make distinctions for me, but still see men in herds for all them. A familiar name cannot make a man less strange to me. It may be given to a savage who retains in secret his own wild title earned in the woods. We have a wild savage in us, and a savage name is perchance somewhere recorded as ours. I see that my neighbor, who bears the familiar epithet William or Edwin, takes it off with his jacket. It does not adhere to him when asleep or in anger, or aroused by any passion or inspiration. I seem to hear pronounced by some of his kin at such a time his original wild name in some jaw-breaking or else melodious tongue.

Here is this vast, savage, howling mother of ours, Nature, lying all around, with such beauty, and such affection for her children, as the leopard; and yet we are so early weaned from her breast to society, to that culture which is exclusively an interaction of man on man,—a sort of breeding in and in, which produces at most a merely English nobility, a civilization destined to have a speedy limit.

In society, in the best institutions of men, it is easy to detect a certain precocity. When we should still be growing children, we are already little men. Give me a culture which imports much muck from the meadows, and deepens the soil,—not that which trusts to heating manures, and improved implements and modes of culture only!

Many a poor sore-eyed student that I have heard would grew faster, both intellectually and physically, if, instead of sitting up so very late, he honestly slumbered a fool's allowance.

There may be an excess even of informing light. Niepce, a Frenchman, discovered "actinism," that power in the sun's rays which produces a chemical effect; that granite rocks, and stone structures, and statues of metal "are all alike destructively acted upon during the hours of sunshine, and, but for provisions of Nature no less wonderful, would soon perish under the delicate touch of the most subtile of the agencies of the universe." But he observed that "those bodies which underwent this change during the daylight possessed the power of restoring themselves to their original conditions during the hours of night, when this excitement was no longer influencing them." Hence it has been inferred that "the hours of darkness are as necessary to the inorganic creation as we know night and sleep are to the organic kingdom." Not even does the moon shine every night, but gives place to darkness.

I would not have every man nor every part of a man cultivated, any more than I would have every acre of earth cultivated: part will be tillage, but the greater part will be meadow and forest, not only serving an immediate use, but preparing a mould against a distant future, by the annual decay of the vegetation which it supports.

There are other letters for the child to learn than those which Cadmus invented. The Spaniards have a good term to express this wild and dusky knowledge, *Gramatica parda*, tawny grammar, a kind of mother-wit derived from that same leopard to which I have referred.

We have heard of a Society for the Diffusion of Useful Knowledge. It is said that knowledge is power, and the like. Methinks there is equal need of a Society for the Diffusion of Useful Ignorance, what we will call Beautiful Knowledge, a knowledge useful in a higher sense: for what is most of our boasted so-called knowledge but a conceit that we know something, which robs us of the advantage of our actual ignorance? What we call knowledge is often our positive ignorance; ignorance our negative knowledge. By long years of patient industry and reading of the newspapers,—for what are the libraries of science but files of newspapers?—a man accumulates a myriad facts, lays them up in his memory, and then when in some spring of his life he saunters abroad into the Great Fields of thought, he, as it were, goes to grass like a horse and leaves all his harness behind in the stable. I would say to the Society for the Diffusion of Useful Knowledge, sometimes,—Go to grass. You have eaten hay long enough. The spring has come with its green crop. The very cows are driven to their country pastures before the end of May; though I have heard of one unnatural farmer who kept his cow in the barn and fed her on hay all the year round. So, frequently, the Society for the Diffusion of Useful Knowledge treats its cattle.

A man's ignorance sometimes is not only useful, but beautiful,—while his knowledge, so called, is oftentimes worse than useless, besides being ugly. Which is the best man to deal with,—he who knows nothing about a subject, and, what is extremely rare, knows that he knows nothing, or he who really knows something about it, but thinks that he knows all?

My desire for knowledge is intermittent, but my desire to bathe my head in atmospheres unknown to my feet is perennial and constant. The highest that we can attain to is not Knowledge, but Sympathy with Intelligence. I do not know that this higher knowledge amounts to anything more definite than a novel and grand surprise on a sudden revelation of the insufficiency of all that we called Knowledge before,—a discovery that there are more things in heaven and earth than are dreamed of in our philosophy. It is the lighting up of the mist by the sun. Man cannot *know* in any higher sense than this, any more than he can look serenely and with impunity in the face of the sun: Ὡς τι νοων, ου κεινον νοησεις, "You will not perceive that, as perceiving a particular thing," say the Chaldean Oracles.

There is something servile in the habit of seeking after a law which we may obey. We may study the laws of matter at and for our convenience, but a successful life knows no law. It is an unfortunate discovery certainly, that of a law which binds us where we did not know before that we were bound. Live free, child of the mist, —and with respect to knowledge we are all children of the mist. The man who takes the liberty to live is superior to all the laws, by virtue of his relation to the law-maker. "That is active duty," says the Vishnu Purana, "which is not for our bondage; that is knowledge which is for our libera-tion: all other duty is good only unto weariness; all other knowl-edge is only the cleverness of an artist."

It is remarkable how few events or crises there are in our histories, how little exercised we have been in our minds, how few experiences we have had. I would fain be assured that I am growing apace and rankly, though my very growth disturb this dull equanimity,—though it be with struggle through long, dark, muggy nights or seasons of gloom. It would be well if all our lives were a divine tragedy even, instead of this trivial comedy or farce. Dante, Bunyan, and others appear to have been exer-cised in their minds more than we: they were subjected to a kind of culture such as our district schools and colleges do not con-template. Even Mahomet, though many may scream at his name, had a good deal more to live for, aye, and to die for, than they have commonly.

When, at rare intervals, some thought visits one, as per-chance he is walking on a railroad, then, indeed, the cars go by without his hearing them. But soon, by some inexorable law, our life goes by and the cars return.

> "Gentle breeze, that wanderest unseen,
> And bendest the thistles round Loira of storms,
> Traveler of the windy glens,
> Why hast thou left my ear so soon?"

While almost all men feel an attraction drawing them to society, few are attracted strongly to Nature. In their reaction to Nature men appear to me for the most part, notwithstanding their arts, lower than the animals. It is not often a beautiful rela-tion, as in the case of the animals. How little appreciation of the beauty of the landscape there is among us! We have to be told that the Greeks called the world Κοσμος, Beauty, or Order, but we do not see clearly why they did so, and we esteem it at best only a curious philological fact.

For my part, I feel that with regard to Nature I live a sort of border life, on the confines of a world into which I make occasional and transient forays only, and my patriotism and allegiance to the state into whose territories I seem to retreat are those of a moss-trooper. Unto a life which I call natural I would gladly follow even a will-o'-the-wisp through bogs and sloughs unimaginable, but no moon nor firefly has shown me the causeway to it. Nature is a personality so vast and universal that we have never seen one of her features. The walker in the familiar fields which stretch around my native town sometimes finds himself in another land than is described in their owners' deeds, as it were in some faraway field on the confines of the actual Concord, where her jurisdiction ceases, and the idea which the word Concord suggests ceases to be suggested. These farms which I have myself surveyed, these bounds which I have set up, appear dimly still as through a mist; but they have no chemistry to fix them; they fade from the surface of the glass, and the picture which the painter painted stands out dimly from beneath. The world with which we are commonly acquainted leaves no trace, and it will have no anniversary.

I took a walk on Spaulding's Farm the other afternoon. I saw the setting sun lighting up the opposite side of a stately pine wood. Its golden rays straggled into the aisles of the wood as into some noble hall. I was impressed as if some ancient and altogether admirable and shining family had settled there in that part of the land called Concord, unknown to me,—to whom the sun was servant,—who had not gone into society in the village,—who had not been called on. I saw their park, their pleasure-ground, beyond through the wood, in Spaulding's cranberry-meadow. The pines furnished them with gables as they grew. Their house was not obvious to vision; the trees grew through it. I do not know whether I heard the sounds of a suppressed hilarity or not. They seemed to recline on the sunbeams. They have sons and daughters. They are quite well. The farmer's cart-path, which leads directly through their hall, does not in the least put them out, as the muddy bottom of a pool is sometimes seen through the reflected skies. They never heard of Spaulding, and do not know that he is their neighbor,—notwithstanding I heard him whistle as he drove his team through the house. Nothing can equal the serenity of their

lives. Their coat-of-arms is simply a lichen. I saw it painted on
the pines and oaks. Their attics were in the tops of the trees.
They are of no politics. There was no noise of labor. I did not
perceive that they were weaving or spinning. Yet I did detect,
when the wind lulled and hearing was done away, the finest
imaginable sweet musical hum,—as of a distant hive in May,—
which perchance was the sound of their thinking. They had no
idle thoughts, and no one without could see their work, for their
industry was not as in knots and excrescences embayed.

But I find it difficult to remember them. They fade irre-
vocably out of my mind even now while I speak, and endeavor
to recall them and recollect myself. It is only after a long and serious effort to recollect my best thoughts that I become again
aware of their cohabitancy. If it were not for such families as
this, I think I should move out of Concord.

We are accustomed to say in New England that few and
fewer pigeons visit us every year. Our forests furnish no mast
for them. So, it would seem, few and fewer thoughts visit each
growing man from year to year, for the grove in our minds is
laid waste,—sold to feed unnecessary fires of ambition, or sent to
mill,—and there is scarcely a twig left for them to perch on.
They no longer build nor breed with us. In some more genial
season, perchance, a faint shadow flits across the landscape of the
mind, cast by the *wings* of some thought in its vernal or autumnal migration, but, looking up, we are unable to detect the substance of the thought itself. Our winged thoughts are turned to
poultry. They no longer soar, and they attain only to a Shanghai
and Cochin-China grandeur. Those *gra-a-ate thoughts*, those
gra-a-ate men you hear of!

We hug the earth,—how rarely we mount! Methinks we
might elevate ourselves a little more. We might climb a tree, at
least. I found my account in climbing a tree once. It was a tall
white pine, on the top of a hill; and though I got well pitched, I
was well paid for it, for I discovered new mountains in the horizon which I had never seen before,—so much more of the earth
and the heavens. I might have walked about the foot of the tree

for threescore years and ten, and yet I certainly should never have seen them. But, above all, I discovered around me,—it was near the end of June,—on the ends of the topmost branches only, a few minute and delicate red cone-like blossoms, the fertile flower of the white pine looking heavenward. I carried straightway to the village the topmost spire, and showed it to stranger jurymen who walked the streets,—for it was court week,—and to farmers and lumber-dealers and wood-choppers and hunters, and not one had ever seen the like before, but they wondered as at a star dropped down. Tell of ancient architects finishing their works on the tops of columns as perfectly as on the lower and more visible parts! Nature has from the first expanded the minute blossom of the forest only toward the heavens, above men's heads and unobserved by them. We see only the flowers that are under our feet in the meadows. The pines have developed their delicate blossoms on the highest twigs of the wood every summer for ages, as well over the heads of Nature's red children as of her white ones; yet scarcely a farmer or hunter in the land has ever seen them.

Above all, we cannot afford not to live in the present. He is blessed over all mortals who loses no moment of the passing life in remembering the past. Unless our philosophy hears the cock crow in every barn-yard within our horizon, it is belated. That sound commonly reminds us that we are growing rusty and antique in our employments and habits of thought. His philosophy comes down to a more recent time than ours. There is something suggested by it that is a newer testament,—the gospel according to this moment. He has not fallen astern; he has got up early and kept up early, and to be where he is is to be in season, in the foremost rank of time. It is an expression of the health and soundness of Nature, a brag for all the world,— healthiness as of a spring burst forth, a new fountain of the Muses, to celebrate this last instant of time. Where he lives no fugitive slave laws are passed. Who has not betrayed his master many times since last he heard that note?

The merit of this bird's strain is in its freedom from all plaintiveness. The singer can easily move us to tears or to laughter, but where is he who can excite in us a pure morning joy? When, in doleful dumps, breaking the awful stillness of

our wooden sidewalk on a Sunday, or, perchance, a watcher in
the house of mourning, I hear a cockerel crow far or near, I think
to myself, "There is one of us well, at any rate,"—and with a
sudden gush return to my senses.

We had a remarkable sunset one day last November. I
was walking in a meadow, the source of a small brook, when the
sun at last, just before setting, after a cold, gray day, reached a
clear stratum in the horizon, and the softest, brightest morning
sunlight fell on the dry grass and on the stems of the trees in the
opposite horizon and on the leaves of the shrub oaks on the
hillside, while our shadows stretched long over the meadow
eastward, as if we were the only motes in its beams. It was such a
light as we could not have imagined a moment before, and the
air also was so warm and serene that nothing was wanting to
make a paradise of that meadow. When we reflected that this
was not a solitary phenomenon, never to happen again, but that
it would happen forever and ever, an infinite number of
evenings, and cheer and reassure the latest child that walked
there, it was more glorious still.

The sun sets on some retired meadow, where no house is
visible, with all the glory and splendor that it lavishes on cities,
and perchance as it has never set before,—where there is but a
solitary marsh hawk to have his wings gilded by it, or only a
musquash looks out from his cabin, and there is some little
black-veined brook in the midst of the marsh, just beginning to
meander, winding slowly round a decaying stump. We walked
in so pure and bright a light, gilding the withered grass and
leaves, so softly and serenely bright, I thought I had never bathed
in such a golden flood, without a ripple or a murmur to it. The
west side of every wood and rising ground gleamed like the
boundary of Elysium, and the sun on our backs seemed like a
gentle herdsman driving us home at evening.

So we saunter toward the Holy Land, till one day the sun
shall shine more brightly than ever he has done, shall perchance
shine into our minds and hearts, and light up our whole lives
with a great awakening light, as warm and serene and golden as
on a bankside in autumn.

Section III
Natural History Essays

THE NATURAL HISTORY OF MASSACHUSETTS[1]
1842

Books of natural history make the most cheerful winter reading. I read in Audubon with a thrill of delight, when the snow covers the ground, of the magnolia, and the Florida Keys, and their warm sea-breezes; of the fence-rail, and the cotton-tree, and the migrations of the rice-bird; of the breaking up of winter in Labrador, and the melting of the snow on the forks of the Missouri; and owe an accession of health to these reminiscences of luxuriant nature.

> Within the circuit of this plodding life,
> There enter moments of an azure hue,
> Untarnished fair as is the violet
> Or anemone, when the spring strews them
> By some meandering rivulet, which make
> The best philosophy untrue that aims
> But to console man for his grievances.
> I have remembered, when the winter came,
> High in my chamber in the frosty nights,
> When in the still light of the cheerful moon,
> On every twig and rail and jutting spout,
> The icy spears were adding to their length
> Against the arrows of the coming sun,
> How in the shimmering noon of summer past
> Some unrecorded beam slanted across
> The upland pastures where the Johnswort grew;
> Or heard, amid the verdure of my mind,
> The bee's long smothered hum, on the blue flag
> Loitering midst the mead; or busy rill,
> Which now through all its course stands still and dumb,
> Its own memorial,—purling at its play
> Along the slopes, and through the meadows next,
> Until its youthful sound was hushed at last
> In the staid current of the lowland stream;

Or seen the furrows shine but late upturned,
And where the fieldfare followed in the rear,
When all the fields around lay bound and hoar
Beneath a thick integument of snow.
So by God's cheap economy made rich
To go upon my winter's task again.

I am singularly refreshed in winter when I hear of service-berries, poke-weed, juniper. Is not heaven made up of these cheap summer glories? There is a singular health in those words, Labrador and East Main, which no desponding creed recognizes. How much more than Federal are these States! If there were no other vicissitudes than the seasons, our interest would never tire. Much more is adoing than Congress wots of. What journal do the persimmon and the buckeye keep, and the sharp-shinned hawk? What is transpiring from summer to winter in the Carolinas, and the Great Pine Forest, and the Valley of the Mohawk? The merely political aspect of the land is never very cheering; men are degraded when considered as the members of a political organization. On this side all lands present only the symptoms of decay. I see but Bunker Hill and Sing-Sing, the District of Columbia and Sullivan's Island, with a few avenues connecting them. But paltry are they all beside one blast of the east or the south wind which blows over them.

In society you will not find health, but in nature. Unless our feet at least stood in the midst of nature, all our faces would he pale and livid. Society is always diseased, and the best is the most so. There is no scent in it so wholesome as that of the pines, nor any fragrance so penetrating and restorative as the life-everlasting in high pastures. I would keep some book of natural history always by me as a sort of elixir, the reading of which should restore the tone of the system. To the sick, indeed, nature is sick, but to the well, a fountain of health. To him who contemplates a trait of natural beauty no harm nor disappointment can come. The doctrines of despair, of spiritual or political tyranny or servitude, were never taught by such as shared the serenity of nature. Surely good courage will not flag here on the Atlantic border, as long as we are flanked by the Fur Countries. There is enough in that sound to cheer one under any circumstances. The spruce, the hemlock, and the pine will not countenance despair. Methinks some creeds in vestries and churches do forget the hunter wrapped in furs by the Great Slave Lake, and that the Esquimaux sledges are drawn by dogs, and in the

twilight of the northern night the hunter does not give over to
follow the seal and walrus on the ice. They are of sick and diseased imaginations who would toll the world's knell so soon.
Cannot these sedentary sects do better than prepare the shrouds
and write the epitaphs of those other busy living men? The
practical faith of all men belies the preacher's consolation. What
is any man's discourse to me, if I am not sensible of something
in it as steady and cheery as the creak of crickets? In it the woods
must be relieved against the sky. Men tire me when I am not
constantly greeted and refreshed as by the flux of sparkling
streams. Surely joy is the condition of life. Think of the young
fry that leap in ponds, the myriads of insects ushered into being
on a summer evening, the incessant note of the hyla with which
the woods ring in the spring, the nonchalance of the butterfly
carrying accident and change painted in a thousand hues upon
its wings, or the brook minnow stoutly stemming the current,
the lustre of whose scales, worn bright by the attrition, is reflected upon the bank!

We fancy that this din of religion, literature, and philosophy, which is heard in pulpits, lyceums, and parlors, vibrates
through the universe, and is as catholic a sound as the creaking
of the earth's axle; but if a man sleep soundly, he will forget it all
between sunset and dawn. It is the three-inch swing of a pendu-
lum in a cupboard, which the great pulse of nature vibrates by
and through each instant. When we lift our eyelids and open
our ears, it disappears with smoke and rattle like the cars on a
railroad. When I detect a beauty in any of the recesses of nature,
I am reminded, by the serene and retired spirit in which it requires to be contemplated, of the inexpressible privacy of a life,—
how silent and unambitious it is. The beauty there is in mosses
must be considered from the holiest, quietest nook. What an
admirable training is science for the more active warfare of life!
Indeed, the unchallenged bravery which these studies imply, is
far more impressive than the trumpeted valor of the warrior. I
am pleased to lean that Thales was up and stirring by night not
unfrequently, as his astronomical discoveries prove. Linnæus,
setting out for Lapland, surveys his "comb" and "spare shirt,"
"leathern breeches" and "gauze cap to keep off gnats," with as
much complacency as Bonaparte a park of artillery for the Rus-
sian campaign. The quiet bravery of the man is admirable. His
eye is to take in fish, flower, and bird, quadruped and biped. Science is always brave; for to know is to know good; doubt and

danger quail before her eye. What the coward overlooks in his hurry, she calmly scrutinizes, breaking ground like a pioneer for the array of arts that follow in her train. But cowardice is unscientific; for there cannot be a science of ignorance. There may be a science of bravery, for that advances; but a retreat is rarely well conducted; if it is, then is it an orderly advance in the face of circumstances.

But to draw a little nearer to our promised topics. Entomology extends the limits of being in a new direction, so that I walk in nature with a sense of greater space and freedom. It suggests besides, that the universe is not rough-hewn, but perfect in its details. Nature will bear the closest inspection; she invites us to lay our eye level with the smallest leaf, and take an insect view of its plain. She has no interstices; every part is full of life. I explore, too, with pleasure, the sources of the myriad sounds which crowd the summer noon, and which seem the very grain and stuff of which eternity is made. Who does not remember the shrill roll-call of the harvest-fly? There were ears for these sounds in Greece long ago, as Anacreon's ode will show.

> "We pronounce thee happy, Cicada,
> For on the tops of the trees,
> Drinking a little dew,
> Like any king thou singest,
> For thine are they all,
> Whatever thou seest in the fields,
> And whatever the woods bear.
> Thou art the friend of the husbandmen,
> In no respect injuring any one;
> And thou art honored among men,
> Sweet prophet of summer.
> The Muses love thee,
> And Phœbus himself loves thee,
> And has given thee a shrill song;
> Age does not wrack thee,
> Thou skillful, earthborn, song-loving,
> Unsuffering, bloodless one;
> Almost thou art like the gods."

In the autumn days, the creaking of crickets is heard at noon over all the land, and as in summer they are heard chiefly at nightfall, so then by their incessant chirp they usher in the evening of the year. Nor can all the vanities that vex the world alter one whit the measure that night has chosen. Every pulse-

beat is in exact time with the cricket's chant and the tickings of
the death-watch in the wall. Alternate with these if you can.

About two hundred and eighty birds either reside permanently in the State, or spend the summer only, or make us a
passing visit. Those which spend the winter with us have obtained our warmest sympathy. The nuthatch and chickadee flitting in company through the dells of the wood, the one harshly
scolding at the intruder, the other with a faint lisping note entic-
ing him on; the jay screaming in the orchard; the crow cawing in
unison with the storm; the partridge, like a russet link extended
over from autumn to spring, preserving unbroken the chain of
summers; the hawk with warrior-like firmness abiding the blasts
of winter; the robin[2] and lark lurking by warm springs in the
woods; the familiar snowbird culling a few seeds in the garden
or a few crumbs in the yard; and occasionally the shrike, with
heedless and unfrozen melody bringing back summer again:—

> His steady sails he never furls
> At any time o' year,
> And perching now on Winter's curls,
> He whistles in his ear.

As the spring advances, and the ice is melting in the river,
our earliest and straggling visitors make their appearance.
Again does the old Teian poet sing as well for New England as
for Greece, in the

RETURN OF SPRING

> Behold, how, Spring appearing,
> The Graces send forth roses;
> Behold, how the wave of the sea
> Is made smooth by the calm;
> Behold, how the duck dives;
> Behold, how the crane travels;
> And Titan shines constantly bright.
> The shadows of the clouds are moving;
> The works of man shine;
> The earth puts forth fruits;
> The fruit of the olive puts forth.
> The cup of Bacchus is crowned,
> Along the leaves, along the branches,
> The fruit, bending them down, flourishes.

The ducks alight at this season in the still water, in company with the gulls, which do not fail to improve an east wind to visit our meadows, and swim about by twos and threes, pluming themselves, and diving to peck at the root of the lily, and the cranberries which the frost has not loosened. The first flock of geese is seen beating to north, in long harrows and waving lines; the jingle of the song sparrow salutes us from the shrubs and fences; the plaintive note of the lark comes clear and sweet from the meadow; and the bluebird, like an azure ray, glances past us in our walk. The fish hawk, too, is occasionally seen at this season sailing majestically over the water, and he who has once observed it will not soon forget the majesty of its flight. It sails the air like a ship of the line, worthy to struggle with the elements, falling back from time to time like a ship on its beam ends, and holding its talons up as if ready for the arrows, in the attitude of the national bird. It is a great presence, as of the master of river and forest. Its eye would not quail before the owner of the soil, but make him feel like an intruder on its domains. And then its retreat, sailing so steadily away, is a kind of advance. I have by me one of a pair of ospreys, which have for some years fished in this vicinity, shot by a neighboring pond, measuring more than two feet in length, and six in the stretch of its wings. Nuttall mentions that "the ancients, particularly Aristotle, pretended that the ospreys taught their young to gaze at the sun, and those who were unable to do so were destroyed. Linnæus even believed, on ancient authority, that one of the feet of this bird had all the toes divided, while the other was partly webbed, so that it could swim with one foot, and grasp a fish with the other." But that educated eye is now dim, and those talons are nerveless. Its shrill scream seems yet to linger in its throat, and the roar of the sea in its wings. There is the tyranny of Jove in its claws, and his wrath in the erectile feathers of the head and neck. It reminds me of the Argonautic expedition, and would inspire the dullest to take flight over Parnassus.

The booming of the bittern, described by Goldsmith and Nuttall, is frequently heard in our fens, in the morning and evening, sounding like a pump, or the chopping of wood in a frosty morning in some distant farm-yard. The manner in which this sound is produced I have not seen anywhere described. On one occasion, the bird has been seen by one of my neighbors to thrust its bill into the water, and suck up as much as it could hold, then, raising its head, it pumped it out again with four or five heaves of the neck, throwing it two or three feet, and making the sound each time.

At length the summer's eternity is ushered in by the cackle of the flicker among the oaks on the hillside, and a new dynasty begins with calm security.

In May and June the woodland quire is in full tune, and, given the immense spaces of hollow air, and this curious human ear, one does not see how the void could be better filled.

> Each summer sound
> Is a summer round.

As the season advances, and those birds which make us but a passing visit depart, the woods become silent again, and but few feathers ruffle the drowsy air. But the solitary rambler may still find a response and expression for every mood in the depths of the wood.

> Sometimes I hear the veery's[3] clarion,
> Or brazen trump of the impatient jay,
> And in secluded woods the chickadee
> Doles out her scanty notes, which sing the praise
> Of heroes, and set forth the loveliness
> Of virtue evermore.

The phœbe still sings in harmony with the sultry weather by the brink of the pond, nor are the desultory hours of noon in the midst of the village without their minstrel.

> Upon the lofty elm-tree sprays
> The vireo rings the changes sweet,
> During the trivial summer days,
> Striving to lift our thoughts above the street.

With the autumn begins in some measure a new spring. The plover is heard whistling high in the air over the dry pastures, the finches flit from tree to tree, the bobolinks and flickers fly in flocks, and the goldfinch rides on the earliest blast, like a winged hyla peeping amid the rustle of the leaves. The crows, too, begin now to congregate; you may stand and count them as they fly low and straggling over the landscape, singly or by twos and threes, at intervals of half a mile, until a hundred have passed.

I have seen it suggested somewhere that the crow was brought to this country by the white man; but I shall as soon believe that the white man planted these pines and hemlocks. He is no spaniel to follow our steps; but rather flits about the clearings like the dusky spirit of the Indian, reminding me oftener of Philip and Powhatan than of Winthrop and Smith. He is of the dark ages. By just so slight, by just so lasting tenure does superstition hold the world ever; there is the rook in England, and the crow in New England.

> Thou dusky spirit of the wood,
> Bird of an ancient brood,
> Flitting thy lonely way,
> A meteor in the summer's day,
> From wood to wood, from hill to hill,
> Low over forest, field, and rill,
> What wouldst thou say?
> Why shouldst thou haunt the day?
> What makes thy melancholy float?
> What bravery inspires thy throat,
> And bears thee up above the clouds,
> Over desponding human crowds,
> Which far below
> Lay thy haunts low?

The late walker or sailor, in the October evenings, may hear the murmurings of the snipe, circling over the meadows, the most spirit-like sound in nature; and still later in the autumn, when the frosts have tinged the leaves, a solitary loon pays a visit to our retired ponds, where he may lurk undisturbed till the season of moulting is passed, making the woods ring with his wild laughter. This bird, the Great Northern Diver, well deserves its name; for when pursued with a boat, it will dive, and swim like a fish under water, for sixty rods or more, as fast as a boat can be paddled, and its pursuer, if he would discover his game again, must put his ear to the surface to hear where it comes up. When it comes to the surface, it throws the water off with one shake of its wings, and calmly swims about until again disturbed.

These are the sights and sounds which reach our senses oftenest during the year. But sometimes one hears a quite new note, which has for background other Carolinas and Mexicos than the books describe, and learns that his ornithology has done him no service.

It appears from the Report that there are about forty quadrupeds belonging to the State, and among these one is glad to hear of a few bears, wolves, lynxes, and wildcats.

When our river overflows its banks in the spring, the wind from the meadows is laden with a strong scent of musk, and by its freshness advertises me of an unexplored wildness. Those backwoods are not far off then. I am affected by the sight of the cabins of the muskrat, made of mud and grass, and raised three or four feet along the river, as when I read of the barrows of Asia. The muskrat is the beaver of the settled States. Their number has even increased within a few years in this vicinity. Among the rivers which empty into the Merrimack, the Concord is known to the boatmen as a dead stream. The Indians are said to have called it Musketaquid, or Prairie River. Its current being much more sluggish and its water more muddy than the rest, it abounds more in fish and game of every kind. According to the History of the town, "The fur-trade was here once very important. As early as 1641, a company was formed in the colony, of which Major Willard of Concord was superintendent, and had the exclusive right to trade with the Indians in furs and other articles; and for this right they were obliged to pay into the public treasury one twentieth of all the furs they obtained." There are trappers in our midst still, as well as on the streams of the far West, who night and morning go the round of their traps, without fear of the Indian. One of these takes from one hundred and fifty to two hundred muskrats in a year, and even thirty-six have been shot by one man in a day. Their fur, which is not nearly as valuable as formerly, is in good condition in the winter and spring only; and upon the breaking up of the ice, when they are driven out of their holes by the water, the greatest number is shot from boats, either swimming or resting on their stools, or slight supports of grass and reeds, by the side of the stream. Though they exhibit considerable cunning at other times, they are easily taken in a trap, which has only to be placed in their holes, or wherever they frequent, without any bait being used, though it is sometimes rubbed with their musk. In the winter the hunter cuts holes in the ice, and shoots them when they come to the surface. Their burrows are usually in the high banks of the river, with the entrance under water, and rising within to above the level of high water. Sometimes their nests, composed of dried meadow-grass and flags, may be discovered where the bank is low and spongy, by the yielding of the ground under the feet. They have from three to seven or eight young in the spring.

Frequently, in the morning or evening, a long ripple is seen in the still water, where a muskrat is crossing the stream, with only its nose above the surface, and sometimes a green bough in its mouth to build its house with. When it finds itself observed, it will dive and swim five or six rods under water, and at length conceal itself in its hole, or the weeds. It will remain under water for ten minutes at a time, and on one occasion has been seen, when undisturbed, to form an air-bubble under the ice, which contracted and expanded as it breathed at leisure. When it suspects danger on shore, it will stand erect like a squirrel, and survey its neighborhood for several minutes, without moving.

In the fall, if a meadow intervene between their burrows and the stream, they erect cabins of mud and grass, three or four feet high, near its edge. These are not their breeding-places, though young are sometimes found in them in late freshets, but rather their hunting-lodges, to which they resort in the winter with their food, and for shelter. Their food consists chiefly of flags and fresh-water mussels, the shells of the latter being left in large quantifies around their lodges in the spring.

The Penobscot Indian wears the entire skin of a muskrat, with the legs and tail dangling, and the head caught under his girdle, for a pouch, into which he puts his fishing-tackle, and essences to scent his traps with.

The bear, wolf, lynx, wildcat, deer, beaver, and marten have disappeared; the otter is rarely if ever seen here at present; and the mink is less common than formerly.

Perhaps of all our untamed quadrupeds, the fox has obtained the widest and most familiar reputation, from the time of Pilpay and Æsop to the present day. His recent tracks still give variety to a winter's walk. I tread in the steps of the fox that has gone before me by some hours, or which perhaps I have started, with such a tip-toe of expectation as if I were on the trail of the Spirit itself which resides in the wood, and expected soon to catch it in its lair. I am curious to know what has determined its graceful curvatures, and how surely they were coincident with the fluctuations of some mind. I know which way a mind wended, what horizon it faced, by the setting of these tracks, and whether it moved slowly or rapidly, by their greater or less intervals and distinctness; for the swiftest step leaves yet a lasting trace. Sometimes you will see the trails of many together, and where they have gamboled and gone through a hundred evolutions, which testify to a singular listlessness and leisure in nature.

When I see a fox run across the pond on the, snow, with the carelessness of freedom, or at intervals trace his course in the sunshine along the ridge of a hill, I give up to him sun and earth as to their true proprietor. He does not go in the sun, but it seems to follow him, and there is a visible sympathy between him and it. Sometimes, when the snow lies light and but five or six inches deep, you may give chase and come up with one on foot. In such a case he will show a remarkable presence of mind, choosing only the safest direction, though he may lose ground by it. Notwithstanding his fright, he will take no step which is not beautiful. His pace is a sort of leopard canter, as if he were in no wise impeded by the snow, but were husbanding his strength all the while. When the ground is uneven, the course is a series of graceful curves, conforming to the shape of the surface. He runs as though there were not a bone in his back. Occasionally dropping his muzzle to the ground for a rod or two, and then tossing his head aloft, when satisfied of his course. When he comes to a declivity, he will put his fore feet together, and slide swiftly down it, shoving the snow before him. He treads so softly that you would hardly hear it from any nearness, and yet with such expression that it would not be quite inaudible at any distance.

Of fishes, seventy-five genera and one hundred and seven species are described in the Report. The fisherman will be startled to learn that there are but about a dozen kinds in the ponds and streams of any inland town; and almost nothing is known of their habits. Only their names and residence make one love fishes. I would know even the number of their fin-rays, and how many scales compose the lateral line. I am the wiser in respect to all knowledges, and the better qualified for all fortunes, for knowing that there is a minnow in the brook. Methinks I have need even of his sympathy, and to be his fellow in a degree.

I have experienced such simple delight in the trivial matters of fishing and sporting, formerly, as might have inspired the muse of Homer or Shakespeare; and now, when I turn the pages and ponder the plates of the Angler's Souvenir, I am fain to exclaim,—

> "Can such things be,
> And overcome us like a summer's cloud?"

Next to nature, it seems as if man's actions were the most natural, they so gently accord with her. The small seines of flax stretched across the shallow and transparent parts of our river are no more intrusion than the cobweb in the sun. I stay my boat in mid-current, and look down in the sunny water to see the civil meshes of his nets, and wonder how the blustering people of the town could have done this elfish work. The twine looks like a new river-weed, and is to the river as a beautiful memento of man's presence in nature, discovered as silently and delicately as a footprint in the sand.

When the ice is covered with snow, I do not suspect the wealth under my feet; that there is as good as a mine under me wherever I go. How many pickerel are poised on easy fin fathoms below the loaded wain! The revolution of the seasons must be a curious phenomenon to them. At length the sun and wind brush aside their curtain, and they see the heavens again.

Early in the spring, after the ice has melted, is the time for spearing fish. Suddenly the wind shifts from northeast and east to west and south, and every icicle, which has tinkled on the meadow grass so long, trickles down its stem, and seeks its level unerringly with a million comrades. The steam curls up from every roof and fence.

> I see the civil sun drying earth's tears,
> Her tears of joy, which only faster flow.

In the brooks is heard the slight grating sound of small cakes of ice, floating with various speed, full of content and promise, and where the water gurgles under a natural bridge, you may hear these hasty rafts hold conversation in an undertone. Every rill is a channel for the juices of the meadow. In the ponds the ice cracks with a merry and inspiriting din, and down the larger streams is whirled grating hoarsely, and crashing its way along, which was so lately a highway for the woodman's team and the fox, sometimes with the tracks of the skaters still fresh upon it, and the holes cut for pickerel. Town committees anxiously inspect the bridges and causeways, as if by mere eye-force to intercede with the ice and save the treasury.

> The river swelleth more and more,
> Like some sweet influence stealing o'er
> The passive town; and for a while
> Each tussock makes a tiny isle,

Where, on some friendly Ararat,
Resteth the weary water-rat.

No ripple shows Musketaquid,
Her very current e'en is hid,
As deepest souls do calmest rest
When thoughts are swelling in the breast,
And she that in the summer's drought
Doth make a rippling and a rout,
Sleeps from Nahshawtuck to the Cliff,
Unruffled by a single skiff.
But by a thousand distant hills
The louder roar a thousand rills,
And many a spring which now is dumb,
And many a stream with smothered hum.
Doth swifter well and faster glide,
Though buried deep beneath the tide.
Our village shows a rural Venice,
Its broad lagoons where yonder fen is;
As lovely as the Bay of Naples
Yon placid cove amid the maples;
And in my neighbor's field of corn
I recognize the Golden Horn.

Here Nature taught from year to year,
When only red men came to hear,—
Methinks 't was in this school of art
Venice and Naples learned their part;
But still their mistress, to my mind,
Her young disciples leaves behind.

The fisherman now repairs and launches his boat. The best time for spearing is at this season, before the weeds have begun to grow, and while the fishes lie in the shallow water, for in summer they prefer the cool depths, and in the autumn they are still more or less concealed by the grass. The first requisite is fuel for your crate; and for this purpose the roots of the pitch pine are commonly used, found under decayed stumps, where the trees have been felled eight or ten years.

With a crate, or jack, made of iron hoops, to contain your fire, and attached to the bow of your boat about three feet from the water, a fish-spear with seven tines and fourteen feet long, a large basket or barrow to carry your fuel and bring back your fish, and a thick outer garment, you are equipped for a cruise. It should be a warm and still evening; and then, with a fire crackling merrily at the prow, you may launch forth like a cucullo into the night. The dullest soul cannot go upon such an expedition without some of the spirit of adventure; as if he had stolen the boat of Charon and gone down the Styx on a midnight expedition into the realms of Pluto. And much speculation does this wandering star afford to the musing night-walker, leading him on and on, jack-o'-lantern-like, over the meadows; or, if he is wiser, he amuses himself with imagining what of human life, far in the silent night, is flitting moth-like round its candle. The silent navigator shoves his craft gently over the water, with a smothered pride and sense of benefaction, as if he were the phosphor, or light-bringer, to these dusky realms, or some sister moon, blessing the spaces with her light. The waters, for a rod or two on either hand and several feet in depth, are lit up with more than noonday distinctness, and he enjoys the opportunity which so many have desired, for the roofs of a city are indeed raised, and he surveys the midnight economy of the fishes. There they lie in every variety of posture; some on their backs, with their white bellies uppermost, some suspended in mid-water, some sculling gently along with a dreamy motion of the fins, and others quite active and wide awake,—a scene not unlike what the human city would present. Occasionally he will encounter a turtle selecting the choicest morsels, or a muskrat resting on a tussock. He may exercise his dexterity, if he sees fit, on the more distant and active fish, or fork the nearer into his boat, as potatoes out of a pot, or even take the sound sleepers with his hands. But these last accomplishments he will soon learn to dispense with, distinguishing the real object of his pursuit, and find compensation in the beauty and never-ending novelty of his position. The pines growing down to the water's edge will show newly as in the glare of a conflagration; and as he floats under the willows with his light, the song sparrow will often wake on her perch, and sing that strain at midnight which she had meditated for the morning. And when he has done, he may have to steer his way home through the dark by the north star, and he will feel himself some degrees nearer to it for having lost his way on the earth.

The fishes commonly taken in this way are pickerel, suckers, perch, eels, pouts, breams, and shiners,—from thirty to sixty weight in a night. Some are hard to be recognized in the unnatural light, especially the perch, which, his dark bands being exaggerated, acquires a ferocious aspect. The number of these transverse bands, which the Report states to be seven, is, however, very variable, for in some of our ponds they have nine and ten even.

It appears that we have eight kinds of tortoises, twelve snakes,—but one of which is venomous,—nine frogs and toads, nine salamanders, and one lizard, for our neighbors.

I am particularly attracted by the motions of the serpent tribe. They make our hands and feet, the wings of the bird, and the fins of the fish seem very superfluous, as if Nature had only indulged her fancy in making them. The black snake will dart into a bush when pursued, and circle round and round with an easy and graceful motion, amid the thin and bare twigs, five or six feet from the ground, as a bird flits from bough to bough, or hang in festoons between the forks. Elasticity and flexibleness in the simpler forms of animal life are equivalent to a complex system of limbs in the higher; and we have only to be as wise and wily as the serpent, to perform as difficult feats without the vulgar assistance of hands and feet.

In May, the snapping turtle (*Emysaurus serpentina*) is frequently taken on the meadows and in the river. The fisherman, taking sight over the calm surface, discovers its snout projecting above the water, at the distance of many rods, and easily secures his prey through its unwillingness to disturb the water by swimming hastily away, for, gradually drawing its head under, it remains resting on some limb or dump of grass. Its eggs, which are buried at a distance from the water, in some soft place, as a pigeon-bed, are frequently devoured by the skunk. It will catch fish by daylight, as a toad catches flies, and is said to emit a transparent fluid from its mouth to attract them.

Nature has taken more care than the fondest parent for the education and refinement of her children. Consider the silent influence which flowers exert, no less upon the ditcher in the meadow than the lady in the bower. When I walk in the woods, I am reminded that a wise purveyor has been there before me; my most delicate experience is typified there. I am struck with the pleasing friendships and unanimities of nature, as when the lichen on the trees takes the form of their leaves. In the most stupendous scenes you will see delicate and fragile features, as slight wreaths of vapor, dew-lines, feathery sprays, which suggest a high refinement, a noble blood and breeding, as it were. It is not hard to account for elves and fairies; they represent this light grace, this ethereal gentility. Bring a spray from the wood, or a crystal from the brook, and place it on your mantel, and your household ornaments will seem plebeian beside its nobler fashion and bearing. It will wave superior there, as if used to a more refined and polished circle. It has a salute and a response to all your enthusiasm and heroism.

In the winter, I stop short in the path to admire how the trees grow up without forethought, regardless of the time and circumstances. They do not wait as man does, but now is the golden age of the sapling. Earth, air, sun, and rain are occasion enough; they were no better in primeval centuries. The "winter of *their* discontent" never comes. Witness the buds of the native poplar standing gayly out to the frost on the sides of its bare switches. They express a naked confidence. With cheerful heart one could be a sojourner in the wilderness, if he were sure to find there the catkins of the willow or the alder. When I read of them in the accounts of northern adventurers, by Baffin's Bay or Mackenzie's River, I see how even there, too, I could dwell. They are our little vegetable redeemers. Methinks our virtue will hold out till they come again. They are worthy to have had a greater than Minerva or Ceres for their inventor. Who was the benignant goddess that bestowed them on mankind?

Nature is mythical and mystical always, and works with the license and extravagance of genius. She has her luxurious and florid style as well as art. Having a pilgrim's cup to make, she gives to the whole—stem, bowl, handle, and nose—some fantastic shape, as if it were to be the car of some fabulous marine deity, a Nereus or Triton.

In the winter, the botanist need not confine himself to his books and herbarium, and give over his outdoor pursuits, but may study a new department of vegetable physiology, what may be called crystalline botany, then. The winter of 1837 was unusually favorable for this. In December of that year, the Genius of vegetation seemed to hover by night over its summer haunts with unusual persistency. Such a hoar-frost as is very uncommon here or anywhere, and whose full effects can never be witnessed after sunrise, occurred several times. As I went forth early on a still and frosty morning, the trees looked like airy creatures of darkness caught napping; on this side huddled together, with their gray hairs streaming, in a secluded valley which the sun had not penetrated; on that, hurrying off in Indian file along some watercourse, while the shrubs and grasses, like elves and fairies of the night, sought to hide their diminished heads in the snow. The river, viewed from the high bank, appeared of a yellowish-green color, though all the landscape was white. Every tree, shrub, and spire of grass, that could raise its head above the snow, was covered with a dense ice-foliage, answering, as it were, leaf for leaf to its summer dress. Even the fences had put forth leaves in the night. The centre, diverging, and more minute fibres were perfectly distinct, and the edges regularly indented. These leaves were on the side of the twig or stubble opposite to the sun, meeting it for the most part at right angles, and there were others standing out at all possible angles upon these and upon one another, with no twig or stubble supporting them. When the first rays of the sun slanted over the scene, the grasses seemed hung with innumerable jewels, which jingled merrily as they were brushed by the foot of the traveler, and reflected all the hues of the rainbow, as he moved from side to side. It struck me that these ghost leaves, and the green ones whose forms they assume, were the creatures of but one law; that in obedience to the same law the vegetable juices swell gradually into the perfect leaf, on the one hand, and the crystalline particles troop to their standard in the same order, on the other. As if the material were indifferent, but the law one and invariable, and every plant in the spring but pushed up into and filled a permanent and eternal mould, which, summer and winter forever, is waiting to be filled.

This foliate structure is common to the coral and the plumage of birds, and to how large a port of animate and inanimate nature. The same independence of law on matter is observable in many other instances, as in the natural rhymes, when some animal form, color, or odor has its counterpart in some vegetable. As, indeed, all rhymes imply an eternal melody, independent of any particular sense.

As confirmation of the fact that vegetation is but a kind of crystallization, every one may observe how, upon the edge of the melting frost on the window, the needle-shaped particles are bundled together so as to resemble fields waving with grain, or shocks rising here and there from the stubble; on one side the vegetation of the torrid zone, high-towering palms and widespread banyans, such as are seen in pictures of oriental scenery; on the other, arctic pines stiff frozen, with downcast branches.

Vegetation has been made the type of all growth; but as in crystals the law is more obvious, their material being more simple, and for the most part more transient and fleeting, would it not be as philosophical as convenient to consider all growth, all filling up within the limits of nature, but a crystallization more or less rapid?

On this occasion, in the side of the high bank of the river, wherever the water or other cause had formed a cavity, its throat and outer edge, like the entrance to a citadel, bristled with a glistening ice-armor. In one place you might see minute ostrich-feathers, which seemed the waving plumes of the warriors filing into the fortress; in another, the glancing, fan-shaped banners of the Lilliputian host; and in another, the needle-shaped particles collected into bundles, resembling the plumes of the pine, might pass for a phalanx of spears. From the under side of the ice in the brooks, where there was a thicker ice below, depended a mass of crystallization, four or five inches deep, in the form of prisms, with their lower ends open, which, when the ice was laid on its smooth side, resembled the roofs and steeples of a Gothic city, or the vessels of a crowded haven under a press of canvas. The very mud in the road, where the ice had melted, was crystallized with deep rectilinear fissures, and the crystalline masses in the sides of the ruts resembled exactly asbestos in the disposition of their needles. Around the roots of the stubble and flower-stalks, the frost was gathered into the form of irregular conical shells, or fairy rings. In some places the ice-crystals were lying upon granite rocks, directly over crystals of quartz, the frostwork of a longer night, crystals of a longer period, but, to some eye unprejudiced by the short term of human life, melting as fast as the former.

In the Report on the Invertebrate Animals, this singular fact is recorded, which teaches us to put a new value on time and space: "The distribution of the marine shells is well worthy of notice as a geological fact. Cape Cod, the right arm of the Commonwealth, reaches out into the ocean, some fifty or sixty miles. It is nowhere many miles wide; but this narrow point of land has hitherto proved a barrier to the migrations of many species of Mollusca. Several genera and numerous species, which are separated by the intervention of only a few miles of land, are effectually prevented from mingling by the Cape, and do not pass from one side to the other. . . . Of the one hundred and ninety-seven marine species, eighty-three do not pass to the south shore, and fifty are not found on the north shore of the Cape."

That common mussel, the *Unio complanatus*, or more properly *fluviatilis*, left in the spring by the muskrat upon rocks and stumps, appears to have been an important article of food with the Indians. In one place, where they are said to have

feasted, they are found in large quantifies, at an elevation of
thirty feet above the river, filling the soil to the depth of a foot,
and mingled with ashes and Indian remains.

The works we have placed at the head of our chapter, with
as much license as the preacher selects his text, are such as imply
more labor than enthusiasm. The State wanted complete cata-
logues of its natural riches, with such additional facts merely as
would be directly useful.

The reports on Fishes, Reptiles, Insects, and Invertebrate
Animals, however, indicate labor and research, and have a
value independent of the object of the legislature.

Those on Herbaceous Plants and Birds cannot be of much
value, as long as Bigelow and Nuttall are accessible. They serve
but to indicate, with more or less exactness, what species are
found in the State. We detect several errors ourselves, and a
more practiced eye would no doubt expand the list.

The Quadrupeds deserved a more final and instructive
report than they have obtained.

These volumes deal much in measurements and minute
descriptions, not interesting to the general reader, with only here
and there a colored sentence to allure him, like those plants
growing in dark forests, which bear only leaves without blossoms. But the ground was comparatively unbroken, and we will
not complain of the pioneer, if he raises no flowers with his
first crop. Let us not underrate the value of a fact; it will one day
flower in a truth. It is astonishing how few facts of importance
are added in a century to the natural history of any animal. The
natural history of man himself is still being gradually written.
Men are knowing enough after their fashion. Every countryman and dairy-maid knows that the coats of the fourth stomach
of the calf will curdle milk, and what particular mushroom is a
safe and nutritious diet. You cannot go into any field or wood,
but it will seem as if every stone had been turned, and the bark
on every tree ripped up. But, after all, it is much easier to discover than to see when the cover is off. It has been well said that
"the attitude of inspection is prone." Wisdom does not inspect,
but behold. We must look a long time before we can see. Slow
are the beginnings of philosophy. He has something demoniacal
in him, who can discern a law or couple two facts. We can imagine a time when "Water runs down hill" may have been taught
in the schools. The true man of science will know nature better
by his finer organization; he will smell, taste, see, hear, feel, bet-

ter than other men. His will be a deeper and finer experience.
We do not learn by inference and deduction and the application
of mathematics to philosophy, but by direct intercourse and
sympathy. It is with science as with ethics,—we cannot know
truth by contrivance and method; the Baconian is as false as any
other, and with all the helps of machinery and the arts, the most
scientific will still be the healthiest and friendliest man, and possess a more perfect Indian wisdom.

Notes

¹ *Reports—on the Fishes, Reptiles, and Birds; the Herbaceous Plants
and Quadrupeds; the Insects Injurious to Vegetation; and the Invertebrate Animals of Massachusetts.* Published agreeably to an Order of the Legislature, by
the Commissioners on the Zoölogical and Botanical Survey of the State.
² A white robin and a white quail have occasionally been seen. It is
mentioned in Audubon as remarkable that the nest of a robin should be found on
the ground; but this bird seems to be less particular than most in the choice of a
building-spot. I have seen its nest placed under the thatched roof of a deserted
barn, and in one instance, where the adjacent country was nearly destitute of
trees, together with two of the phœbe, upon the end of a board in the loft of a
sawmill, but a few feet from the saw, which vibrated several inches with the
motion of the machinery.
³ This bird, which in so well described by Nuttall, but is apparently
unknown by the author of the Report, is one of the most common in the woods in
this vicinity, and in Cambridge I have heard the college yard ring with its
trill. The boys call it "yorrick," from the sound of its querulous and chiding
note, as it flits near the traveler through the underwood. The cowbird's egg is
occasionally found in its nest, as mentioned by Audubon.

THE SUCCESSION OF FOREST TREES[1]
1860

Every man is entitled to come to Cattle-Show, even a transcendentalist; and for my part I am more interested in the men than in the cattle. I wish to see once more those old familiar faces, whose names I do not know, which for me represent the Middlesex country, and come as near being indigenous to the soil as a white man can; the men who are not above their business, whose coats are not too black, whose shoes do not shine very much, who never wear gloves to conceal their hands. It is true, there are some queer specimens of humanity attracted to our festival, but all are welcome. I am pretty sure to meet once more that weak-minded and whimsical fellow, generally weak-bodied too, who prefers a crooked stick for a cane; perfectly useless, you would say, only bizarre, fit for a cabinet, like a petrified snake. A ram's horn would be as convenient, and is yet more curiously twisted. He brings that much indulged bit of the country with him, from some town's end or other, and introduces it to Concord groves, as if he had promised it so much sometime. So some, it seems to me, elect their rulers for their crookedness. But I think that a straight stick makes the best cane, and an upright man the best ruler. Or why choose a man to do plain work who is distinguished for his oddity? However, I do not know but you will think that they have committed this mistake who invited me to speak to you to-day.

In my capacity of surveyor, I have often talked with some of you, my employers, at your dinner-tables, after having gone round and round and behind your farming, and ascertained exactly what its limits were. Moreover, taking a surveyor's and a naturalist's liberty, I have been in the habit of going across your lots much oftener than is usual, as many of you, perhaps to your sorrow, are aware. Yet many of you, to my relief, have seemed not to be aware of it; and, when I came across you in some out-of-the-way nook of your farms, have inquired, with an air of surprise, if I were not lost, since you had never seen me in that part of the town or county before; when, if the truth were known, and it had not been for betraying my secret, I might with more propriety have inquired if *you* were not lost, since I had never seen you there before. I have several times shown the proprietor the shortest way out of his wood-lot.

Therefore, it would seem that I have some title to speak to you to-day; and considering what that title is, and the occasion that has called us together, I need offer no apology if I invite your attention, for the few moments that are allotted me, to a purely scientific subject.

At those dinner-tables referred to, I have often been asked, as many of you have been, if I could tell how it happened, that when a pine wood was cut down an oak one commonly sprang up, and *vice versa*. To which I have answered, and now answer, that I can tell,—that it is no mystery to me. As I am not aware that this has been clearly shown by any one, I shall lay the more stress on this point. Let me lead you back into your wood-lots again.

When, hereabouts, a single forest tree or a forest springs up naturally where none of its kind grew before, I do not hesitate to say, though in some quarters still it may sound paradoxical, that it came from a seed. Of the various ways by which trees are *known* to be propagated,—by transplanting, cuttings, and the like,—this is the only supposable one under these circumstances. No such tree has ever been known to spring from anything else. If any one asserts that it sprang from something else, or from nothing, the burden of proof lies with him.

It remains, then, only to show how the seed is transported from where it grows to where it is planted. This is done chiefly by the agency of the wind, water, and animals. The lighter seeds, as those of pines and maples, are transported chiefly by wind and water; the heavier, as acorns and nuts, by animals.

In all the pines, a very thin membrane, in appearance much like an insect's wing, grows over and around the seed, and independent of it, while the latter is being developed within its base. Indeed this is often perfectly developed, though the seed is abortive; nature being, you would say, more sure to provide the means of transporting the seed, than to provide the seed to be transported. In other words, a beautiful thin sack is woven around the seed, with a handle to it such as the wind can take hold of, and it is then committed to the wind, expressly that it may transport the seed and extend the range of the species; and this it does, as effectually as when seeds are sent by mail in a different kind of sack from the Patent Office. There is a patent office at the seat of government of the universe, whose managers are as much interested in the dispersion of seeds as anybody at Washington can be, and their operations are infinitely more extensive and regular.

There is, then, no necessity for supposing that the pines have sprung up from nothing, and I am aware that I am not at all peculiar in asserting that they come from seeds, though the mode of their propagation *by nature* has been but little attended to. They are very extensively raised from the seed in Europe, and are beginning to be here.

When you cut down an oak wood, a pine wood will not *at once* spring up there unless there are, or have been quite recently, seed-bearing pines near enough for the seeds to be blown from them. But, adjacent to a forest of pines, if you prevent other crops from growing there, you will surely have an extension of your pine forest, provided the soil is suitable.

As for the heavy seeds and nuts which are not furnished with wings, the notion is still a very common one that, when the trees which bear these spring up where none of their kind were noticed before, they have come from seeds or other principles spontaneously generated there in an unusual manner, or which have lain dormant in the soil for centuries, or perhaps been called into activity by the heat of a burning. I do not believe these assertions, and I will state some of the ways in which, according to my observation, such forests are planted and raised.

Every one of these seeds, too, will be found to be winged or legged in another fashion. Surely it is not wonderful that cherry trees of all kinds are widely dispersed, since their fruit is well known to be the favorite food of various birds. Many kinds are called bird cherries, and they appropriate many more kinds, which are not so called. Eating cherries is a bird-like employment, and unless we disperse the seeds occasionally, as they do, I shall think that the birds have the best right to them. See how artfully the seed of a cherry is placed in order that a bird may be compelled to transport it,—in the very midst of a tempting pericarp, so that the creature that would devour this must commonly take the stone also into its mouth or bill. If you ever ate a

cherry, and did not make two bites of it, you must have perceived it,—right in the centre of the luscious morsel, a large
earthy residuum left on the tongue. We thus take into our
mouths cherry-stones as big as peas, a dozen at once, for Nature
can persuade us to do almost anything when she would compass
her ends. Some wild men and children instinctively swallow
these, as the birds do when in a hurry, it being the shortest way
to get rid of them. Thus, though these seeds are not provided
with vegetable wings, Nature has impelled the thrush tribe to
take them into their bills and fly away with them; and they are
winged in another sense, and more effectually than the seeds of
pines, for these are carried even against the wind. The consequence is, that cherry trees grow not only here but there. The
same is true of a great many other seeds.

But to come to the observation which suggested these remarks. As I have said, I suspect that I can throw some light on
the fact that when hereabouts a dense pine wood is cut down,
oaks and other hard woods may at once take its place. I have got
only to show that the acorns and nuts, provided they are grown
in the neighborhood, are regularly planted in such woods; for I
assert that if an oak tree has not grown within ten miles, and
man has not carried acorns thither, then an oak wood will not
spring up *at once*, when a pine wood is cut down.

Apparently, there were only pines there before. They are
cut off, and after a year or two you see oaks and other hard
woods springing up there, with scarcely a pine amid them, and
the wonder commonly is, the seed could have lain in the
ground so long without decaying. But the truth is, that it has not
lain in the ground so long, but is regularly planted each year by
various quadrupeds and birds.

In this neighborhood, where oaks and pines are about
equally dispersed, if you look through the thickest pine wood,
even the seemingly unmixed pitch pine ones, you will commonly detect many little oaks, birches, and other hard woods,
sprung from seeds carried into the thicket by squirrels and other
animals, and also blown thither, but which are overshadowed
and choked by the pines. The denser the evergreen wood, the
more likely it is to be well planted with these seeds, because the
planters incline to resort with their forage to the closest covert.
They also carry it into birch and other woods. This planting is
carried on annually, and the oldest seedlings annually die; but
when the pines are cleared off, the oaks, having got just the start

they want, and now secured favorable conditions, immediately spring up to trees.

The shade of a dense pine wood is more unfavorable to the springing up of pines of the same species than of oaks within it, though the former may come up abundantly when the pines are cut, if there chance to be sound seed in the ground.

But when you cut off a lot of hard wood, very often the little pines mixed with it have a similar start, for the squirrels have carried off the nuts to the pines, and not to the more open wood, and they commonly make pretty clean work of it; and moreover, if the wood was old, the sprouts will be feeble or entirely fail; to say nothing about the soil being, in a measure, exhausted for this kind of crop.

If a pine wood is surrounded by a white oak one chiefly, white oaks may be expected to succeed when the pines are cut. If it is surrounded instead by an edging of shrub oaks, then you will probably have a dense shrub oak thicket.

I have no time to go into details, but will say, in a word, that while the wind is conveying the seeds of pines into hard woods and open lands, the squirrels and other animals are conveying the seeds of oaks and walnuts into the pine woods, and thus a rotation of crops is kept up.

I affirmed this confidently many years ago, and an occasional examination of dense pine woods confirmed me in my opinion. It has long been known to observers that squirrels bury nuts in the ground, but I am not aware that any one has thus accounted for the regular succession of forests.

On the 24th of September, in 1857, as I was paddling down the Assabet, in this town, I saw a red squirrel run along the bank under some herbage, with something large in its mouth. It stopped near the foot of a hemlock, within a couple of rods of me, and, hastily pawing a hole with its fore feet, dropped its booty into it, covered it up, and retreated part way up the trunk of the tree. As I approached the shore to examine the deposit, the squirrel, descending part way, betrayed no little anxiety about its treasure, and made two or three motions to recover it before it finally retreated. Digging there, I found two green pignuts joined together, with the thick husks on, buried about an inch and a half under the reddish soil of decayed hemlock leaves,— just the right depth to plant it. In short, this squirrel was then engaged in accomplishing two objects, to wit, laying up a store of winter food for itself, and planting a hickory wood for all creation. If the squirrel was killed, or neglected its deposit, a hickory would spring up. The nearest hickory tree was twenty rods distant. These nuts were there still just fourteen days later, but were gone when I looked again, November 21st, or six weeks later still.

I have since examined more carefully several dense woods, which are said to be, and are apparently, exclusively pine, and always with the same result. For instance, I walked the same day to a small but very dense and handsome white pine grove, about fifteen rods square, in the east part of this town. The trees are large for Concord, being from ten to twenty inches in diameter, and as exclusively pine as any wood that I know. Indeed, I selected this wood because I thought it the least likely to contain anything else. It stands on an open plain or pasture, except that it adjoins another small pine wood, which has a few little oaks in it, on the southeast side. On every other side, it was at least thirty rods from the nearest woods. Standing on the edge of this grove and looking through it, for it is quite level and free from underwood, for the most part bare, red-carpeted ground, you would have said that there was not a hardwood tree in it, young or old. But on looking carefully along over its floor I discovered, though it was not till my eye had got used to the search, that, alternating with thin ferns, and small blueberry bushes, there was, not merely here and there, but as often as every five feet and with a degree of regularity, a little oak, from three to twelve inches high, and in one place I found a green acorn dropped by the base of a pine.

I confess I was surprised to find my theory so perfectly proved in this case. One of the principal agents in this planting, the red squirrels, were all the while curiously inspecting me, while I was inspecting their plantation. Some of the little oaks had been browsed by cows, which resorted to this wood for shade.

After seven or eight years, the hard woods evidently find such a locality unfavorable to their growth, the pines being allowed to stand. As an evidence of this, I observed a diseased red maple twenty-five feet long, which had been recently prostrated, though it was still covered with green leaves, the only maple in any position in the wood.

But although these oaks almost invariably die if the pines are not cut down, it is probable that they do better for a few years under their shelter than they would anywhere else.

The very extensive and thorough experiments of the English have at length led them to adopt a method of raising oaks almost precisely like this which somewhat earlier had been adopted by Nature and her squirrels here; they have simply rediscovered the value of pines as nurses for oaks. The English experimenters seem, early and generally, to have found out the importance of using trees of some kind as nurse-plants for the young oaks. I quote from Loudon what he describes as "the ultimatum on the subject of planting and sheltering oaks,"—"an abstract of the practice adopted by the government officers in the national forests" of England, prepared by Alexander Milne.

At first some oaks had been planted by themselves, and others mixed with Scotch pines; "but in all cases," says Mr. Milne, "where oaks were planted actually among the pines and surrounded by them [though the soil might be inferior], the oaks were found to be much the best." "For several years past, the plan pursued has been to plant the enclosures with Scotch pines only [a tree very similar to our pitch pine], and when the pines have got to the height of five or six feet, then to put in good strong oak plants of about four or five years' growth among the pines,—not cutting away any pines at first, unless they happen to be so strong and thick as to overshadow the oaks. In about two years it becomes necessary to shred the branches of the pines, to give light and air to the oaks, and in about two or three more years to begin gradually to remove the pines altogether, taking out a certain number each year, so that, at the end of twenty or twenty-five years, not a single Scotch pine shall be left; although, for the first ten or twelve years, the plantation may have appeared to contain nothing else but pine. The advantage of this mode of planting has been found to be that the pines dry and ameliorate the soil, destroying the coarse grass and brambles which frequently choke and injure oaks; and that no mending over is necessary, as scarcely an oak so planted is found to fail."

Thus much the English planters have discovered by patient experiment, and, for aught I know, they have taken out a patent for it; but they appear not to have discovered that it was discovered before, and that they are merely adopting the method of Nature, which she long ago made patent to all. She is all the while planting the oaks amid the pines without our knowledge, and at last, instead of government officers, we send a party of wood-choppers to cut down the pines, and so rescue an oak forest, at which we wonder as if it had dropped from the skies.

As I walk amid hickories, even in August, I hear the sound of green pignuts falling from time to time, cut off by the chickaree over my head. In the fall, I notice on the ground, either within or in the neighborhood of oak woods, on all sides of the town, stout oak twigs three or four inches long, bearing half a dozen empty acorn-cups, which twigs have been gnawed off by squirrels, on both sides of the nuts, in order to make them more portable. The jays scream and the red squirrels scold while you are clubbing and shaking the chestnut trees, for they are there on the same errand, and two of a trade never agree. I frequently see a red or gray squirrel cast down a green chestnut bur, as I am going through the woods, and I used to think, sometimes, that they were cast at me. In fact, they are so busy about it, in the midst of the chestnut season, that you cannot stand long in the woods without hearing one fall. A sportsman told me that he had, the day before,—that was in the middle of October,—seen a green chestnut bur dropped on our great river meadow, fifty rods from the nearest wood, and much further from the nearest chestnut tree, and he could not tell how it came there. Occasionally, when chestnutting in midwinter, I find thirty or forty nuts in a pile, left in its gallery, just under the leaves, by the common wood mouse (*Mus leucopus*).

But especially, in the winter, the extent to which this transportation and planting of nuts is carried on is made apparent by the snow. In almost every wood, you will see where the red or gray squirrels have pawed down through the snow in a hundred places, sometimes two feet deep, and almost always directly to a nut or a pine cone, as directly as if they had started from it and bored upward,—which you and I could not have done. It would be difficult for us to find one before the snow falls. Commonly, no doubt, they had deposited them there in the fall. You wonder if they remember the localities, or discover them by the scent. The red squirrel commonly has its winter abode in the earth under a thicket of evergreens, frequently under a small clump of evergreens in the midst of a deciduous wood. If there are any nut trees which still retain their nuts standing at a distance without the wood, their paths often lead directly to and from them. We therefore need not suppose an oak standing here and there *in* the wood in order to seed it, but if a few stand within twenty or thirty rods of it, it is sufficient.

I think that I may venture to say that every white pine cone that falls to the earth naturally in this town, before opening and losing its seeds, and almost every pitch pine one that falls at all, is cut off by a squirrel, and they begin to pluck them long before they are ripe, so that when the crop of white pine cones is a small one, as it commonly is, they cut off thus almost every one of these before it fairly ripens. I think, moreover, that their design, if I may so speak, in cutting them off green, is, partly, to prevent their opening and losing their seeds, for these are the ones for which they dig through the snow, and the only white pine cones which contain anything then. I have counted in one heap, within a diameter of four feet, the cores of 239 pitch pine cones which had been cut off and stripped by the red squirrel the previous winter.

The nuts thus left on the surface, or buried just beneath it, are placed in the most favorable circumstances for germinating. I have sometimes wondered how those which merely fell on the surface of the earth got planted; but, by the end of December, I find the chestnut of the same year partially mixed with the mould, as it were, under the decaying and mouldy leaves, where there is all the moisture and manure they want, for the nuts fall fast. In a plentiful year, a large proportion of the nuts are thus covered loosely an inch deep, and are, of course, somewhat concealed from squirrels. One winter, when the crop had been abundant, I got, with the aid of a rake, many quarts of these nuts as late as the tenth of January, and though some bought at the store the same day were more than half of them mouldy, I did not find a single mouldy one among these which I picked from under the wet and mouldy leaves, where they had been snowed on once or twice. Nature knows how to pack them best. They were still plump and tender. Apparently, they do not heat there, though wet. In the spring they were all sprouting.

Loudon says that "when the nut [of the common walnut of Europe] is to be preserved through the winter for the purpose of planting in the following spring, it should be laid in a rot-heap, as soon as gathered, with the husk on, and the heap should be turned over frequently in the course of the winter."

Here, again, he is stealing Nature's "thunder." How can a poor mortal do otherwise? for it is she that finds fingers to steal with, and the treasure to be stolen. In the planting of the seeds of most trees, the best gardeners do no more than follow Nature, though they may not know it. Generally, both large and small ones are most sure to germinate, and succeed best, when only beaten into the earth with the back of a spade, and then covered with leaves or straw. These results to which planters have arrived remind us of the experience of Kane and his companions at the north, who, when learning to live in that climate, were surprised to find themselves steadily adopting the customs of the natives, simply becoming Esquimaux. So, when we experiment in planting forests, we find ourselves at last doing as Nature does. Would it not be well to consult with Nature in the outset? for she is the most extensive and experienced planter of us all, not excepting the Dukes of Athol.

In short, they who have not attended particularly to this subject are but little aware to what an extent quadrupeds and birds are employed, especially in the fall, in collecting, and so disseminating and planting, the seeds of trees. It is the almost constant employment of the squirrels at that season, and you rarely meet with one that has not a nut in its mouth, or is not just going to get one. One squirrel-hunter of this town told me that he knew of a walnut tree which bore particularly good nuts, but that on going to gather them one fall, he found that he had been anticipated by a family of a dozen red squirrels. He took out of the tree, which was hollow, one bushel and three pecks by measurement, without the husks, and they supplied him and his family for the winter. It would be easy to multiply instances of this kind. How commonly in the fall you see the cheek-pouches of the striped squirrel distended by a quantity of nuts! This species gets its scientific name, *Tamias*, or the steward, from its habit of storing up nuts and other seeds. Look under a nut tree a month after the nuts have fallen, and see what proportion of sound nuts to the abortive ones and shells you will find ordinarily. They have been already eaten, or dispersed far and wide. The ground looks like a platform before a grocer, where the gossips of the village sit to crack nuts and less savory jokes. You have come, you would say, after the feast was over, and are presented with the shells only.

Occasionally, when threading the woods in the fall, you will hear a sound as if some one had broken a twig, and, looking up, see a jay pecking at an acorn, or you will see a flock of them at once about it, in the top of an oak, and hear them break them off. They then fly to a suitable limb, and placing the acorn under one foot, hammer away at it busily, making a sound like a woodpecker's tapping, looking round from time to time to see if any foe is approaching, and soon reach the meat, and nibble at it, holding up their heads to swallow, while they hold the remain-

der very firmly with their claws. Nevertheless it often drops to
the ground before the bird has done with it. I can confirm what
William Bartram wrote to Wilson, the ornithologist, that "the
jay is one of the most useful agents in the economy of nature, for
disseminating forest trees and other nuciferous and hard-seeded
vegetables on which they feed. Their chief employment during
the autumnal season is foraging to supply their winter stores. In
performing this necessary duty they drop abundance of seed in
their flight over fields, hedges, and by fences, where they alight
to deposit them in the post-holes, etc. It is remarkable what
numbers of young trees rise up in fields and pastures after a wet
winter and spring. These birds alone are capable, in a few years'
time, to replant all the cleared lands."

I have noticed that squirrels also frequently drop their
nuts in open land, which will still further account for the oaks
and walnuts which spring up in pastures, for, depend on it, every new tree comes from a seed. When I examine the little oaks,
one or two years old, in such places, I invariably find the empty
acorn from which they sprung.

So far from the seed having lain dormant in the soil since
oaks grew there before, as many believe, it is well known that it
is difficult to preserve the vitality of acorns long enough to
transport them to Europe; and it is recommended in Loudon's
"Arboretum," as the safest course, to sprout them in pots on the
voyage. The same authority states that "very few acorns of any
species will germinate after having been kept a year," that beech
mast "only retains its vital properties one year," and the black
walnut "seldom more than six months after it has ripened." I
have frequently found that in November almost every acorn left
on the ground had sprouted or decayed. What with frost,
drouth, moisture, and worms, the greater part are soon destroyed. Yet it is stated by one botanical writer that "acorns that
have lain for centuries, on being ploughed up, have soon vege-
tated."

Mr. George B. Emerson, in his valuable Report on the
Trees and Shrubs of this State, says of the pines: "The tenacity of
life of the seeds is remarkable. They will remain for many years
unchanged in the ground, protected by the coolness and deep
shade of the forest above them. But when the forest is removed,
and the warmth of the sun admitted, they immediately vege-
tate." Since he does not tell us on what observation his remark

is rounded, I must doubt its truth. Besides, the experience of nursery-men makes it the more questionable.

The stories of wheat raised from seed buried with an ancient Egyptian, and of raspberries raised from seed found in the stomach of a man in England, who is supposed to have died sixteen or seventeen hundred years ago, are generally discredited, simply because the evidence is not conclusive.

Several men of science, Dr. Carpenter among them, have used the statement that beach plums sprang up in sand which was dug up forty miles inland in Maine, to prove that the seed had lain there a very long time, and some have inferred that the coast has receded so far. But it seems to me necessary to their argument to show, first, that beach plums grow only on a beach. They are not uncommon here, which is about half that distance from the shore; and I remember a dense patch a few miles north of us, twenty-five miles inland, from which the fruit was annually carried to market. How much further inland they grow, I know not. Dr. Charles T. Jackson speaks of finding "beach plums" (perhaps they were this kind) more than one hundred miles inland in Maine.

It chances that similar objections lie against all the more notorious instances of the kind on record.

Yet I am prepared to believe that some seeds, especially small ones, may retain their vitality for centuries under favorable circumstances. In the spring of 1859, the old Hunt house, so called, in this town, whose chimney bore the date 1703, was taken down. This stood on land which belonged to John Winthrop, the first governor of Massachusetts, and a part of the house was evidently much older than the above date, and belonged to the Winthrop family. For many years I have ransacked this neighborhood for plants, and I consider my-self familiar with its productions. Thinking of the seeds which are said to be sometimes dug up at an unusual depth in the earth, and thus to reproduce long extinct plants, it occurred to me last fall that some new or rare plants might have sprung up in the cellar of this house, which had been covered from the light so long. Searching there on the 22d of September, I found, among other rank weeds, a species of nettle (*Urtica urens*) which I had not found before; dill, which I had not seen growing spontaneously; the Jerusalem oak (*Chenopodium Botrys*), which I had seen wild in but one place; black nightshade (*Solanum nigrum*), which is quite rare hereabouts, and common tobacco, which, though it was often cultivated here in the last century, has for fifty years been an unknown plant in this town, and a few months before this not even I had heard that one man, in the north part of the town, was cultivating a few plants for his own use. I have no doubt that some or all of these plants sprang from seeds which had long been buried under or about that house, and that that tobacco is an additional evidence that the plant was formerly cultivated here. The cellar has been filled up this year, and four of those plants, including the tobacco, are now again extinct in that locality.

It is true, I have shown that the animals consume a great part of the seeds of trees, and so, at least, effectually prevent their becoming trees; but in all these cases, as I have said, the consumer is compelled to be at the same time the disperser and planter, and this is the tax which he pays to Nature. I think it is Linnæus who says that while the swine is rooting for acorns he is planting acorns.

Though I do not believe that a plant will spring up where no seed has been, I have great faith in a seed,—a, to me, equally mysterious origin for it. Convince me that you have a seed there, and I am prepared to expect wonders. I shall even believe that the millennium is at hand, and that the reign of justice is about to commence, when the Patent Office, or Government, begins to distribute, and the people to plant, the seeds of these things.

In the spring of 1857 I planted six seeds sent to me from the Patent Office, and labeled, I think, *Poitrine jaune grosse*, large yellow squash. Two came up, and one bore a squash which weighed 123 1/2 pounds, the other bore four, weighing together 186 1/2 pounds. Who would have believed that there was 310 pounds of *poitrine jaune grosse* in that corner of my garden? These seeds were the bait I used to catch it, my ferrets which I sent into its burrow, my brace of terriers which unearthed it. A little mysterious hoeing and manuring was all the *abracadabra presto-change* that I used, and lo! true to the label, they found for me 810 pounds of *poitrine jaune grosse* there, where it never was known to be, nor was before. These talismans had perchance sprung from America at first, and returned to it with unabated force. The big squash took a premium at your fair that fall, and I understood that the man who bought it, intended to sell the seeds for ten cents apiece. (Were they not cheap at that?) But I have more hounds of the same breed. I learn that one which I despatched to a distant town, true to its instincts, points to the large yellow squash there, too, where no hound ever found it before, as its ancestors did here and in France.

Other seeds I have which will find other things in that corner of my garden, in like fashion, almost any fruit you wish, every year for ages, until the crop more than fills the whole garden. You have but little more to do than throw up your cap for entertainment these American days. Perfect alchemists I keep who can transmute substances without end, and thus the corner of my garden is an inexhaustible treasure-chest. Here you can dig, not gold, but the value which gold merely represents; and there is no Signor Blitz about it. Yet farmers' sons will stare by the hour to see a juggler draw ribbons from his throat, though he tells them it is all deception. Surely, men love darkness rather than light.

Note

[1] An Address read to the Middlesex Agricultural Society in Concord, September 1860.

AUTUMNAL TINTS
1862

Europeans coming to America are surprised by the brilliancy of our autumnal foliage. There is no account of such a phenomenon in English poetry, because the trees acquire but few bright colors there. The most that Thomson says on this subject in his "Autumn" is contained in the lines,—

> "But see the fading many-colored woods
> Shade deepening over shade, the country round
> Imbrown; a crowded umbrage, dusk and dun,
> Of every hue, from wan declining green
> To sooty dark;"

and in the line in which he speaks of

> "Autumn beaming o'er the yellow woods."

The autumnal change of our woods has not made a deep impression on our own literature yet. October has hardly tinged our poetry.

A great many, who have spent their lives in cities, and have never chanced to come into the country at this season, have never seen this, the flower, or rather the ripe fruit, of the year. I remember riding with one such citizen, who, though a fortnight too late for the most brilliant tints, was taken by surprise, and would not believe that there had been any brighter. He had never heard of this phenomenon before. Not only many in our towns have never witnessed it, but it is scarcely remembered by the majority from year to year.

Most appear to confound changed leaves with withered ones, as if they were to confound ripe apples with rotten ones. I think that the change to some higher color in a leaf is an evidence that it has arrived at a late and perfect maturity, answering to the maturity of fruits. It is generally the lowest and oldest leaves which change first. But as the perfect-winged and usually bright-colored insect is short-lived, so the leaves ripen but to fall.

Generally, every fruit, on ripening, and just before it falls, when it commences a more independent and individual existence, requiring less nourishment from any source, and that not so much from the earth through its stem as from the sun and air, acquires a bright tint. So do leaves. The physiologist says it is "due to an increased absorption of oxygen." That is the scientific account of the matter,—only a reassertion of the fact. But I am more interested in the rosy cheek than I am to know what particular diet the maiden fed on. The very forest and herbage, the pellicle of the earth, must acquire a bright color, an evidence of its ripeness,—as if the globe itself were a fruit on its stem, with ever a cheek toward the sun.

Flowers are but colored leaves, fruits but ripe ones. The edible part of most fruits is, as the physiologist says, "the parenchyma or fleshy tissue of the leaf," of which they are formed.

Our appetites have commonly confined our views of ripeness and its phenomena, color, mellowness, and perfectness, to the fruits which we eat, and we are wont to forget that an immense harvest which we do not eat, hardly use at all, is annually ripened by Nature. At our annual cattle-shows and horticultural exhibitions, we make, as we think, a great show of fair fruits, destined, however, to a rather ignoble end, fruits not valued for their beauty chiefly. But round about and within our towns there is annually another show of fruits, on an infinitely grander scale, fruits which address our taste for beauty alone.

October is the month for painted leaves. Their rich glow now flashes round the world. As fruits and leaves and the day itself acquire a bright tint just before they fall, so the year near its setting. October is its sunset sky; November the later twilight.

I formerly thought that it would be worth the while to get a specimen leaf from each changing tree, shrub, and herbaceous plant, when it had acquired its brightest characteristic color, in its transition from the green to the brown state, outline it, and copy its color exactly, with paint, in a book, which should be entitled "October, or Autumnal Tints,"—beginning with the earliest reddening woodbine and the lake of radical leaves, and coming down through the maples, hickories, and sumachs, and many beautifully freckled leaves less generally known, to the latest oaks and aspens. What a memento such a book would be! You would need only to turn over its leaves to take a ramble through the autumn woods whenever you pleased. Or if I could preserve the leaves themselves, unfaded, it would be better still. I have made but little progress toward such a book, but I have endeavored, instead, to describe all these bright tints in the order in which they present themselves. The following are some extracts from my notes.

THE PURPLE GRASSES

By the twentieth of August, everywhere in woods and swamps we are reminded of the fall, both by the richly spotted sarsaparilla leaves and brakes, and the withering and blackened skunk-cabbage and helle-bore, and, by the riverside, the already blackening pontederia.

The purple grass (*Eragrostis pectinacea*) is now in the height of its beauty. I remember still when I first noticed this grass particularly. Standing on a hillside near our river, I saw, thirty or forty rods off, a stripe of purple half a dozen rods long, under the edge of a wood, where the ground sloped toward a meadow. It was as high-colored and interesting, though not quite so bright, as the patches of rhexia, being a darker purple to and examining it, I found it to be a kind of grass in bloom, hardly a foot high, with but few green blades, and a fine spreading panicle of purple flowers, a shallow, purplish mist trembling around me. Close at hand it appeared but a dull purple, and made little impression on the eye; it was even difficult to detect; and if you plucked a single plant, you were surprised to find how thin it was, and how little color it had. But viewed at a distance in a favorable light, it was of a fine lively purple, flower-like, enriching the earth. Such puny causes combine to produce these decided effects. I was the more surprised and charmed because grass is commonly of a sober and humble color.

With its beautiful purple blush it reminds me, and supplies the place, of the rhexia, which is now leaving off, and it is one of the most interesting phenomena of August. The finest patches of it grow on waste strips or selvages of land at the base of dry hills, just above the edge of the meadows, where the greedy mower does not deign to swing his scythe; for this is a thin and poor grass, beneath his notice. Or, it may be, cause it is so beautiful he does not know that it exists; for the same eye does not see this and timothy. He carefully gets the meadow-hay and the more nutritious grasses which grow next to that, but he leaves this fine purple mist for the walker's harvest,—fodder for his fancy stock. Higher up the hill, perchance, grow also black-berries, John's-wort, and neglected, withered, and wiry June-grass. How fortunate that it grows in such places, and not in the midst of the rank grasses which are annually cut! Nature thus keeps use and beauty distinct. I know many such localities, where it does not fail to present itself annually, and paint the earth with its blush. It grows on the gentle slopes, either in a continuous patch or in scattered and rounded tufts a foot in di-ameter, and it lasts till it is killed by the first smart frosts.

In most plants the corolla or calyx is the part which attains the highest color, and is the most attractive; in many it is the seed-vessel or fruit; in others, as the red maple, the leaves; and in others still it is the very culm itself which is the principal flower or blooming part.

The last is especially the case with the poke or garget (*Phytolacca decandra*). Some which stand under our cliffs quite dazzle me with their purple stems now and early in September. They are as interesting to me as most flowers, and one of the most important fruits of our autumn. Every part is flower (or fruit), such is its superfluity of color,—stem, branch, peduncle, pedicel, petiole, and even the at length yellowish, purple-veined leaves. Its cylindrical racemes of berries of various hues, from green to dark purple, six or seven inches long, are gracefully drooping on all sides, offering repasts to the birds; and even the sepals from which the birds have picked the berries are a bril-liant lake red, with crimson flame-like reflections, equal to any-thing of the kind,—all on fire with ripeness. Hence the *lacca*, from *lac*, lake. There are at the same time flower buds, flowers, green berries, dark-purple or ripe ones, and these flower-like sepals, all on the same plant.

We love to see any redness in the vegetation of the tem-perate zone. It is the color of colors. This plant speaks to our blood. It asks a bright sun on it to make it show to best advan-tage, and it must be seen at this season of the year. On warm hillsides its stems are ripe by the twenty-third of August. At that date I walked through a beautiful grove of them, six or seven feet high, on the side of one of our cliffs, where they ripen early. Quite to the ground they were a deep, brilliant purple, with a bloom contrasting with the still clear green leaves. It appears a rare triumph of Nature to have produced and perfected such a plant, as if this were enough for a summer. What a perfect maturity it arrives at! It is the emblem of a successful life concluded by a death not premature, which is an ornament to Nature. What if we were to mature as perfectly, root and branch, glowing in the midst of our decay, like the poke! I confess that it excites me to behold them. I cut one for a cane, for I would fain handle and lean on it. I love to press the berries between my fingers, and see their juice staining my hand. To walk amid these upright, branching casks of purple wine, which retain and diffuse a sunset glow, tasting each one with your eye, instead of counting the pipes on a London dock, what a privilege! For Nature's vintage is not confined to the vine. Our poets have sung of wine, the product of a foreign plant which commonly they never saw, as if our own plants had no juice in them more than the singers. Indeed, this has been called by some the American grape, and, though a native of America, its juices are used in some foreign countries to improve the color of the wine; so that the poetaster may be celebrating the virtues of the poke without knowing it. Here are berries enough to paint afresh the western sky, and play the bacchanal with, if you will. And what flutes its ensanguined stems would make, to be used in such a dance! It is truly a royal plant. I could spend the evening of the year musing amid the poke stems. And perchance amid these groves might arise at last a new school of philosophy or poetry. It lasts all through September.

At the same time with this, or near the end of August, a to me very interesting genus of grasses, andropogons, or beard-grasses, is in its prime: *Andropogon furcatus*, forked beard-grass, or call it purple-fingered grass; *Andropogon scoparius*, purple wood-grass; and *Andropogon* (now called *Sorghum*) *nutans*, Indian-grass. The first is a very tall and slender-culmed grass, three to seven feet high, with four or five purple finger-like spikes raying upward from the top. The second is also quite slender, growing in tufts two feet high by one wide, with culms often somewhat curving, which, as the spikes go out of bloom, have a whitish, fuzzy look. These two are prevailing grasses at this season on dry and sandy fields and hillsides. The culms of both, not to mention their pretty flowers, reflect a purple tinge, and help to declare the ripeness of the year. Perhaps I have the more sympathy with them because they are despised by the farmer, and occupy sterile and neglected soil. They are high-colored, like ripe grapes, and express a maturity which the spring did not suggest. Only the August sun could have thus burnished these culms and leaves. The farmer has long since done his upland haying, and he will not condescend to bring his scythe to where these slender wild grasses have at length flowered thinly; you often see spaces of bare sand amid them. But I walk encouraged between the tufts of purple wood-grass over the sandy fields, and along the edge of the shrub oaks, glad to recognize these simple contemporaries. With thoughts cutting a broad swathe I "get" them, with horse-raking thoughts I gather them into windrows. The fine-eared poet may hear the whetting of my scythe. These two were almost the first grasses that I learned to distinguish, for I had not known by how many friends I was surrounded; I had seen them simply as grasses standing. The purple of their culms also excites me like that of the poke-weed stems.

Think what refuge there is for one, before August is over, from college commencements and society that isolates! I can skulk amid the tufts of purple wood-grass on the borders of the "Great Fields." Wherever I walk these afternoons, the purple-fingered grass also stands like a guide-board, and points my thoughts to more poetic paths than they have lately traveled.

A man shall perhaps rush by and trample down plants as high as his head, and cannot be said to know that they exist, though he may have cut many tons of them, littered his stables with them, and fed them to his cattle for years. Yet, if he ever favorably attends to them, he may be overcome by their beauty. Each humblest plant, or weed, as we call it, stands there to express some thought or mood of ours; and yet how long it stands in vain! I had walked over those Great Fields so many Augusts, and never yet distinctly recognized these purple companions that I had there. I had brushed against them and trodden on them, forsooth; and now, at last, they, as it were, rose up and blessed me. Beauty and true wealth are always thus cheap and despised. Heaven might be defined as the place which men avoid. Who can doubt that these grasses, which the farmer says are of no account to him, find some compensation in your appreciation of them? I may say that I never saw them before; though, when I came to look them face to face, there did come down to me a purple gleam from previous years; and now, wherever I go, I see hardly anything else. It is the reign and presidency of the andropogons.

Almost the very sands confess the ripening influence of the August sun, and methinks, together with the slender grasses waving over them, reflect a purple tinge. The impurpled sands! Such is the consequence of all this sunshine absorbed into the pores of plants and of the earth. All sap or blood is now wine-colored. At last we have not only the purple sea, but the purple land.

The chestnut beard-grass, Indian-grass, or wood-grass, growing here and there in waste places, but more rare than the former (from two to four or five feet high), is still handsomer and of more vivid colors than its congeners, and might well have caught the Indian's eye. It has a long, narrow, one-sided, and slightly nodding panicle of bright purple and yellow flowers, like a banner raised above its reedy leaves. These bright standards are now advanced on the distant hillsides, not in large armies, but in scattered troops or single file, like the red men. They stand thus fair and bright, representative of the race which they are named after, but for the most part unobserved as they. The expression of this grass haunted me for a week, after I first passed and noticed it, like the glance of an eye. It stands like an Indian chief taking a last look at his favorite hunting-grounds.

THE RED MAPLE

By the twenty-fifth of September, the red maples generally are beginning to be ripe. Some large ones have been conspicuously changing for a week, and some single trees are now very brilliant. I notice a small one, half a mile off across a meadow, against the green woodside there, a far brighter red than the blossoms of any tree in summer, and more conspicuous. I have observed this tree for several autumns invariably changing earlier than its fellows, just as one tree ripens its fruit earlier than another. It might serve to mark the season, perhaps. I should be sorry if it were cut down. I know of two or three such trees in different parts of our town, which might, perhaps, be propagated from, as early ripeners or September trees, and their seed be advertised in the market, as well as that of radishes, if we cared as much about them.

At present these burning bushes stand chiefly along the edge of the meadows, or I distinguish them afar on the hillsides here and there. Sometimes you will see many small ones in a swamp turned quite crimson when all other trees around are still perfectly green, and the former appear so much the brighter for it. They take you by surprise, as you are going by on one side, across the fields, thus early in the season, as if it were some gay encampment of the red men, or other foresters, of whose arrival you had not heard.

Some single trees, wholly bright scarlet; seen against others of their kind still freshly green, or against evergreens, are more memorable than whole groves will be by and by. How beautiful, when a whole tree is like one great scarlet fruit full of ripe juices, every leaf, from lowest limb to topmost spire, all aglow, especially if you look toward the sun! What more remarkable object can there be in the landscape? Visible for miles, too fair to be believed. If such a phenomenon occurred but once, it would be handed down by tradition to posterity, and get into the mythology at last.

The whole tree thus ripening in advance of its fellows attains a singular preëminence, and sometimes maintains it for a week or two. I am thrilled at the sight of it, bearing aloft its scarlet standard for the regiment of green-clad foresters around, and I go half a mile out of my way to examine it. A single tree becomes thus the crowning beauty of some meadowy vale, and the expression of the whole surrounding forest is at once more spirited for it.

A small red maple has grown, perchance, far away at the head of some retired valley, a mile from any road, unobserved. It has faithfully discharged the duties of a maple there, all winter and summer, neglected none of its economies, but added to its stature in the virtue which belongs to a maple, by a steady growth for so many months, never having gone gadding abroad, and is nearer heaven than it was in the spring. It has faithfully husbanded its sap, and afforded a shelter to the wandering bird, has long since ripened its seeds and committed them to the winds, and has the satisfaction of knowing, perhaps, that a thousand little well-behaved maples are already settled in life somewhere. It deserves well of Mapledom. Its leaves have been asking it from time to time, in a whisper, "When shall we redden?"

And now, in this month of September, this month of traveling, when men are hastening to the seaside, or the mountains, or the lakes, this modest maple, still without budging an inch, travels in its reputation,—runs up its scarlet flag on that hillside, which shows that it has finished its summer's work before all other trees, and withdraws from the contest. At the eleventh hour of the year, the tree which no scrutiny could have detected here when it was most industrious is thus, by the tint of its maturity, by its very blushes, revealed at last to the careless and distant traveler, and leads his thoughts away from the dusty road into those brave solitudes which it inhabits. It flashes out conspicuous with all the virtue and beauty of a maple,—*Acer rubrum*. We may now read its title, or *rubric*, clear. Its *virtues*, not its sins, are as scarlet.

Notwithstanding the red maple is the most intense scarlet of any of our trees, the sugar maple has been the most celebrated, and Michaux in his "Sylva" does not speak of the autumnal color of the former. About the second of October, these trees, both large and small, are most brilliant, though many are still green. In "sprout-lands" they seem to vie with one another, and ever some particular one in the midst of the crowd will be of a peculiarly pure scarlet, and by its more intense color attract our eye even at a distance, and carry off the palm. A large red maple swamp, when at the height of its change, is the most obviously brilliant of all tangible things, where I dwell, so abundant is this tree with us. It varies much both in form and color. A great many are merely yellow; more, scarlet; others, scarlet deepening into crimson, more red than common. Look at yonder swamp of maples mixed with pines, at the base of a pine-clad hill, a quarter of a mile off, so that you get the full effect of the bright colors, without detecting the imperfections of the leaves, and see their yellow, scarlet, and crimson fires, of all tints, mingled and contrasted with the green. Some maples are yet green, only yellow or crimson-tipped on the edges of their flakes, like the edges of a hazelnut bur; some are wholly brilliant scarlet, raying out regularly and finely every way, bilaterally, like the veins of a leaf; others, of more irregular form, when I turn my head slightly, emptying out some of its earthiness and concealing the trunk of the tree, seem to rest heavily flake on flake, like yellow and scarlet clouds, wreath upon wreath, or like snow-drifts driving through the air, stratified by the wind. It adds greatly to the beauty of such a swamp at this season, that, even though there may be no other trees interspersed, it is not seen as a simple mass of color, but, different trees being of different colors and hues, the outline of each crescent treetop is distinct, and where one laps on to another. Yet a painter would hardly venture to make them thus distinct a quarter of a mile off.

As I go across a meadow directly toward a low rising ground this bright afternoon, I see, some fifty rods off toward the sun, the top of a maple swamp just appearing over the sheeny russet edge of the hill, a stripe apparently twenty rods long by ten feet deep, of the most intensely brilliant scarlet, orange, and yellow, equal to any flowers or fruits, or any tints ever painted. As I advance, lowering the edge of the hill which makes the firm foreground or lower frame of the picture, the depth of the brilliant grove revealed steadily increases, suggesting that the whole of the inclosed valley is filled with such color. One wonders that the tithing-men and fathers of the town are not out to see what the trees mean by their high colors and exuberance of spirits, fearing that some mischief is brewing. I do not see what the Puritans did at this season, when the maples blaze out in scarlet. They certainly could not have worshipped in groves then. Perhaps that is what they built meeting houses and fenced them round with horse-sheds for.

THE ELM

Now too, the first of October, or later, the elms are at the height of their autumnal beauty,—great brownish-yellow masses, warm from their September oven, hanging over the highway. Their leaves are perfectly ripe. I wonder if there is any answering ripeness in the lives of the men who live beneath them. As I look down our street, which is lined with them, they remind me both by their form and color of yellowing sheaves of grain, as if the harvest had indeed come to the village itself, and we might expect to find some maturity and flavor in the thoughts of the villagers at last. Under those bright rustling yellow piles just ready to fall on the heads of the walkers, how can any crudity or greenness of thought or act prevail? When I stand where half a dozen large elms droop over a house, it is as if I stood within a ripe pumpkin-rind, and I feel as mellow as if I were the pulp, though I may be somewhat stringy and seedy withal. What is the late greenness of the English elm, like a cucumber out of season, which does not know when to have done, compared with the early and golden maturity of the American tree? The street is the scene of a great harvest-home. It would be worth the while to set out these trees, if only for their autumnal value. Think of these great yellow canopies or parasols held over our heads and houses by the mile together, making the village all one and compact,—an *ulmarium*, which is at the same time a nursery of men! And then how gently and unobserved they drop their burden and let in the sun when it is wanted, their leaves not heard when they fall on our roofs and in our streets; and thus the village parasol is shut up and put away! I see the market-man driving into the village, and disappearing under its canopy of elm-tops, with *his* crop, as into a great granary or barnyard. I am tempted to go thither as to a husking of thoughts, now dry and ripe, and ready to be separated from their integuments; but, alas! I foresee that it will be chiefly husks and little thought, blasted pig-corn, fit only for cob-meal,—for, as you sow, so shall you reap.

FALLEN LEAVES

By the sixth of October the leaves generally begin to fall, in successive showers, after frost or rain; but the principal leaf-harvest, the acme of the *Fall*, is commonly about the sixteenth. Some morning at that date there is perhaps a harder frost than we have seen, and ice formed under the pump, and now, when the morning wind rises, the leaves come down in denser showers than ever. They suddenly form thick beds or carpets on the ground, in this gentle air, or even without wind, just the size and form of the tree above. Some trees, as small hickories, appear to have dropped their leaves instantaneously, as a soldier grounds arms at a signal; and those of the hickory, being bright yellow still, though withered, reflect a blaze of light from the ground where they lie. Down they have come on all sides, at the first earnest touch of autumn's wand, making a sound like rain.

Or else it is after moist and rainy weather that we notice how great a fall of leaves there has been in the night, though it may not yet be the touch that loosens the rock maple leaf. The streets are thickly strewn with the trophies, and fallen elm leaves make a dark brown pavement under our feet. After some remarkably warm Indian-summer day or days, I perceive that it is the unusual heat which, more than anything, causes the leaves to fall, there having been, perhaps, no frost nor rain for some time. The intense heat suddenly ripens and wilts them, just as it softens and ripens peaches and other fruits, and causes them to drop.

The leaves of late red maples, still bright, strew the earth, often crimson-spotted on a yellow ground, like some wild apples,—though they preserve these bright colors on the ground but a day or two, especially if it rains. On causeways I go by trees here and there all bare and smoke-like, having lost their brilliant clothing; but there it lies, nearly as bright as ever, on the ground on one side, and making nearly as regular a figure as lately on the tree. I would rather say that I first observe the trees thus flat on the ground like a permanent colored shadow, and they suggest to look for the boughs that bore them. A queen might be proud to walk where these gallant trees have spread their bright cloaks in the mud. I see wagons roll over them as a shadow or a reflection, and the drivers heed them just as little as they did their shadows before.

Birds' nests, in the huckleberry and other shrubs, and in trees, are already being filled with the withered leaves. So many have fallen in the woods that a squirrel cannot run after a falling nut without being heard. Boys are raking them in the streets, if only for the pleasure of dealing with such clean, crisp substances. Some sweep the paths scrupulously neat, and then stand to see the next breath strew them with new trophies. The swamp floor is thickly covered, and the *Lycopodium lucidulum* looks suddenly greener amid them. In dense woods they half cover pools that are three or four rods long. The other day I could hardly find a well-known spring, and even suspected that it had dried up, for it was completely concealed by freshly fallen leaves; and when I swept them aside and revealed it, it was like striking the earth, with Aaron's rod, for a new spring. Wet grounds about the edges of swamps look dry with them. At one swamp, where I was surveying, thinking to step on a leafy shore from a rail, I got into the water more than a foot deep.

When I go to the river the day after the principal fall of leaves, the sixteenth, I find my boat all covered, bottom and seats, with the leaves of the golden willow under which it is moored, and I set sail with a cargo of them rustling under my feet. If I empty it, it will be full again to-morrow. I do not regard them as litter, to be swept out, but accept them as suitable straw or matting for the bottom of my carriage. When I turn up into the mouth of the Assabet, which is wooded, large fleets of leaves are floating on its surface, as it were getting out to sea, with room to tack; but next the shore, a little farther up, they are thicker than foam, quite concealing the water for a rod in width, under and amid the alders, button-bushes, and maples, still perfectly light and dry, with fibre unrelaxed; and at rocky bend where they are met and stopped by the morning wind, they sometimes form a broad and dense crescent quite across the river. When I turn my prow that way, and the wave which it makes strikes them, list what a pleasant rustling from these dry substances getting on one another! Often it is their undulation only which reveals the water beneath them. Also every motion of the wood turtle on the shore is betrayed by their rustling there. Or even in mid-channel, when the wind rises, I hear them blown with a rustling sound. Higher up they are slowly moving round and round in some great eddy which the river makes, as that at the "Leaning Hemlocks," where the water is deep, and the current is wearing into the bank.

Perchance, in the afternoon of such a day, when the water is perfectly calm and full of reflections, I paddle gently down the main stream, and, turning up the Assabet, reach a quiet cove, where I unexpectedly find myself surrounded by myriads of leaves, like fellow-voyagers, which seem to have the same purpose, or want of purpose, with myself. See this great fleet of scattered leaf-boats which we paddle amid, in this smooth river-bay, each one curled up on every side by the sun's skill, each nerve a stiff spruce knee,—like boats of hide, and of all patterns,— Charon's boat probably among the rest,—and some with lofty prows and poops, like the stately vessels of the ancients, scarcely moving in the sluggish current,—like the great fleets, the dense Chinese cities of boats, with which you mingle on entering some great mart, some New York or Canton, which we are all steadily approaching together. How gently each has been deposited on the water! No violence has been used towards them yet, though, perchance, palpitating hearts were present at the launching. And painted ducks, too, the splendid wood duck among the rest, often come to sail and float amid the painted leaves,—barks of a nobler model still!

What wholesome herb drinks are to be had in the swamps now! What strong medicinal but rich scents from the decaying leaves! The rain falling on the freshly dried herbs and leaves, and filling the pools and ditches into which they have dropped thus clean and rigid, will soon convert them into tea,—green, black, brown, and yellow teas, of all degrees of strength, enough to set all Nature a-gossiping. Whether we drink them or not, as yet, before their strength is drawn, these leaves, dried on great Nature's coppers, are of such various pure and delicate tints as might make the fame of Oriental teas.

How they are mixed up, of all species, oak and maple and chestnut and birch! But Nature is not cluttered with them; she is a perfect husbandman; she stores them all. Consider what a vast crop is thus annually shed on the earth! This, more than any mere grain or seed, is the great harvest of the year. The trees are now repaying the earth with interest what they have taken from it. They are discounting. They are about to add a leaf's thickness to the depth of the soil. This is the beautiful way in which Nature gets her muck, while I chaffer with this man and that, who talks to me about sulphur and the cost of carting. We are all the richer for their decay. I am more interested in this crop than in the English grass alone or in the corn. It prepares the virgin mould for future corn-fields and forests, on which the earth fattens. It keeps our homestead in good heart.

For beautiful variety no crop can be compared with this. Here is not merely the plain yellow of the grains, but nearly all the colors that we know, the brightest blue not excepted: the early blushing maple, the poison sumach blazing its sins as scarlet, the mulberry ash, the rich chrome yellow of the poplars, the brilliant red huckleberry, with which the hills' backs are painted, like those of sheep. The frost touches them, and, with the slightest breath of returning day or jarring of earth's axle, see in what showers they come floating down! The ground is all particolored with them. But they still live in the soil, whose fertility and bulk they increase, and in the forests that spring from it. They stoop to rise, to mount higher in coming years, by subtle chemistry, climbing by the sap in the trees; and the sapling's first fruits thus shed, transmuted at last, may adorn its crown, when, in after years, it has become the monarch of the forest.

It is pleasant to walk over the beds of these fresh, crisp, and rustling leaves. How beautifully they go to their graves! how gently lay themselves down and turn to mould!—painted of a thousand hues, and fit to make the beds of us living. So they troop to their last resting-place, light and frisky. They put on no weeds, but merrily they go scampering over the earth, selecting the spot, choosing a lot, ordering no iron fence, whispering all through the woods about it,—some choosing the spot where the bodies of men are mouldering beneath, and meeting them half-way. How many flutterings before they rest quietly in their graves! They that soared so loftily, how contentedly they return to dust again, and are laid low, resigned to lie and decay at the foot of the tree, and afford nourishment to new generations of their kind, as well as to flutter on high! They teach us how to die. One wonders if the time will ever come when men, with their boasted faith in immortality, will lie down as gracefully and as ripe,—with such an Indian-summer serenity will shed their bodies, as they do their hair and nails.

When the leaves fall, the whole earth is a cemetery pleasant to walk in. I love to wander and muse over them in their graves. Here are no lying nor vain epitaphs. What though you own no lot at Mount Auburn? Your lot is surely cast somewhere in this vast cemetery, which has been consecrated from of old. You need attend no auction to secure a place. There is room enough here. The loose strife shall bloom and the huckleberry-bird sing over your bones. The woodsman and hunter shall be your sextons, and the children shall tread upon the borders as much as they will. Let us walk in the cemetery of the leaves; this is your true Greenwood Cemetery.

THE SUGAR MAPLE

But think not that the splendor of the year is over; for as one leaf does not make a summer, neither does one falling leaf make an autumn. The smallest sugar maples in our streets make a great show as early as the fifth of October, more than any other trees there. As I look up the main street, they appear like painted screens standing before the houses; yet many are green. But now, or generally by the seventeenth of October, when almost all red maples and some white maples are bare, the large sugar maples also are in their glory, glowing with yellow and red, and show unexpectedly bright and delicate tints. They are remarkable for the contrast they often afford of deep blushing red on one half and green on the other. They become at length

dense masses of rich yellow with a deep scarlet blush, or more
than blush, on the exposed surfaces, They are the brightest trees
now in the street.

The large ones on our Common are particularly beautiful.
A delicate but warmer than golden yellow is now the prevailing
color, with scarlet cheeks. Yet, standing on the east side of the
Common just before sundown, when the western light is
transmitted through them, I see that their yellow even, compared with the pale lemon yellow of an elm close by, amounts to
a scarlet, without noticing the bright scarlet portions. Generally,
they are great regular oval masses of yellow and scarlet. All the
sunny warmth of the season, the Indian summer, seems to be
absorbed in their leaves. The lowest and inmost leaves next the
bole are, as usual, of the most delicate yellow and green, like the
complexion of young men brought up in the house. There is an
auction on the Common to-day, but its red flag is hard to be dis-
cerned amid this blaze of color.

Little did the fathers of the town anticipate this brilliant
success, when they caused to be imported from farther in the
country some straight poles with their tops cut off, which they
called sugar maples; and, as I remember, after they were set out, a
neighboring merchant's clerk, by way of jest, planted beans about
them. Those which were then jestingly called bean-poles are to-
day far the most beautiful objects noticeable in our streets. They
are worth all and more than they have cost,—though one of the
selectmen, while setting them out, took the cold which occasioned his death,—if only because they have filled the open eyes
of children with their rich color unstintedly so many Octobers.
We will not ask them to yield us sugar in the spring, while they
afford us so fair a prospect in the autumn. Wealth indoors may
be the inheritance of few, but it is, equally distributed on the
Common. All children alike can revel in this golden harvest.

Surely trees should be set in our streets with a view to
their October splendor, though I doubt whether this is ever considered by the "Tree Society." Do you not think it will make
some odds to these children that they were brought up under the
maples? Hundreds of eyes are steadily drinking in this color,
and by these teachers even the truants are caught and educated
the moment they step abroad. Indeed, neither the truant nor the
studious is at present taught color in the schools. These are instead of the bright colors in apothecaries' shops and city windows. It is a pity that we have no more *red* maples, and some

hickories, in our streets as well. Our paint-box is very imper-
fectly filled. Instead of, or beside, supplying such paint-boxes as
we do, we might supply these natural colors to the young.
Where else will they study color under greater advantages?
What School of Design can vie with this? Think how much the
eyes of painters of all kinds, and of manufacturers of cloth and
paper, and paper-stainers, and countless others, are to be educated by these autumnal colors. The stationer's envelopes may
be of very various tints, yet not so various as those of the leaves
of a single tree. If you want a different shade or tint of a particular color, you have only to look farther within or without the
tree or the wood. These leaves are not many dipped in one dye,
as at the dye-house, but they are dyed in light of infinitely various degrees of strength and left to set and dry there.

Shall the names of so many of our colors continue to be
derived from those of obscure foreign localities, as Naples yellow, Prussian blue, raw Sienna, burnt Umber, Gamboge? (surely
the Tyrian purple must have faded by this time), or from comparatively trivial articles of commerce,—chocolate, lemon, cof-
fee, cinnamon, claret? (shall we compare our hickory to a lemon,
or a lemon to a hickory?) or from ores and oxides which few
ever see? Shall we so often, when describing to our neighbors
the color of something we have seen, refer them, not to some
natural object in our neighborhood, but perchance to a bit of
earth fetched from the other side of the planet, which possibly
they may find at the apothecary's, but which probably neither
they nor we ever saw? Have we not an *earth* under our feet,
—aye, and a sky over our heads? Or is the last *all* ultramarine?
What do we know of sapphire, amethyst, emerald, ruby, amber,
and the like,—most of us who take these names in vain? Leave
these precious words to cabinet-keepers, virtuosos, and maids-of-
honor,—to the Nabobs, Begums, and Chobdars of Hindostan, or
wherever else. I do not see why, since America and her autumn
woods have been discovered, our leaves should not compete
with the precious stones in giving names to colors; and, indeed, I
believe that in course of time the names of some of our trees and
shrubs, as well as flowers, will get into our popular chromatic
nomenclature.

But of much more importance than a knowledge of the
names and distinctions of color is the joy and exhilaration which
these colored leaves excite. Already these brilliant trees
throughout the street, without any more variety, are at least

equal to an annual festival and holiday, or a week of such.
These are cheap and innocent gala-days, celebrated by one and all
without the aid of committees or marshals, such a show as may
safely be licensed, not attracting gamblers or rum-sellers, not requiring any special police to keep the peace. And poor indeed
must be that New England village's October which has not the
maple in its streets. This October festival costs no powder, nor
ringing of bells, but every tree is a living liberty-pole on which a
thousand bright flags are waving.

No wonder that we must have our annual cattle-show,
and fall training, and perhaps cornwallis, our September courts,
and the like. Nature herself holds her annual fair in October,
not only in the streets, but in every hollow and on every hillside. When lately we looked into that red maple swamp all
ablaze, where the trees were clothed in their vestures of most
dazzling tints, did it not suggest a thousand gypsies beneath,—a
race capable of wild delight,—or even the fabled fauns, satyrs,
and wood-nymphs come back to earth? Or was it only a congregation of wearied wood-choppers, or of proprietors come to inspect their lots, that we thought of? Or, earlier still, when we
paddled on the river through that fine-grained September air,
did there not appear to be something new going on under the
sparkling surface of the stream, a shaking of props, at least, so
that we made haste in order to be up in time? Did not the rows
of yellowing willows and button-bushes on each side seem like
rows of booths, under which, perhaps, some fluviatile egg-pop
equally yellow was effervescing? Did not all these suggest that
man's spirits should rise as high as Nature's,—should hang out
their flag, and the routine of his life be interrupted by an analogous expression of joy and hilarity?

No annual training or muster of soldiery, no celebration
with its scarfs and banners, could import into the town a hun-
dredth part of the annual splendor of our October. We have
only to set the trees, or let them stand, and Nature will find the
colored drapery,—flags of all her nations, some of whose private
signals hardly the botanist can read,—while we walk under the
triumphal arches of the elms. Leave it to Nature to appoint the
days, whether the same as in neighboring States or not, and let
the clergy read her proclamations, if they can understand them.
Behold what a brilliant drapery is her woodbine flag! What pub-
lic-spirited merchant, think you, has contributed this part of the
show? There is no handsomer shingling and paint than this

vine, at present covering a whole side of some houses. I do not believe that the ivy *never sere* is comparable to it. No wonder it has been extensively introduced into London. Let us have a good many maples and hickories and scarlet oaks, then, I say. Blaze away! Shall that dirty roll of bunting in the gun-house be all the colors a village can display? A village is not complete, unless it have these trees to mark the season in it. They are important, like the town clock. A village that has them not will not be found to work well. It has a screw loose, an essential part is wanting. Let us have willows for spring, elms for summer, maples and walnuts and tupeloes for autumn, evergreens for winter, and oaks for all seasons. What is a gallery in a house to a gallery in the streets, which every marketman rides through, whether he will or not? Of course, there is not a picture-gallery in the country which would be worth so much to us as is the western view at sunset under the elms of our main street. They are the frame to a picture which is daily painted behind them. An avenue of elms as large as our largest and three miles long would seem to lead to some admirable place, though only C—— were at the end of it.

A village needs these innocent stimulants of bright and cheering prospects to keep off melancholy and superstition. Show me two villages, one embowered in trees and blazing with all the glories of October, the other a merely trivial and treeless waste, or with only a single tree or two for suicides, and I shall he sure that in the latter will be found the most starved and bigoted religionists and the most desperate drinkers. Every washtub and milk-can and gravestone will be exposed. The inhabitants will disappear abruptly behind their barns and houses, like desert Arabs amid their rocks, and I shall look to see spears in their hands. They will be ready to accept the most barren and forlorn doctrine,—as that the world is speedily coming to an end, or has already got to it, or that they themselves are turned wrong side outward. They will perchance crack their dry joints at one another and call it a spiritual communication.

But to confine ourselves to the maples. What if we were to take half as much pains in protecting them as we do in setting them out,—not stupidly tie our horses to our dahlia stems?

What meant the fathers by establishing this *perfectly living* institution before the church,—this institution which needs no repairing nor repainting, which is continually enlarged and repaired by its growth? Surely they

"Wrought in a sad sincerity;
Themselves from God they could not free;
They *planted* better than they knew;—
The conscious *trees* to beauty grew."

Verily these maples are cheap preachers, permanently settled, which preach their half-century, and century, aye, and cen-
tury-and-a-half sermons, with constantly increasing unction and
influence, ministering to many generations of men; and the
least we can do is to supply them with suitable colleagues as they
grow infirm.

THE SCARLET OAK

Belonging to a genus which is remarkable for the beautiful form of its leaves, I suspect that some scarlet oak leaves surpass those of all other oaks in the rich and wild beauty of their
outlines. I judge from an acquaintance with twelve species, and
from drawings which I have seen of many others.

Stand under this tree and see how finely its leaves are cut
against the sky,—as it were, only a few sharp points extending
from a midrib. They look like double, treble, or quadruple
crosses. They are far more ethereal than the less deeply scalloped
oak leaves. They have so little leafy *terra firma* that they appear
melting away in the light, and scarcely obstruct our view. The
leaves of very young plants are, like those of full-grown oaks of
other species, more entire, simple, and lumpish in their outlines, but these, raised high on old trees, have solved the leafy
problem. Lifted higher and higher, and sublimated more and
more, putting off some earthiness and cultivating more inti-
macy with the light each year, they have at length the least possible amount of earthy matter, and the greatest spread and grasp
of skyey influences. There they dance, arm in arm with the
light,—tripping it on fantastic points, fit partners in those aerial
halls. So intimately mingled are they with it, that, what with
their slenderness and their glossy surfaces, you can hardly tell at
last what in the dance is leaf and what is light. And when no
zephyr stirs, they are at most but a rich tracery to the forest windows.

I am again struck with their beauty, when, a month later,
they thickly strew the ground in the woods, piled one upon an-

other under my feet. They are then brown above, but purple beneath. With their narrow lobes and their bold, deep scallops
reaching almost to the middle, they suggest that the material
must be cheap, or else there has been a lavish expense in their
creation, as if so much had been cut out. Or else they seem to us
the remnants of the stuff out of which leaves have been cut with
a die. Indeed, when they lie thus one upon another, they remind me of a pile of scrap-tin.

Or bring one home, and study it closely at your leisure, by
the fireside. It is a type, not from any Oxford font, not in the
Basque nor the arrow-headed character, not found on the
Rosetta Stone, but destined to be copied in sculpture one day, if
they ever get to whittling stone here. What a wild and pleasing
outline, a combination of graceful curves and angles! The eye
rests with equal delight on what is not leaf and on what is leaf,—
on the broad, free, open sinuses, and on the long, sharp, bristle-
pointed lobes. A simple oval outline would include it all, if you
connected the points of the leaf; but how much richer is it than
that, with its half-dozen deep scallops, in which the eye and
thought of the beholder are embayed! If I were a drawing-mas-
ter, I would set my pupils to copying these leaves, that they
might learn to draw firmly and gracefully.

Regarded as water, it is like a pond with half a dozen
broad rounded promontories extending nearly to its middle, half
from each side, while its watery bays extend far inland, like sharp
friths, at each of whose heads several fine streams empty in,—
almost a leafy archipelago.

But it oftener suggests land, and, as Dionysius and Pliny
compared the form of the Morea to that of the leaf of the Oriental plane tree, so this leaf reminds me of some fair wild island in
the ocean, whose extensive coast, alternate rounded bays with
smooth strands, and sharp-pointed rocky capes, mark it as fitted
for the habitation of man, and destined to become a centre of civilization at last. To the sailor's eye, it is a much indented shore.
Is it not, in fact, a shore to the aerial ocean, on which the windy
surf beats? At sight of this leaf we are all mariners,—if not
vikings, buccaneers, and filibusters. Both our love of repose and
our spirit of adventure are addressed. In our most casual glance,
perchance, we think that if we succeed in doubling those sharp
capes we shall find deep, smooth, and secure havens in the ample bays. How different from the white oak leaf, with its
rounded headlands, on which no lighthouse need be placed!

That is an England, with its long civil history, that may be read. This is some still unsettled New-found Island or Celebes. Shall we go and be rajahs there?

By the twenty-sixth of October the large scarlet oaks are in their prime, when other oaks are usually withered. They have been kindling their fires for a week past, and now generally burst into a blaze. This alone of *our* indigenous deciduous trees (excepting the dogwood, of which I do not know half a dozen, and they are but large bushes) is now in its glory. The two aspens and the sugar maple come nearest to it in date, but they have lost the greater part of their leaves. Of evergreens, only the pitch pine is still commonly bright.

But it requires a particular alertness, if not devotion to these phenomena, to appreciate the wide-spread, but late and unexpected glory of the scarlet oaks. I do not speak here of the small trees and shrubs, which are commonly observed, and which are now withered, but of the large trees. Most go in and shut their doors, thinking that bleak and colorless November has already come, when some of the most brilliant and memorable colors are not yet lit.

This very perfect and vigorous one, about forty feet high, standing in an open pasture, which was quite glossy green on the twelfth, is now, the twenty-sixth, completely changed to bright dark-scarlet,—every leaf, between you and the sun, as if it had been dipped into a scarlet dye. The whole tree is much like a heart in form, as well as color. Was not this worth waiting for? Little did you think, ten days ago, that that cold green tree would assume such color as this. Its leaves are still firmly attached, while those of other trees are falling around it. It seems to say: "I am the last to blush, but I blush deeper than any of ye. I bring up the rear in my red coat. We scarlet ones, alone of oaks, have not given up the fight."

The sap is now, and even far into November, frequently flowing fast in these trees, as in maples in the spring; and apparently their bright tints, now that most other oaks are withered, are connected with this phenomenon. They are full of life. It has a pleasantly astringent, acorn-like taste, this strong oak wine, as I find on tapping them with my knife.

Looking across this woodland valley, a quarter of a mile wide, how rich those scarlet oaks embosomed in pines, their bright red branches intimately intermingled with them! They have their full effect there. The pine boughs are the green calyx

to their red petals. Or, as we go along a road in the woods, the
sun striking endwise through it, and lighting up the red tents of
the oaks, which on each side are mingled with the liquid green
of the pines, makes a very gorgeous scene. Indeed, without the
evergreens for contrast, the autumnal tints would lose much of
their effect.

The scarlet oak asks a clear sky and the brightness of late
October days. These bring out its colors. If the sun goes into a
cloud they become comparatively indistinct. As I sit on a cliff in
the southwest part of our town, the sun is now getting low, and
the woods in Lincoln, south and east of me, are lit up by its more
level rays; and in the scarlet oaks, scattered so equally over the
forest, there is brought out a more brilliant redness than I had
believed was in them. Every tree of this species which is visible
in those directions, even to the horizon, now stands out distinctly red. Some great ones lift their red backs high above the
woods, in the next town, like huge roses with a myriad of fine
petals; and some more slender ones, in a small grove of white
pines on Pine Hill in the east, on the very verge of the horizon,
alternating with the pines on the edge of the grove, and shoul-
dering them with their red coats, look like soldiers in red amid
hunters in green. This time it is Lincoln green, too. Till the sun
got low, I did not believe that there were so many redcoats in the
forest army. Theirs is an intense, burning red, which would lose
some of its strength, methinks, with every step you might take
toward them; for the shade that lurks amid their foliage does not
report itself at this distance, and they are unanimously red. The
focus of their reflected color is in the atmosphere far on this side.
Every such tree becomes a nucleus of red, as it were, where, with
the declining sun, that color grows and glows. It is partly borrowed fire, gathering strength from the sun on its way to your
eye. It has only some comparatively dull red leaves for a rally-
ing-point, or kindling-stuff, to start it, and it becomes an intense
scarlet or red mist, or fire, which finds fuel for itself in the very
atmosphere. So vivacious is redness. The very rails reflect a
rosy light at this hour and season. You see a redder tree than exists.

If you wish to count the scarlet oaks, do it now. In a clear
day stand thus on a hilltop in the woods, when the sun is an
hour high, and every one within range of your vision, excepting
in the west, will be revealed. You might live to the age of
Methuselah and never find a tithe of them, otherwise. Yet

sometimes even in a dark day I have thought them as bright as I ever saw them. Looking westward, their colors are lost in a blaze of light; but in other directions the whole forest is a flower-garden, in which these late roses burn, alternating with green, while the so-called "gardeners," walking here and there, perchance, beneath, with spade and water-pot, see only a few little asters amid withered leaves.

These are *my* China-asters, *my* late garden-flowers. It costs me nothing for a gardener. The falling leaves, all over the forest, are protecting the roots of my plants. Only look at what is to be seen, and you will have garden enough, without deepening the soil in your yard. We have only to elevate our view a little, to see the whole forest as a garden. The blossoming of the scarlet oak,—the forest-flower, surpassing all in splendor (at least since the maple)! I do not know but they interest me more than the maples, they are so widely and equally dispersed throughout the forest; they are so hardy, a nobler tree on the whole; our chief November flower, abiding the approach of winter with us, imparting warmth to early November prospects. It is remarkable that the latest bright color that is general should be this deep, dark scarlet and red, the intensest of colors. The ripest fruit of the year; like the cheek of a hard, glossy red apple, from the cold Isle of Orleans, which will not be mellow for eating till next spring! When I rise to a hilltop, a thousand of these great oak roses, distributed on every side, as far as the horizon! I admire them four or five miles off! This my unfailing prospect for a fortnight past! This late forest-flower surpasses all that spring or summer could do. Their colors were but rare and dainty specks comparatively (created for the nearsighted, who walk amid the humblest herbs and underwoods), and made no impression on a distant eye. Now it is an extended forest or a mountain-side, through or along which we journey from day to day, that bursts into bloom. Comparatively, our gardening is on a petty scale,— the gardener still nursing a few asters amid dead weeds, ignorant of the gigantic asters and roses which, as it were, overshadow him, and ask for none of his care. It is like a little red paint ground on a saucer, and held up against the sunset sky. Why not take more elevated and broader views, walk in the great garden; not skulk in a little "debauched" nook of it? consider the beauty of the forest, and not merely of a few impounded herbs?

Let your walks now be a little more adventurous; ascend the hills. If, about the last of October, you ascend any hill in the

outskirts of our town, and probably of yours, and look over the
forest, you may see—well, what I have endeavored to describe.
All this you surely *will* see, and much more, if you are prepared
to see it,—if you *look* for it. Otherwise, regular and universal as
this phenomenon is, whether you stand on the hilltop or in the
hollow, you will think for threescore years and ten that all the
wood is, at this season, sere and brown. Objects are concealed
from our view, not so much because they are out of the course of
our visual ray as because we do not bring our minds and eyes to
bear on them, for there is no power to see in the eye itself, any
more than in any other jelly. We do not realize how far and
widely, or how near and narrowly, we are to look. The greater
part of the phenomena of Nature are for this reason concealed
from us all our lives. The gardener sees only the gardener's garden. Here, too, as in political economy, the supply answers to
the demand. Nature does not cast pearls before swine. There is
just as much beauty visible to us in the landscape as we are prepared to appreciate,—not a grain more. The actual objects which
one man will see from a particular hilltop are just as different
from those which another will see as the beholders are different.
The scarlet oak must, in a sense, be in your eye when you go
forth. We cannot see anything until we are possessed with the
idea of it, take it into our heads,—and then we can hardly see
anything else. In my botanical rambles I find that, first, the idea,
or image, of a plant occupies my thoughts, though it may seem
very foreign to this locality,—no nearer than Hudson's Bay,—
and for some weeks or months I go thinking of it, and expecting
it, unconsciously, and at length I surely see it. This is the history
of my finding a score or more of rare plants which I could name.
A man sees only what concerns him. A botanist absorbed in the
study of grasses does not distinguish the grandest pasture oaks.
He, as it were, tramples down oaks unwittingly in his walk, or at
most sees only their shadows. I have found that it required a different intention of the eye, in the same locality, to see different
plants, even when they were closely allied, as *Juncaceae* and
Gramineae: when I was looking for the former, I did not see the
latter in the midst of them. How much more, then, it requires
different intentions of the eye and of the mind to attend to different departments of knowledge! How differently the poet and
the naturalist look at objects!

　　Take a New England selectman, and set him on the highest of our hills, and tell him to look,—sharpening his sight to

the utmost, and putting on the glasses that suit him best (aye, using a spy-glass, if he likes),—and make a full report. What, probably, will he *spy*?—what will he *select* to look at? Of course, he will see a Brocken spectre of himself. He will see several meeting-houses, at least, and, perhaps, that somebody ought to be assessed higher than he is, since he has so handsome a wood-lot. Now take Julius Cæsar, or Emanuel Swedenborg, or a Fiji-Islander, and set him up there. Or suppose all together, and let them compare notes afterward. Will it appear that they have enjoyed the same prospect? What they will see will be as different as Rome was from heaven or hell, or the last from the Fiji Islands. For aught we know, as strange a man as any of these is always at our elbow.

Why, it takes a sharpshooter to bring down even such trivial game as snipes and woodcocks; he must take very particular aim, and know what he is aiming at. He would stand a very small chance, if he fired at random into the sky, being told that snipes were flying there. And so is it with him that shoots at beauty; though he wait till the sky falls, he will not bag any, if he does not already know its seasons and haunts, and the color of its wing,—if he has not dreamed of it, so that he can *anticipate* it; then, indeed, he flushes it at every step, shoots double and on the wing, with both barrels, even in corn-fields. The sportsman trains himself, dresses, and watches unweariedly, and loads and primes for his particular game. He prays for it, and offers sacrifices, and so he gets it. After due and long preparation, schooling his eye and hand, dreaming awake and asleep, with gun and paddle and boat, he goes out after meadow-hens, which most of his townsmen never saw nor dreamed of, and paddles for miles against a head wind, and wades in water up to his knees, being out all day without his dinner, and *therefore* he gets them. He had them half-way into his bag when he started, and has only to shove them down. The true sportsman can shoot you almost any of his game from his windows: what else has he windows or eyes for? It comes and perches at last on the barrel of his gun; but the rest of the world never see it *with the feathers on*. The geese fly exactly under his zenith, and honk when they get there, and he will keep himself supplied by firing up his chimney; twenty musquash have the refusal of each one of his traps before it is empty. If he lives, and his game spirit increases, heaven and earth shall fail him sooner than game; and when he dies, he will go to more extensive and, perchance, happier hunting-grounds.

The fisherman, too, dreams of fish, sees a bobbing cork in his dreams, till he can almost catch them in his sink-spout. I knew a girl who, being sent to pick huckleberries, picked wild gooseberries by the quart, where no one else knew that there were any, because she was accustomed to pick them upcountry where she came from. The astronomer knows where to go star-gathering, and sees one clearly in his mind before any have seen it with a glass. The hen scratches and finds her food right under where she stands; but such is not the way with the hawk.

These bright leaves which I have mentioned are not the exception, but the rule; for I believe that all leaves, even grasses and mosses, acquire brighter colors just before their fall. When you come to observe faithfully the changes of each humblest plant, you find that each has, sooner or later, its peculiar autumnal tint; and if you undertake to make a complete list of the bright tints, it will be nearly as long as a catalogue of the plants in your vicinity.

WILD APPLES
1862

THE HISTORY OF THE APPLE TREE

It is remarkable how closely the history of the apple tree is connected with that of man. The geologist tells us that the order of the *Rosaceae*, which includes the apple, also the true grasses, and the *Labiatae*, or mints, were introduced only a short time previous to the appearance of man on the globe.

It appears that apples made a part of the food of that unknown primitive people whose traces have lately been found at the bottom of the Swiss lakes, supposed to be older than the foundation of Rome, so old that they had no metallic implements. An entire black and shriveled crab-apple has been recovered from their stores.

Tacitus says of the ancient Germans that they satisfied their hunger with wild apples (*agrestia poma*), among other things.

Niebuhr observes that "the words for a house, a field, a plow, plowing, wine, oil, milk, sheep, apples, and others relating to agriculture and the gentler way of life, agree in Latin and Greek, while the Latin words for all objects pertaining to war or the chase are utterly alien from the Greek." Thus the apple tree may be considered a symbol of peace no less than the olive.

The apple was early so important, and generally distributed, that its name traced to its root in many languages signifies fruit in general. Μηλον, in Greek, means an apple, also the fruit of other trees, also a sheep and any cattle, and finally riches in general.

The apple tree has been celebrated by the Hebrews, Greeks, Romans, and Scandinavians. Some have thought that the first human pair were tempted by its fruit. Goddesses are labeled to have contended for it, dragons were set to watch it, and heroes were employed to pluck it.

The tree is mentioned in at least three places in the Old Testament, and its fruit in two or three more. Solomon sings, "As the apple-tree among the trees of the wood, so is my beloved among the sons." And again, "Stay me with flagons, comfort me with apples." The noblest part of man's noblest feature is named from this fruit, "the apple of the eye."

The apple tree is also mentioned by Homer and Herodotus. Ulysses saw in the glorious garden of Alcinoüs "pears and pomegranates, and apple trees bearing beautiful fruit" (και μηλεαι αγλαοκαρποι). And according to Homer, apples were among the fruits which Tantalus could not pluck, the wind ever blowing their boughs away from him. Theophrastus knew and described the apple tree as a botanist.

According to the Prose Edda, "Iduna keeps in a box the apples which the gods, when they feel old age approaching, have only to taste of to become young again. It is in this manner that they will be kept in renovated youth until Ragnarök" (or the destruction of the gods).

I learn from Loudon that "the ancient Welsh bards were rewarded for excelling in song by the token of the apple-spray;" and "in the Highlands of Scotland the apple-tree is the badge of the clan Lamont."

The apple tree (*Pyrus malus*) belongs chiefly to the northern temperate zone. Loudon says that "it grows spontaneously in every part of Europe except the frigid zone, and throughout Western Asia, China, and Japan." We have also two or the varieties of the apple indigenous in North America. The cultivated apple tree was first introduced into this country by the earliest settlers, and is thought to do as well or better here than anywhere else. Probably some of the varieties which are now cultivated were first introduced into Britain by the Romans.

Pliny, adopting the distinction of Theophrastus, says, "Of trees there are some which are altogether wild (*sylvestres*), some more civilized (*urbaniores*)." Theophrastus includes the apple among the last; and, indeed, it is in this sense the most civilized of all trees. It is as harmless as a dove, as beautiful as a rose, and as valuable as flocks and herds. It has been longer cultivated than any other, and so is more humanized; and who knows but, like the dog, it will at length be no longer traceable to its wild original? It migrates with man, like the dog and horse and cow:

first, perchance, from Greece to Italy, thence to England, thence
to America; and our Western emigrant is still marching steadily
toward the setting sun with the seeds of the apple in his pocket,
or perhaps a few young trees strapped to his load. At least a million apple trees are thus set farther westward this year than any
cultivated ones grew last year.   Consider how the Blossom
Week, like the Sabbath, is thus annually spreading over the
prairies; for when man migrates, he carries with him not only
his birds, quadrupeds, insects, vegetables, and his very sward, but
his orchard also.

The leaves and tender twigs are an agreeable food to many
domestic animals, as the cow, horse, sheep, and goat; and the
fruit is sought after by the first, as well as by the hog. Thus there
appears to have existed a natural alliance between these animals
and this tree from the first. "The fruit of the crab in the forests of
France" is said to be "a great resource for the wild boar."

Not only the Indian, but many indigenous insects, birds,
and quadrupeds, welcomed the apple tree to these shores. The
tent caterpillar saddled her eggs on the very first twig that was
formed, and it has since shared her affections with the wild
cherry; and the canker-worm also in a measure abandoned the
elm to feed on it. As it grew apace, the bluebird, robin, cherry-
bird, kingbird, and many more came with haste and built their
nests and warbled in its boughs, and so became orchard-birds,
and multiplied more than ever. It was an era in the history of
their race. The downy woodpecker found such a savory morsel
under its bark that he perforated it in a ring quite round the tree,
before he left it,—a thing which he had never done before, to my
knowledge. It did not take the partridge long to find out how
sweet its buds were, and every winter eve she flew, and still flies,
from the wood, to pluck them, much to the farmer's sorrow.
The rabbit, too, was not slow to learn the taste of its twigs and
bark; and when the fruit was ripe, the squirrel half rolled, half
carried it to his hole; and even the musquash crept up the bank
from the brook at evening, and greedily devoured it, until he
had worn a path in the grass there; and when it was frozen and
thawed, the crow and the jay were glad to taste it occasionally.
The owl crept into the first apple tree that became hollow, and
fairly hooted with delight, finding it just the place for him; so,
settling down into it, he has remained there ever since.

My theme being the Wild Apple, I will merely glance at some of the seasons in the annual growth of the cultivated apple, and pass on to my special province.

The flowers of the apple are perhaps the most beautiful of any tree's, so copious and so delicious to both sight and scent. The walker is frequently tempted to turn and linger near some more than usually handsome one, whose blossoms are two-thirds expanded. How superior it is in these respects to the pear, whose blossoms are neither colored nor fragrant!

By the middle of July, green apples are so large as to remind us of coddling, and of the autumn. The sward is commonly strewed with little ones which fall stillborn, as it were,— Nature thus thinning them for us. The Roman writer Palladius said, "If apples are inclined to fall before their time, a stone placed in a split root will retain them." Some such notion, still surviving, may account for some of the stones which we see placed, to be overgrown, in the forks of trees. They have a saying in Suffolk, England,—

"At Michaelmas time, or a little before,
Half an apple goes to the core."

Early apples begin to be ripe about the first of August; but I think that none of them are so good to eat as some to smell. One is worth more to scent your handkerchief with than any perfume which they sell in the shops. The fragrance of some fruits is not to be forgotten, along with that of flowers. Some gnarly apple which I pick up in the road reminds me by its fragrance of all the wealth of Pomona,—carrying me forward to those days when they will be collected in golden and ruddy heaps in the orchards and about the cider-mills.

A week or two later, as you are going by orchards or gardens, especially in the evenings, you pass through a little region possessed by the fragrance of ripe apples, and thus enjoy them without price, and without robbing anybody.

There is thus about all natural products a certain volatile and ethereal quality which represents their highest value, and which cannot be vulgarized, or bought and sold. No mortal has ever enjoyed the perfect flavor of any fruit, and only the godlike among men begin to taste its ambrosial qualities. For nectar and ambrosia are only those fine flavors of every earthly fruit which our coarse palates fail to perceive,—just as we occupy the heaven

of the gods without knowing if. When I see a particularly mean
man carrying a load of fair and fragrant early apples to market, I
seem to see a contest going on between him and his horse, on
the one side, and the apples on the other, and, to my mind, the
apples always gain it. Pliny says that apples are the heaviest of
all things, and that the oxen begin to sweat at the mere sight of a
load of them. Our driver begins to lose his load the moment he
tries to transport them to where they do not belong, that is, to
any but the most beautiful. Though he gets out from time to
time, and feels of them, and thinks they are all there, I see the
stream of their evanescent and celestial qualities going to
heaven from his cart, while the pulp and skin and core only are
going to market. They are not apples, but pomace. Are not these
still Iduna's apples, the taste of which keeps the gods forever
young? and think you that they will let Loki or Thjassi carry
them off to Jotunheim, while they grow wrinkled and gray? No,
for Ragnarök, or the destruction of the gods, is not yet.

There is another thinning of the fruit, commonly near the
end of August or in September, when the ground is strewn with
windfalls; and this happens especially when high winds occur after rain. In some orchards you may see fully three quarters of
the whole crop on the ground, lying in a circular form beneath
the trees, yet hard and green, or, if it is a hillside, rolled far down
the hill. However, it is an ill wind that blows nobody any good.
All the country over, people are busy picking up the windfalls,
and this will make them cheap for early apple pies.

In October, the leaves falling, the apples are more distinct
on the trees. I saw one year in a neighboring town some trees
fuller of fruit than I remember to have ever seen before, small
yellow apples hanging over the road. The branches were gracefully drooping with their weight, like a barberry bush, so that the
whole tree acquired a new character. Even the topmost
branches, instead of standing erect, spread and drooped in all directions; and there were so many poles supporting the lower
ones that they looked like pictures of banyan trees. As an old
English manuscript says, "The mo appelen the tree bereth the
more sche boweth to the folk."

Surely the apple is the noblest of fruits. Let the most
beautiful or the swiftest have it. That should be the "going"
price of apples.

Between the 5th and 20th of October I see the barrels lie
under the trees. And perhaps I talk with one who is selecting

some choice barrels to fulfill an order. He turns a specked one over many times before he leaves it out. If I were to tell what is passing in my mind, I should say that every one was specked which he had handled; for he rubs off all the bloom, and those fugacious ethereal qualities leave it. Cool evenings prompt the farmers to make haste, and at length I see only the ladders here and there left leaning against the trees.

It would be well, if we accepted these gifts with more joy and gratitude, and did not think it enough simply to put a fresh load of compost about the tree. Some old English customs are suggestive at least. I find them described chiefly in Brand's "Popular Antiquities." It appears that "on Christmas Eve the farmers and their men in Devonshire take a large bowl of cider, with a toast in it, and carrying it in state to the orchard, they salute the apple-trees with much ceremony, in order to make them bear well the next season." This salutation consists in "throwing some of the cider about the roots of the tree, placing bits of the toast on the branches," and then, "encircling one of the best bearing trees in the orchard, they drink the following toast three several times:—

> 'Here's to thee, old apple tree,
> Whence thou mayst bud, and whence thou mayst blow,
> And whence thou mayst bear apples enow!
>   Hats-full! caps-full!
>   Bushel, bushel, sacks-full!
>   And my pockets full, too! Hurra!'"

Also what was called "apple-howling" used to be practiced in various counties of England on New Year's Eve. A troop of boys visited the different orchards, and, encircling the apple trees, repeated the following words:—

> "Stand fast, root! bear well, top!
> Pray God send us a good howling crop:
> Every twig, apples big;
> Every bough, apples enow!"

"They then shout in chorus, one of the boys accompanying them on a cow's horn. During this ceremony they rap the trees with their sticks." This is called "wassailing" the trees, and is thought by some to be "a relic of the heathen sacrifice to Pomona."

Herrick sings,—

> "Wassaile the trees that they may beare
> You many a plum and many a peare;
> For more or less fruits they will bring
> As you so give them wassailing."

Our poets have as yet a better right to sing of cider than of wine; but it behooves them to sing better than English Phillips did, else they will do no credit to their Muse.

THE WILD APPLE

So much for the more civilized apple trees (*urbaniores*, as Pliny calls them). I love better to go through the old orchards of ungrafted apple trees, at what ever season of the year,—so irregularly planted: sometimes two trees standing close together; and the rows so devious that you would think that they not only had grown while the owner was sleeping, but had been set out by him in a somnambulic state. The rows of grafted fruit will never tempt me to wander amid them like these. But I now, alas, speak rather from memory than from any recent experience, such ravages have been made!

Some soils, like a rocky tract called the Easterbrooks Country in my neighborhood, are so suited to the apple, that it will grow faster in them without any care, or if only the ground is broken up once a year, than it will in many places with any amount of care. The owners of this tract allow that the soil is excellent for fruit, but they say that it is so rocky that they have not patience to plow it, and that, together with the distance, is the reason why it is not cultivated. There are, or were recently, extensive orchards there standing without order. Nay, they spring up wild and bear well there in the midst of pines, birches, maples, and oaks. I am often surprised to see rising amid these trees the rounded tops of apple trees glowing with red or yellow fruit, in harmony with the autumnal tints of the forest.

Going up the side of a cliff about the first of November, I saw a vigorous young apple tree, which, planted by birds or cows, had shot up amid the rocks and open woods there, and had now much fruit on it, uninjured by the frosts, when all cultivated apples were gathered. It was a rank, wild growth, with many green leaves on it still, and made an impression of thorniness. The fruit was hard and green, but looked as if it would be palatable in the winter. Some was dangling on the twigs, but more half buried in the wet leaves under the tree, or rolled far down the hill amid the rocks. The owner knows nothing of it. The day was not observed when it first blossomed, nor when it first bore fruit, unless by the chickadee. There was no dancing on the green beneath it in its honor, and now there is no hand to pluck its fruit,—which is only gnawed by squirrels, as I perceive. It has done double duty,—not only borne this crop, but each twig has grown a foot into the air. And this is *such* fruit! bigger than many berries, we must admit, and carried home will be sound and palatable next spring. What care I for Iduna's apples so long as I can get these?

When I go by this shrub thus late and hardy, and see its dangling fruit, I respect the tree, and I am grateful for Nature's bounty, even though I cannot eat it. Here on this rugged and woody hillside has grown an apple tree, not planted by man, no relic of a former orchard, but a natural growth, like the pines and oaks. Most fruits which we prize and use depend entirely on our care. Corn and grain, potatoes, peaches, melons, etc., depend altogether on our planting; but the apple emulates man's independence and enterprise. It is not simply carried, as I have said, but, like him, to some extent, it has migrated to this New World, and is even, here and there, making its way amid the aboriginal trees; just as the ox and dog and horse sometimes run wild and maintain themselves.

Even the sourest and crabbedest apple, growing in the most unfavorable position, suggests such thoughts as these, it is so noble a fruit.

THE CRAB

Nevertheless, *our* wild apple is wild only like myself, perchance, who belong not to the aboriginal race here, but have strayed into the woods from the cultivated stock. Wilder still, as I have said, there grows elsewhere in this country a native and aboriginal crab-apple, *Malus coronaria*, "whose nature has not yet been modified by cultivation." It is found from western New York to Minnesota, and southward. Michaux says that its ordi-

nary height "is fifteen or eighteen feet, but it is sometimes found
twenty-five or thirty feet high," and that the large ones "exactly
resemble the common apple tree." "The flowers are white mingled with rose color, and are collected in corymbs." They are remarkable for their delicious odor. The fruit, according to him, is
about an inch and a half in diameter, and is intensely acid. Yet
they make fine sweetmeats and also cider of them. He concludes
that "if, on being cultivated, it does not yield new and palatable
varieties, it will at least be celebrated for the beauty of its flowers,
and for the sweetness of its perfume."

I never saw the crab-apple till May 1861. I had heard of it
through Michaux, but more modern botanists, so far as I
know, have not treated it as of any peculiar importance. Thus it
was a half-fabulous tree to me. I contemplated a pilgrimage to
the "Glades," a portion of Pennsylvania where it was said to
grow to perfection. I thought of sending to a nursery for it, but
doubted if they had it, or would distinguish it from European
varieties. At last I had occasion to go to Minnesota, and on
entering Michigan I began to notice from the cars a tree with
handsome rose-colored flowers. At first I thought it some
variety of thorn; but it was not long before the truth flashed on
me, that this was my long-sought crab-apple. It was the
prevailing flowering shrub or tree to be seen from the cars at that
season of the year,—about the middle of May. But the cars never
stopped before one, and so I was launched on the bosom of the
Mississippi without having touched one, experiencing the fate of
Tantalus. On arriving at St. Anthony's Falls, I was sorry to be
told that I was too far north for the crab-apple. Nevertheless I
succeeded in finding it about eight miles west of the Falls;
touched it and smelled it, and secured a lingering corymb of
flowers for my herbarium. This must have been near its northern limit.

HOW THE WILD APPLE GROWS

But though these are indigenous, like the Indians, I doubt
whether they are any hardier than those backwoodsmen among
the apple trees, which, though descended from cultivated stocks,
plant themselves in distant fields and forests, where the soil is
favorable to them. I know of no trees which have more difficul-

ties to contend with, and which more sturdily resist their foes.
These are the ones whose story we have to tell. It oftentimes
reads thus:—

Near the beginning of May, we notice little thickets of apple trees just springing up in the pastures where cattle have
been,—as the rocky ones of our Easterbrooks Country, or the top
of Nobscot Hill, in Sudbury. One or two of these, perhaps, survive the drought and other accidents,—their very birthplace defending them against the encroaching grass and some other dangers, at first.   .

> In two years' time 't had thus
>   Reached the level of the rocks,
> Admired the stretching world,
>   Nor feared the wandering flocks.
>
> But at this tender age
>   Its sufferings began:
> There came a browsing ox
>   And cut it down a span.

This time, perhaps, the ox does not notice it amid the grass; but
the next year, when it has grown more stout, he recognizes it for
a fellow-emigrant from the old country, the flavor of whose
leaves and twigs he well knows; and though at first he pauses to
welcome it, and express his surprise, and gets for answer, "The
same cause that brought you here brought me," he nevertheless
browses it again, reflecting, it may be, that he has some title to it.

Thus cut down annually, it does not despair; but, putting
forth two short twigs for every one cut off, it spreads out low
along the ground in the hollows or between the rocks, growing
more stout and scrubby, until it forms, not a tree as yet, but a little pyramidal, stiff, twiggy mass, almost as solid and impenetrable as a rock. Some of the densest and most impenetrable
clumps of bushes that I have ever seen, as well on account of the
closeness and stubbornness of their branches as of their thorns,
have been these wild apple scrubs. They are more like the
scrubby fir and black spruce on which you stand, and sometimes
walk, on the tops of mountains, where cold is the demon they
contend with, than anything else. No wonder they are
prompted to grow thorns at last, to defend themselves against
such foes. In their thorniness, however, there is no malice, only
some malic acid.

The rocky pastures of the tract I have referred to—for they maintain their ground best in a rocky field—are thickly sprinkled with these little tufts, reminding you often of some rigid gray mosses or lichens, and you see thousands of little trees just springing up between them, with the seed still attached to them.

Being regularly clipped all around each year by the cows, as a hedge with shears, they are often of a perfect conical or pyramidal form, from one to four feet high, and more or less sharp, as if trimmed by the gardener's art. In the pastures on Nobscot Hill and its spurs, they make fine dark shadows when the sun is low. They are also an excellent covert from hawks for many small birds that roost and build in them. Whole flocks perch in them at night, and I have seen three robins' nests in one which was six feet in diameter.

No doubt many of these are already old trees, if you reckon from the day they were planted, but infants still when you consider their development and the long life before them. I counted the annual rings of some which were just one foot high, and as wide as high, and found that they were about twelve years old, but quite sound and thrifty! They were so low that they were unnoticed by the walker, while many of their contemporaries from the nurseries were already bearing considerable crops. But what you gain in time is perhaps in this case, too, lost in power,—that is, in the vigor of the tree. This is their pyramidal state.

The cows continue to browse them thus for twenty years or more, keeping them down and compelling them to spread, until at last they are so broad that they become their own fence, when some interior shoot, which their foes cannot reach, darts upward with joy: for it has not forgotten its high calling, and bears its own peculiar fruit in triumph.

Such are the tactics by which it finally defeats its bovine foes. Now, if you have watched the progress of a particular shrub, you will see that it is no longer a simple pyramid or cone, but that out of its apex there rises a sprig or two, growing more lustily perchance than an orchard-tree, since the plant now devotes the whole of its repressed energy to these upright parts. In a short time these become a small tree, an inverted pyramid resting on the apex of the other, so that the whole has now the form of a vast hour-glass. The spreading bottom, having served its purpose, finally disappears, and the generous tree permits the now harmless cows to come in and stand in its shade, and rub against and redden its trunk, which has grown in spite of them, and even to taste a part of its fruit, and so disperse the seed.

Thus the cows create their own shade and food; and the tree, its hour-glass being inverted, lives a second life, as it were.

It is an important question with some nowadays, whether you should trim young apple trees as high as your nose or as high as your eyes. The ox trim them up as high as he can reach, and that is about the right height, I think.

In spite of wandering kine, and other adverse circumstances, that despised shrub, valued only by small birds as a covert and shelter from hawks, has its blossom week at last, and in course of time its harvest, sincere, though small.

By the end of some October, when its leaves have fallen, I frequently see such a central sprig, whose progress I have watched, when I thought it had forgotten its destiny, as I had, bearing its first crop of small green or yellow or rosy fruit, which the cows cannot get at over the bushy and thorny hedge which surrounds it, and I make haste to taste the new and undescribed variety. We have all heard of the numerous varieties of fruit invented by Van Mons and Knight. This is the system of Van Cow, and she has invented far more and more memorable varieties than both of them.

Through what hardships it may attain to bear a sweet fruit! Though somewhat small, it may prove equal, if not superior, in flavor to that which has grown in a garden,—will perchance be all the sweeter and more palatable for the very difficulties it has had to contend with. Who knows but this chance wild fruit, planted by a cow or a bird on some remote and rocky hillside, where it is as yet unobserved by man, may be the choicest of all its kind, and foreign potentates shall hear of it, and royal societies seek to propagate it, though the virtues of the perhaps truly crabbed owner of the soil may never be heard of,—at least, beyond the limits of his village? It was thus the Porter and the Baldwin grew.

Every wild apple shrub excites our expectation thus, somewhat as every wild child. It is, perhaps, a prince in disguise. What a lesson to man! So are human beings, referred to the highest standard, the celestial fruit which they suggest and aspire to bear, browsed on by fate; and only the most persistent and strongest genius defends itself and prevails, sends a tender scion upward at last, and drops its perfect fruit on the ungrateful earth.

Poets and philosophers and statesmen thus spring up in the country pastures, and outlast the hosts of unoriginal men.

Such is always the pursuit of knowledge. The celestial fruits, the golden apples of the Hesperides, are ever guarded by a hundred-headed dragon which never sleeps, so that it is an Herculean labor to pluck them.

This is one, and the most remarkable way in which the wild apple is propagated; but commonly it springs up at wide intervals in woods and swamp, and by the sides of roads, as the soil may suit it, and grows with comparative rapidity. Those which grow in dense woods are very tall and slender. I frequently pluck from these trees a perfectly mild and tamed fruit. As Palladius says, "*Et injussu consternitur ubere mali:*" And the ground is strewn with the fruit of an unbidden apple tree.

It is an old notion that, if these wild trees do not bear a valuable fruit of their own, they are the best stocks by which to transmit to posterity the most highly prized qualities of others. However, I am not in search of stocks, but the wild fruit itself, whose fierce gust has suffered no "inteneration." It is not my

"highest plot
To plant the Bergamot"

THE FRUIT, AND ITS FLAVOR

The time for wild apples is the last of October and the first of November. They then get to be palatable, for they ripen late, and they are still perhaps as beautiful as ever. I make a great account of these fruits, which the farmers do not think it worth the while to gather,—wild flavors of the Muse, vivacious and inspiriting. The farmer thinks that be has better in his barrels, but he is mistaken, unless he has a walker's appetite and imagination, neither of which can he have.

Such as grow quite wild, and are left out till the first of November, I presume that the owner does not mean to gather. They belong to children as wild as themselves,—to certain active boys that I know,—to the wild-eyed woman of the fields, to whom nothing comes amiss, who gleans after all the world, and, moreover, to us walkers. We have met with them, and they are ours. These rights, long enough insisted upon, have come to be

an institution in some old countries, where they have learned
how to live. I hear that "the custom of grippling, which may be
called apple-gleaning, is, or was formerly, practiced in Herefordshire. It consists in leaving a few apples, which are called the
grippies, on every tree, after the general gathering, for the boys,
who go with climbing-poles and bags to collect them."

As for those I speak of, I pluck them as a wild fruit, native
to this quarter of the earth,—fruit of old trees that have been dying ever since I was a boy and are not yet dead, frequented only
by the woodpecker and the squirrel, deserted now by the owner,
who has not faith enough to look under their boughs. From the
appearance of the tree-top, at a little distance, you would expect
nothing but lichens to drop from it, but your faith is rewarded by
finding the ground strewn with spirited fruit,—some of it, perhaps, collected at squirrel-holes, with the marks of their teeth by
which they carried them,—some containing a cricket or two
silently feeding within, and some, especially in damp days, a
shell-less snail. The very sticks and stones lodged in the treetop
might have convinced you of the savoriness of the fruit which
has been so eagerly sought after in past years.

I have seen no account of these among the "Fruits and
Fruit-Trees of America," though they are more memorable to
my taste than the grafted kinds; more racy and wild American
flavors do they possess when October and November, when December and January, and perhaps February and March even,
have assuaged them somewhat. An old farmer in my neighborhood, who always selects the right word, says that "they have a
kind of bow-arrow tang."

Apples for grafting appear to have been selected commonly, not so much for their spirited flavor, as for their mild-
ness, their size, and bearing qualities,—not so much for their
beauty, as for their fairness and soundness. Indeed, I have no
faith in the selected lists of pomological gentlemen. Their "Fa-
vorites" and "None-suches" and "Seek-no-farthers," when I
have fruited them, commonly turn out very tame and forget-
table. They are eaten with comparatively little zest, and have no
real *tang* nor *smack* to them.

What if some of these wildings are acrid and puckery,
genuine *verjuice*, do they not still belong to the *Pomacæ*, which
are uniformly innocent and kind to our race? I still begrudge
them to the cider-mill. Perhaps they are not fairly ripe yet.

No wonder that these small and high-colored apples are thought to make the best cider. Loudon quotes from the "Herefordshire Report," that "apples of a small size are always, if equal in quality, to be preferred to those of a larger size, in order that the rind and kernel may bear the greatest proportion to the pulp, which affords the weakest and most watery juice." And he says that, "to prove this, Dr. Symonds, of Hereford, about the year 1800, made one hogshead of cider entirely from the rinds and cores of apples, and another from the pulp only, when the first was found of extraordinary strength and flavor, while the latter was sweet and insipid."

Evelyn says that the "Red-strake" was the favorite cider-apple in his day; and he quotes one Dr. Newburg as saying, "In Jersey 't is a general observation, as I hear, that the more of red any apple has in its rind, the more proper it is for this use. Pale-faced apples they exclude as much as may be from their cider-vat." This opinion still prevails.

All apples are good in November. Those which the farmer leaves out as unsalable and unpalatable to those who frequent the markets are choicest fruit to the walker. But it is remarkable that the wild apple, which I praise as so spirited and racy when eaten in the fields or woods, being brought into the house has frequently a harsh and crabbed taste. The Saunterer's Apple not even the saunterer can eat in the house. The palate rejects it there, as it does haws and acorns, and demands a tamed one; for there you miss the November air, which is the sauce it is to be eaten with. Accordingly, when Tityrus, seeing the lengthening shadows, invites Meliboeus to go home and pass the night with him, he promises him *mild* apples and soft chest-nuts,—*mitia poma, castaneœ molles.* I frequently pluck wild apples of so rich and spicy a flavor that I wonder all orchardists do not get a scion from that tree, and I fail not to bring home my pockets full. But perchance, when I take one out of my desk and taste it in my chamber, I find it unexpectedly crude,—sour enough to set a squirrel's teeth on edge and make a jay scream.

These apples have hung in the wind and frost and rain till they have absorbed the qualifies of the weather or season, and thus are highly *seasoned*, and they *pierce* and *sting* and *permeate* us with their spirit. They must be eaten in *season*, accordingly,—that is, out-of-doors.

To appreciate the wild and sharp flavors of these October fruits, it is necessary that you be breathing the sharp October or

November air. The outdoor air and exercise which the walker
gets give a different tone to his palate, and he craves a fruit
which the sedentary would call harsh and crabbed. They must
he eaten in the fields, when your system is all aglow with exercise, when the frosty weather nips your fingers, the wind rattles
the bare boughs or rustles the few remaining leaves, and the jay
is heard screaming around. What is sour in the house a bracing
walk makes sweet. Some of these apples might be labeled, "To
be eaten in the wind."

Of course no flavors are thrown away; they are intended
for the taste that is up to them. Some apples have two distinct
flavors, and perhaps one half of them must be eaten in the
house, the other outdoors. One Peter Whitney wrote from
Northborough in 1782, for the Proceedings of the Boston
Academy, describing an apple tree in that town "producing fruit
of opposite qualities, part of the same apple being frequently sour
and the other sweet"; also some all sour, and others all sweet,
and this diversity on all parts of the tree.

There is a wild apple on Nawshawtuct Hill in my town
which has to me a peculiarly pleasant bitter tang, not perceived
till it is three-quarters tasted. It remains on the tongue. As you
eat it, it smells exactly like a squash-bug. It is a sort of triumph to
eat and relish it.

I hear that the fruit of a kind of plum tree in Provence is
"called *Prunes sibarelles,* because it is impossible to whistle after
having eaten them, from their sourness." But perhaps they
were only eaten in the house and in summer, and if tried out-of-
doors in a stinging atmosphere, who knows but you could whistle an octave higher and clearer?

In the fields only are the sours and bitters of Nature ap-
preciated; just as the wood-chopper eats his meal in a sunny
glade, in the middle of a winter day, with tent, basks in a sunny
ray there, and dreams of summer in a degree of cold which, experienced in a chamber, would make a student miserable. They
who are at work abroad are not cold, but rather it is they who sit
shivering in houses. As with temperatures, so with flavors; as
with cold and heat, so with sour and sweet. This natural raci-
ness, the sours and bitters which the diseased palate refuses, are
the true condiments.

Let your condiments be in the condition of your senses.
To appreciate the flavor of these wild apples requires vigorous

and healthy senses, *papillæ* firm and erect on the tongue and palate, not easily flattened and tamed.

From my experience with wild apples, I can understand that there may be reason for a savage's preferring many kinds of food which the civilized man rejects. The former has the palate of an outdoor man. It takes a savage or wild taste to appreciate a wild fruit.

What a healthy out-of-door appetite it takes to relish the apple of life, the apple of the world, then!

> "Nor is it every apple I desire,
>   Nor that which pleases every palate best;
> 'T is not the lasting Deuxan I require,
>   Nor yet the red-cheeked Greening I request,
> Nor that which first beshrewed the name of wife,
>   Nor that whose beauty caused the golden strife:
> No, no! bring me an apple from the tree of life."

So there is one *thought* for the field, another for the house. I would have my thoughts, like wild apples, to be food for walkers, and will not warrant them to be palatable if tasted in the house.

THEIR BEAUTY

Almost all wild apples are handsome. They cannot be too gnarly and crabbed and rusty to look at. The gnarliest will have some redeeming traits even to the eye. You will discover some evening redness dashed or sprinkled on some protuberance or in some cavity. It is rare that the summer lets an apple go without streaking or spotting it on some part of its sphere. It will have some red stains, commemorating the mornings and evenings it has witnessed; some dark and rusty blotches, in memory of the clouds and foggy, mildewy days that have passed over it; and a spacious field of green reflecting the general face of nature,—green even as the fields; or a yellow ground, which implies a milder flavor,—yellow as the harvest, or russet as the hills.

Apples, these I mean, unspeakably fair,—apples not of Discord, but of Concord! Yet not so rare but that the homeliest may have a share. Painted by the frosts, some a uniform clear bright yellow, or red, or crimson, as if their spheres had regularly revolved, and enjoyed the influence of the sun on all sides alike,—some with the faintest pink blush imaginable,—some brindled with deep red streaks like a cow, or with hundreds of fine blood-red rays running regularly from the stem-dimple to the blossom end, like meridional lines, on a straw-colored ground,—some touched with a greenish rust, like a fine lichen, here and there, with crimson blotches or eyes more or less confluent and fiery when wet,—and others gnarly, and freckled or peppered all over on the stem side with fine crimson spots on a white ground, as if accidentally sprinkled from the brush of Him who paints the autumn leaves. Others, again, are sometimes red inside, perfused with a beautiful blush, fairy food, too beautiful to eat,—apple of the Hesperides, apple of the evening sky! But like shells and pebbles on the seashore, they must be seen as they sparkle amid the withering leaves in some dell in the woods, in the autumnal air, or as they lie in the wet grass, and not when they have wilted and faded in the house.

The Naming of Them

It would be a pleasant pastime to find suitable names for the hundred varieties which go to a single heap at the cider-mill. Would it not tax a man's invention,—no one to be named after a man, and all in the *lingua vernacula*? Who shall stand godfather at the christening of the wild apples? It would exhaust the Latin and Greek languages, if they were used, and make the *lingua vernacula* flag. We should have to call in the sunrise and the sunset, the rainbow and the autumn woods and the wildflowers, and the woodpecker and the purple finch and the squirrel and the jay and the butterfly, the November traveler and the truant boy, to our aid.

In 1836 there were in the garden of the London Horticultural Society more than fourteen hundred distinct sorts. But here are species which they have not in their catalogue, not to mention the varieties which our crab might yield to cultivation.

Let us enumerate a few of these. I find myself compelled, after all, to give the Latin names of some for the benefit of those who live where English is not spoken,—for they are likely to have a world-wide reputation.

There is, first of all, the Wood Apple (*Malus sylvatica*); the
Blue-Jay Apple; the Apple which grows in Dells in the Woods
(*sylvestrivallis*), also in Hollows in Pastures (*campestrivallis*);
the Apple that grows in an old Cellar-Hole (*Malus cellaris*); the
Meadow Apple; the Partridge Apple; the Truant's Apple
(*cessatoris*), which no boy will ever go by without knocking off
some, however late it may be; the Saunterer's Apple,—you must
lose yourself before you can find the way to that; the Beauty of
the Air (*decus aëris*); December-Eating; the Frozen-Thawed
(*gelato-soluta*), good only in that state; the Concord Apple, possibly the same with the *Musketaquidensis*; the Assabet Apple; the
Brindled Apple; Wine of New England; the Chickaree Apple; the
Green Apple (*Malus viridis*),—this has many synonyms: in an
imperfect state, it is the *choleramorbifera aut dysenterifera,
puerulis dilectissima*; the Apple which Atalanta stopped to pick
up; the Hedge Apple (*Malus sepium*); the Slug Apple (*limacea*);
the Railroad Apple, which perhaps came from a core thrown out
of the cars; the Apple whose Fruit we tasted in our Youth; our
Particular Apple, not to be found in any catalogue; *pedestrium
solatium*; also the Apple where hangs the Forgotten Scythe;
Iduna's Apples, and the Apples which Loki found in the Wood;
and a great many more I have on my list, too numerous to mention,—all of them good. As Bodæus exclaims, referring to the
cultivated kinds, and adapting Virgil to his case, so I, adapting
Bodæus,—

> "Not if I had a hundred tongues, a hundred mouths,
> An iron voice, could I describe all the forms
> And reckon up all the names of these *wild apples*."

THE LAST GLEANING

By the middle of November the wild apples have lost
some of their brilliancy, and have chiefly fallen. A great part are
decayed on the ground, and the sound ones are more palatable
than before. The note of the chickadee sounds now more distinct, as you wander amid the old trees, and the autumnal dan-
delion is half closed and tearful. But still, if you are a skillful
gleaner, you may get many a pocketful even of grafted fruit, long
after apples are supposed to be gone out-of-doors. I know a Blue
Pearmain tree, growing within the edge of a swamp, almost as

good as wild. You would not suppose that there was any fruit left there, on the first survey, but you must look according to system. Those which lie exposed are quite brown and rotten now, or perchance a few still show one blooming cheek here and there amid the wet leaves. Nevertheless, with experienced eyes, I explore amid the bare alders and the huckleberry bushes and the withered sedge, and in the crevices of the rocks, which are full of leaves, and pry under the fallen and decaying ferns, which, with apple and alder leaves, thickly strew the ground. For I know that they lie concealed, fallen into hollows long since and covered up by the leaves of the tree itself,—a proper kind of packing. From these lurking-places, anywhere within the circumference of the tree, I draw forth the fruit, all wet and glossy, maybe nibbled by rabbits and hollowed out by crickets, and perhaps with a leaf or two cemented to it (as Curzon an old manuscript from a monastery's mouldy cellar), but still with a rich bloom on it, and at least as ripe and well-kept, if not better than those in barrels, more crisp and lively than they. If these resources fail to yield anything, I have learned to look between the bases of the suckers which spring thickly from some horizontal limb, for now and then one lodges there, or in the very midst of an alder-clump, where they are covered by leaves, safe from cows which may have smelled them out. If I am sharp-set, for I do not refuse the Blue Pearmain, I fill my pockets on each side; and as I retrace my steps in the frosty eve, being perhaps four or five miles from home, I eat one first from this side, and then from that, to keep my balance.

I learn from Topsell's Gesner, whose authority appears to be Albertus, that the following is the way in which the hedgehog collects and carries home his apples. He says,—"His meat is apples, worms, or grapes: when he findeth apples or grapes on the earth, he rolleth himself upon them, until he have filled all his prickles, and then carrieth them home to his den, never bearing above one in his mouth; and if it fortune that one of them fall off by the way, he likewise shaketh off all the residue, and walloweth upon them afresh, until they be all settled upon his back again. So, forth he goeth, making a noise like a cart-wheel; and if he have any young ones in his nest, they pull off his load where-withal he is loaded, eating thereof what they please, and laying up the residue for the time to come."

THE "FROZEN-THAWED" APPLE

Toward the end of November, though some of the sound ones are yet more mellow and perhaps more edible, they have generally, like the leaves, lost their beauty, and are beginning to freeze. It is finger-cold, and prudent farmers get in their barreled apples, and bring you the apples and cider which they have engaged; for it is time to put them into the cellar. Perhaps a few on the ground show their red cheeks above the early snow, and occasionally some even preserve their color and soundness under the snow throughout the winter. But generally at the beginning of the winter they freeze hard, and soon, though undecayed, acquire the color of a baked apple.

Before the end of December, generally, they experience their first thawing. Those which a month ago were sour, crabbed, and quite unpalatable to the civilized taste, such at least as were frozen while sound, let a warmer sun come to thaw them,—for they are extremely sensitive to its rays,—are found to be filled with a rich, sweet cider, better than any bottled cider that I know of, and with which I am better acquainted than with wine. All apples are good in this state, and your jaws are the cider-press. Others, which have more substance, are a sweet and luscious food,—in my opinion of more worth than the pineapples which are imported from the West Indies. Those which lately even I tasted only to repent of it,—for I am semi-civilized,—which the farmer willingly left on the tree, I am now glad to find have the property of hanging on like the leaves of the young oaks. It is a way to keep cider sweet without boiling. Let the frost come to freeze them first, solid as stones, and then the rain or a warm winter day to thaw them and they will seem to have borrowed a flavor from heaven through the medium of the air in which they hang. Or perchance you find, when you get home, that those which rattled in your pocket have thawed, and the ice is turned to cider. But after the third or fourth freezing and thawing they will not be found so good.

What are the imported half-ripe fruits of the torrid south, to this fruit matured by the cold of the frigid north? These are those crabbed apples with which I cheated my companion, and kept a smooth face that I might tempt him to eat. Now we both greedily fill our pockets with them,—bending to drink the cup and save our lappets from the overflowing juice,—and grow more social with their wine. Was there one that hung so high and sheltered by the tangled branches that our sticks could not dislodge it?

It is a fruit never carried to market, that I am aware of,—quite distinct from the apple of the markets, as from dried apple and cider,—and it is not every winter that produces it in perfection.

The era of the Wild Apple will soon be past. It is a fruit which will probably become extinct in New England. You may still wander through old orchards of native fruit of great extent, which for the most part went to the cider-mill, now all gone to decay. I have heard of an orchard in a distant town, on the side of a hill, where the apples rolled down and lay four feet deep against a wall on the lower side, and this the owner cut down for fear they should be made into cider. Since the temperance reform and the general introduction of grafted fruit, no native apple trees, such as I see everywhere in deserted pastures, and where the woods have grown up around them, are set out. I fear that he who walks over these fields a century hence will not know the pleasure of knocking off wild apples. Ah, poor man, there are many pleasures which he will not know! Notwithstanding the prevalence of the Baldwin and the Porter, I doubt if so extensive orchards are set out to-day in my town as there were a century ago, when those vast straggling cider-orchards were planted, when men both ate and drank apples, when the pomace-heap was the only nursery, and trees cost nothing but the trouble of setting them out. Men could afford then to stick a tree by every wall-side and let it take its chance. I see nobody planting trees to-day in such out of the way places, along the lonely roads and lanes, and at the bottom of dells in the wood. Now that they have grafted trees, and pay a price for them, they collect them into a plat by their houses, and fence them in, and the end of it all will be that we shall be compelled to look for our apples in a barrel.

This is "The word of the Lord that came to Joel the son of Pethuel.

"Hear this, ye old men, and give ear, all ye inhabitants of the land! Hath this been in your days, or even in the days of your fathers? . . .

"That which the palmerworm hath left hath the locust eaten; and that which the locust hath left hath the cankerworm eaten; and that which the cankerworm hath left hath the caterpillar eaten.

"Awake, ye drunkards, and weep; and howl, all ye drinkers of wine, because of the new wine; for it is cut off from your mouth.

"For a nation is come up upon my land, strong, and without number, whose teeth are the teeth of a lion, and he hath the cheek teeth of a great lion.

"He hath laid my vine waste, and barked my fig tree: he hath made it clean bare, and cast it away; the branches thereof are made white. . . .

"Be ye ashamed, O ye husbandmen; howl, O ye vine-dressers. . . .

"The vine is dried up, and the fig tree languisheth; the pomegranate tree, the palm tree also, and the apple tree, even all the trees of the field, are withered: because joy is withered away from the sons of men."

Index

Printed in the United States
5678R

9 780878 755233